The Personal Social Services

Eric Sainsbury

Professor of Social Administration
Department of Sociological Studies
University of Sheffield

Pitman

PITMAN PUBLISHING LIMITED
39 Parker Street, London WC2B 5PB

Associated Companies
Copp Clark Ltd, Toronto
Fearon-Pitman Publishers Inc, Belmont, California
Pitman Publishing Co. SA (Pty) Ltd, Johannesburg
Pitman Publishing New Zealand Ltd, Wellington
Pitman Publishing Pty Ltd, Melbourne

© E. Sainsbury

First published in Great Britain 1977

Text set in 11/12 pt Photon Times, printed by photolithography,
and bound in Great Britain at The Pitman Press, Bath

ISBN 0 273 01097 2

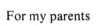

For my parents

Contents

Editor's Introduction

The purpose of this series is to continue Pitman's interest in the field of government and administration which first began by their publication of Clarke's
Outlines of Local Government in 1916. As with the earlier volumes, it is intended that the books in this new series should have a wide appeal. They will be
primarily addressed to students in all forms of higher education, to candidates
for professional examinations and to the practitioners themselves. They will
also provide an essential understanding for the many hundreds of politicians
and elected councillors who have a responsibility for controlling and directing
our public services.

The extensive growth of governmental services, the intricate mechanisms set
up to administer them, and the vast influence which they exercise over the lives
of the citizen and the maintenance of his rights and liberties, the efficient and
effective use of scarce resources, and the ordering and regulation of public
behaviour in a humane and dignified manner are factors which combine to
make it important that both officials and elected representatives shall not only
know their jobs, but shall carry them out competently and with understanding
of the needs of the people they serve. The aim of this series is to provide information about the structure and working of our major governmental institutions
and the services they provide, and to encourage a development of an understanding of the problems and issues they have to handle.

The field is vast—it has increased in size and complexity since the end of the
second world war. The series sets out to deal with the major institutions and services in a logical and easily assimilated manner. The main volumes will deal
with Parliament and the political processes, the central administration and the
civil service; the structure of local government, local government finance, and
the local government service; and with the main social services such as education, the personal social services, social security, housing, the national health
service and town planning.

The authors will represent a wide field of interests. Some come from an
academic background, whilst others are practitioners in the field. They all,

however, come to their task with a long experience of the subject on which they write and all have an established reputation.

WILLIAM THORNHILL
University of Sheffield

Preface

The intention of this book is to offer a brief introduction to the work of the personal social services and to guide the reader towards more detailed studies of particular components of this work. Certain difficulties arise, however, in presenting a succinct account of these social provisions. First, from modest beginnings, they have grown rapidly in size, complexity and power in recent years; they have assumed new functions and, in doing so, they have lost some of their earlier clarity of purpose. Secondly, their acquisition of resources, in money and manpower, has led to the development of managerial hierarchies which are perceived ambivalently by the main grade of their employees—both as a support to their work and as representing some loss of personal autonomy. Thirdly, the work of the personal social services is associated closely with the practice of social work. The rapid growth of the services has coincided with the development of professional aspirations among social workers, and there is at present a lively debate about the relationship between the status of employee and the status of professional.

This introductory book attempts, therefore, to offer not only an outline of the main provisions of the personal social services, but also a brief resumé of the principal issues involved in relating these provisions to professional social work, to dilemmas of organization and administration and to trends in social policy. It reflects the state of current thinking within the services, in that it offers more problems than solutions.

My thanks are due particularly to William Thornhill for his interest and support, and to Glenda Lee and her colleagues for their patient help with the typescript.

E.E.S.

Introduction

Any consideration of the welfare of individuals, and of society as a whole, is today inextricably linked with thoughts about the social services: health, education, income maintenance, housing and the personal social services. This book will be concerned to discuss welfare in relation to the work of the personal social services. But first it is necessary to consider briefly the broader context of the social services as a whole. What do the social services have in common with each other? Do they share certain characteristics which separate them from other kinds of social institutions and organizations and which we can use as a framework for considering the personal social services? What do we mean by 'welfare'?

This chapter will offer a brief guide to current thinking about the nature of the social services as a whole. The following section will then consider more specifically the personal social services and their relationship to the nature and promotion of 'welfare'. This approach may sound somewhat tentative, and indeed it will be. The social services are artefacts of modern society; they cannot be considered in isolation from more extensive social values, practices and institutions; they promote but are also responsive to social change. No artefact, whether it is a discotheque or a washing machine, can be adequately described and defined unless one can say something about its form and its purpose. Social artefacts such as the social services are more difficult to pin down for study because society itself is in constant change.

THE SCOPE AND PURPOSE OF THE SOCIAL SERVICES

There is at present no agreed definition either of the purpose of the social services or of their scope. In very broad terms, they are communal services concerned with meeting certain social needs and alleviating certain kinds of social problems—in particular, needs and problems which require a general public acceptance of mutual responsibility and which depend for their solution on the organizing of social relationships. Forder (1975) has described the social services as based on collective action and provided for social and humanitarian rather than economic motives.

But within statements of this kind there is room for considerable dispute about the meaning of 'collective action' and the place of 'economic motives'. In the provision of services for disabled people, collective action has until recently meant little more than a loosely related patchwork of health and welfare services variously available to those suffering from particular handicaps. We are still a long way from providing the kinds of help necessary to enable the achievement of a personally satisfying mode of life by all disabled people and their families. Neither are our present services for the disabled related simply to a humanitarian concern to meet their needs. They are based, at least in part, on the intention of making disabled people economically productive; the most severely disabled—those least likely to become productive—have hitherto received the least adequate services. Forder's description of the social services leaves room, therefore, for dispute about the sense in which they represent collective action and about the extent to which economic motives are (and should be) influential. Within this description also, there is scope for the implementation of a variety of divergent and incompatible political and moral value systems. For example, where should one strike a balance between the needs and rights of individuals and the protection and 'good order' of society? How is one to resolve dilemmas in which the freedom and autonomy of the individual appear to be at variance with the interests of others? Forder's reference to collective action implies a dilemma also in relation to the organization of services: social problems can be solved only by processes of large-scale organization, planning and regulation; yet the meeting of certain needs may require a high degree of sensitivity to individual variations in suffering. An administrative problem for all services is how to achieve a balance between individual responsiveness and mass provision.

These issues will be considered in detail when we look specifically at the personal social services. They are issues which, of course, find expression in all aspects of our social life; they are not merely problems for the social services. Dealing with inflation may mean an increase in unemployment. If so, the private costs of collective well-being—of solving a social problem—will be high; some would argue that they are too high. In an entirely different context, a man convicted of a criminal act may be treated more harshly than his case, when considered in isolation, appears to warrant in order to deter others from similar acts about which the general public happens to feel strongly. This may happen in cases of football hooliganism or the commission of crimes of violence.

Conflicts between the general good and the individual good, between combating social problems and meeting individual needs, are endemic and of daily concern in the social services. The recipient of supplementary benefit may spend his money in ways of which his neighbours (and his social security officer as a public representative) disapprove, and may be temporarily without food; if he is given an extra amount to meet his needs, this will seem unjust to other recipients who budget their resources differently. This is not *simply* a conflict between ideals of equity and of individualized justice, though this is the form with which employees in the social services are most familiar. The conflict stems from more fundamental political and economic divergences of view. On the one hand it could be argued that the economic progress of the country depends upon some measure of competitive self-help, and that the redistribution of resources by means of the social services in favour of the economically unsuccessful runs counter to social progress insofar as this is related to economic growth. On the other hand, this view would be challenged by those who define social progress in terms of greater equality between people and between classes, and who see the redistributive activities of the social services as an essential component in progress. According to which view one takes, one will tend to define both the purposes of the social services and their proper functioning in different ways. Any attempt to define purpose leads inevitably to broad issues of social relationships and political ideals; and these in turn influence one's further thoughts about purpose and function.

One runs into similar difficulties when one tries to define the scope of the social services and their appropriate auspices. To what extent should services be statutorily provided from public funds, or by voluntary organizations, or by employers, or by self-help groups? There are no ultimate and absolute limits to the number of social conditions which may at some time be defined as social problems which need attention. Similarly, individual human needs are virtually illimitable. There are thus no boundaries to the potential scope of social services. Yet it is clearly not possible to meet all human needs by statutory intervention. Therefore the debate takes on two dimensions: first, which human needs are *properly* the concern of the social services and which are to be left to the economic market—there appears to be general agreement, for example, that if one needs help with one's marriage one should approach a social service but if one needs help to find a marriage partner one should employ a commercial agent; and second, which of the needs falling within the 'social service type' should be met by statutory services, which by voluntary services, and which by a combination of the two sectors. In this last matter, the solution often appears to have been defined more by accident than by coherent policy, particularly in the operations of the personal social services. Responsibilities for the protection of children have become predominantly a statutory concern, probably because inadequacies in parental care have been regarded as a major source of certain social problems, notably juvenile delinquency; on the other hand, responsibility for alleviating the loneliness associated with old age has until recently been exclusively the concern of voluntary organizations; the needs of the handicapped are met by both the statutory and voluntary sectors in some sort of partnership. But there are no agreed guidelines to determine which kinds of services ought to be statutorily provided and which voluntarily: different political and social ideologies would differently define how extensive or restricted the statutory sector should be, and to which problems and needs statutory services should give most weight.

Finally, irrespective of our personal views about the purpose of the social services and the proper responsibilities of the state in meeting needs, there are two practical problems influencing statutory provision: first, the relative importance of the social services in comparison with other areas of national expenditure (for example, the arts, support to industry, national defence); and second, how best to allocate the available resources when there is a change in the demand for services. It is widely recognized that the expansion of services since 1948 has been fundamentally dependent on the maintenance of full employment and economic growth. If there were a major increase in unemployment, the demands on the social services would inevitably increase—particularly on those concerned with income maintenance and family welfare. If at the same time additional resources for the social services could not be made available, the choice would lie between attempting to maintain a broad range of statutory services, under-financed and inadequate in their operations, or restricting the scope of provisions in order to maintain a satisfactory level of service in response to a smaller range of needs. This, as we shall see, is a particularly problematic issue in the personal services at the present time.

No simple formulation of the purpose or scope of the social services is available to us. Part of the interest in studying them lies in these uncertainties and disputes, and in the dynamic for change and development to which they give rise. In the following sections we shall examine these issues and consider how far it is possible to reach agreement on the nature of the social services.

THE NATURE OF THE SOCIAL SERVICES

Richard Titmuss (1958) has described the social services as 'manifestations of society's will to survive as an organic whole and of the expressed wish of all people to assist the survival of some people.' This description draws attention to two aspects of the nature of the social services which may be fundamental: first, that they are an essential and integral part of our social life (not merely a benevolent addition for the exclusive use of minority groups of beneficiaries); but, second, that some people feel the need for them more than others do. The truth of this juxtaposition becomes evident when one considers the health and family services: a complex industrialized society such as our own is built upon economic processes which make it possible to afford adequate health and welfare services, available (more or less freely) to all citizens. At the same time, such a society cannot be maintained without a workforce which is both healthy and capable of the mobility required by industrial organization—a mobility which leads to the increased vulnerability of some citizens, who cannot rely on readily available domiciliary care from members of their own families. Similarly, in relation to educational services, advanced industrialization requires literacy, numeracy and job-specialization: it is incompatible with do-it-yourself education. Thus social services tend to be inter-dependently linked with industrial organization: as Titmuss comments, for many consumers, social services are partial compensation for 'socially generated disservices' and 'socially caused diswelfare'. 'They are part of the price we pay to some people for bearing parts of the costs of other people's progress.' (1968) Thus, there is a social service element in many policies outside the mainstream of the social services, for example in smoke abatement legislation, the provision of recreational facilities, and in government industrial retraining programmes. Compared with the other social services the personal services are specifically tailored to individual or family needs and distress suffered by a minority of citizens. But these again are not merely acts of social benevolence; they represent a complex fusion of two functions: maintaining such standards of social behaviour and efficiency as are thought to be essential to an industrial and urbanized society, and mitigating the disruptions (emotional and material) which such a society generates. All social services, whether uniformly applied (like social insurance) or individually applied (like the legislation in respect of child care and probation), are concerned both with liberating people from socially generated distress and with controlling some aspects of their social circumstances and behaviour. They are mechanisms to promote both social order and individual welfare. One of the principal dilemmas, as we have seen, is where to set the point of balance between these two functions.

It will be apparent from earlier comments that the way one determines this point of balance derives from the values one holds about citizens' rights and obligations in respect of large-scale economic and social processes lying outside their control. (I am assuming that none of us, individually or in like-minded groups, has the power in the short-term to re-order the fabric of society in accordance to his ideals, whatever political views he holds.)

In caricature, there are two extreme and opposed views. On the one hand we might argue that citizens must take the world as they find it, and cope as best they may individually with the pressures they experience, irrespective of the source of those pressures. Thus, if you live under the flight path of Concorde, or rent a damp house in an atmospherically polluted area, or are married to a man who has just been made redundant, or have no control over the behaviour of your unemployed teenage children—then either you have nothing to blame but your own failure to survive in a competitive world, or at best your situation is an unfortunate, unavoidable but temporary by-product of social progress and will improve as we all become richer in later generations. On the other hand, we may argue that social inequalities of the kind described here are not natural and inevitable, and that responsibility for their persistence must be pinned firmly on (e.g.) the landlord, or the manufacturers of Concorde, or on society as a whole which promotes and tolerates such problems as pollution and unemployment. The first viewpoint would define the social services as of an essentially *ad hoc* nature, concerned to reduce the number of social misfits by adjustments to their behaviour or circumstances, and by promoting an ideal of social functioning based on the overriding values of work and personal self-sufficiency. The second viewpoint tends rather to emphasize the rights of people to claim equality with others (equality either of opportunity or of standards of living) and would thus define all social services as a permanent and essential means whereby resources can be redistributed between citizens. Where the first viewpoint would focus the operation of the services on a minority of deprived people, in the hope that the need for service will in time wither away, the second would argue for a steady extension of resources.

In practice, as Titmuss has shown, we tend to achieve a shifting compromise between these extreme views, based not on a clear consensus about long-term purpose but on the achievement of small-scale day-to-day goals: the changes we make in social services tend to be incremental rather than radical, and we set our sights on specific issues (such as better housing, less crime, more responsible family life, lower unemployment rates, less hypothermia among the elderly, home improvements and further education for the handicapped) rather than on major social change or on a major rethinking of value systems. In the absence of agreement about the purpose of social services, Kathleen Bell (1973) has suggested that our achievements in welfare provisions have been based on periodic conflicts of ideologies and interests interspersed with periods of equilibrium. It is fundamental to the nature of the social services at the present time that plans for their development cannot be based exclusively on the strategies of conflict or consensus without affront to the opinions and values of many citizens.

THE CHARACTERISTICS OF THE SOCIAL SERVICES

If it is accepted that the development of social services is based on alternating periods of conflict and equilibrium, then we may expect to discover tensions within the common characteristics shared by the services. For example, social services are concerned to promote the welfare of citizens; but welfare in this context may relate both to the promotion of equality between people (Marshall, 1965) and to the individual's freedom to pursue his own definition of welfare. (The dilemma of matching these two notions of welfare is apparent in the current debates about private beds in National Health Service hospitals and the choice of schools within the educational system.)

Services are based upon collective action, involving the redistribution of a range of material and non-material resources; but this redistribution depends on compromise between the self-interests of different groups—rich and poor, able and disabled.

Services are concerned in part with promoting stability in the organization of an industrial urban society, and thus contain an element of social control over the contributors to and recipients of services (who may often be the same people); but, depending on one's political views and social position, one may regard this control as necessary and beneficial, or as the means whereby certain interest-groups institutionalize and legitimize the maintenance of their own power. Certainly, services can survive only if some measure of goodwill is maintained with the major power groups; yet some services have the potential to promote social change which may over a period involve a shift in power.

Social services are characteristically available to all citizens and, in the statutory sector, must therefore be offered on a large scale; at the same time, they are required to recognize individual differences in circumstances and in the perception and experience of need. They need to combine an equitable discharge of their responsibilities with a recognition of the special needs of those in vulnerable and destructive social situations. Thus, they are variously accountable: to elected representatives for their own internal efficiency; to pressure groups campaigning on behalf of special groups; to individual users applying for discretionary variations in help or requiring a quality of service which extends beyond the formal definitions of entitlement.

Services are established to meet need; yet they are charged with the responsibility also of defining it and of seeking to prevent its emergence. Thus, they seek to extend public knowledge of their availability, and to discover those whose personal resources need to be supplemented or replaced, while at the same time attempting to operate within clearly defined budgets.

Services are, in Romanyshyn's (1971) words, 'people-changing institutions' in that they are instruments of socialization and their employees are invested with authority—authority derived from statutes, professional knowledge and expertise; yet this authority may seem to run counter to the democratic values upon which public support for the social services depends. (See Handler, 1968)

Implicit in each of these characteristics is the necessity to find compromises which will be temporarily acceptable both politically and administratively. Both policy makers and executives must find some means of agreeing priorities in meeting competitive demands for the use of available resources. They must seek to reconcile the professional and career interests of various specialists. They must reconcile the varieties of patterns for the delivery of different services, both internally and in response to the presentation of needs by the consumers (for examples see Donnison et al., 1975). Parker et al. (1975) have suggested that, at central government level, the development of a new social service (or a change in the scope of an existing service) depends upon decisions about its feasibility, the extent to which it is acceptable as a legitimate area for government intervention, and the likely degree of public support both for the service itself and for the government in power. Similar considerations apply at a local level in the planning and operation of any service: is the service feasible in terms of the attitudes and availability of staff to implement it? Will the service be seen as legitimate by local voters and pressure groups, particularly if its financing leads to reductions in other services? Will the public support the service in spite of consequential increases in taxes or rates?

Questions of this kind, and the answers one gives to them, form a prelude to further issues which require administrative, moral and social consideration. These are concerned with how a service should be operated and how it should present itself to the general public. For example, should it be shaped in accordance with public opinion, however one is able to aggregate this? An ideal of democratic accountability would suggest that it should; yet, depending upon the user-group concerned, this principle could lead to liberality or punitiveness in the operation of the service. Alternatively, one may allow the staff of the service to shape it in accordance with their administrative convenience or professional ideology, but at the risk that the service will no longer seem accountable to the general public. Some kind of compromise between these alternatives is achieved when services are governed by elected representatives—as in education, housing and the local authority social services—but even so, 'public opinion' in this context is of a somewhat esoteric kind, based usually on a single political ideology and a better-than-average understanding of the context of a particular provision; neither housing nor personal social services have yet developed equivalents to the parent-teacher association. Income maintenance and health provisions at local level are essentially dominated by administrative and professional interpretations of effective service; public opinion may find greater expression in the latter service than hitherto through the developing activities of Community Health Councils. But it is doubtful how far it can, or even should, find expression in the work of income maintenance services, particularly of the Supplementary Benefits Commission's officers, whose work might easily become intolerable in the cross-fire between pressure groups (such as the Claimants' Union and CPAG) and other expressions of public opinion which seek to reduce payments. Yet the existence of pressure groups and complaints of service-abuse are themselves indications of the anxiety that services are shaped in ways contrary to the wishes of significant sections of the community.

A further dilemma in shaping a service-provision is that of determining how far it should aim to deal with a social problem or need by a quasi-therapeutic concern with those already in difficulty, or should intervene, uninvited, in the lives of those judged to be at risk of future difficulty, or should intervene in a wider social context of prevention. For example, if no services existed for elderly handicapped people, what sort of services should be devised, and how and by whom should the decisions be taken? Should the services be concerned exclusively with the provision of domiciliary and institutional care; or should an effort also be made to identify those who may in the future become handicapped; should wider provisions be made to develop comprehensive 'good neighbour' schemes to offset risks of future loneliness or physical neglect; should public attitudes to the needs of the elderly be subjected to re-education? A simple case of this kind illustrates the complexity of shaping a new service. Whatever decisions are reached, one would need to retain sufficient flexibility to change the priorities and scope of intervention in the light of change in the nature of the problem and in reciprocal response to any later development of other relevant services and resources. Whatever decisions are reached, these would inevitably imply that certain beneficiaries or potential beneficiaries should be given priority over others, however extensive the available resources. These issues may be difficult to resolve in political debate, and may therefore be left for resolution to the administrators and professionals employed in the service; these in turn will devise rules governing entitlement and access to the service and the allocation of resources. But once the rules are devised, it will become all the more difficult to re-open a wider public debate of the questions at issue in providing the service in the first place, and to find fresh answers to those questions. While all services would acknowledge the importance of remaining responsive to changing formulations of need, problem and social values, the inevitability of structures impedes that responsiveness.

Finally, therefore, in considering the general characteristics of the social services, note should be taken of the variety of structures through which they are made available. Within central government administration, responsibility for social services lies with the DHSS, Home Office, Department of Education and Science, Department of the Environment; at local level, services are provided by local authority social services committees, by probation and after-care committees, by structures within the National Health Service, by local offices for employment and income maintenance. At both levels, there is a wide range of voluntary organizations. In the provision of social services, therefore, society makes use of a variety of structures, all autonomous, all influenced and sustained by the traditions evolved during their formation and development. Forder (1975) has pointed out that this structural complexity leads to discontinuities both in the coherence of provisions and in the attitudes and expectations of those who use the 'welfare' services. An applicant to several services may be met by a variety of attitudes when he presents his various needs; he will be uncertain how far the information he gives will be shared; he may detect fundamental divergencies in the objectives of the services in relation to himself. 'The responsibility for co-ordinating services in the promotion of his own welfare lies very largely with the consumer.' Some voluntary organizations (for example, Councils of Voluntary Service, MIND, Age Concern) exist to a considerable extent to promote better co-ordination between services. The need for this voluntary intervention is a constant reminder of the extent of incoherence of policies and practices in the field of social welfare.

SOCIAL POLICY

In the light of this discussion, how far is it possible to speak of 'social policy' as a unitary concept? In one respect the words can be used to describe an argument or process of thinking which offers reasons for establishing and using social institutions as means of ensuring that certain aspects of social life develop in a particular direction. But it cannot be assumed that social policy implies the presence of a substantial majority agreement about the direction to be taken and the goals to be achieved. Different social groups would define different policies and goals, and social policy represents only the partial agreement between, or the overlapping of, sectional interests. Similarly, it is unwise to assume that the formulation and reformulation of social policy necessarily represents a *consistent* movement towards the achievement of long-term goals (goals, for example, like social justice, equality of opportunity or equality of living standards). Even though it is politically expedient always to present each reformulation by reference to words like 'justice', social policy may sometimes tend to re-inforce existing patterns of social and economic power while at other times it challenges these patterns; just as, in individual life, a word like 'benevolence' may be expressed behaviourally in paternalistic, restrictive or egalitarian ways. Furthermore, the institutions and procedures devised to implement social policy may in various subtle ways subvert it. To take a simple example, institutions offering long-stay care may *de facto* acquire responsibilities for the whole life-style of residents and may be regarded as exercising the functions of guardianship. Yet the procedures adopted in caring may be incompatible both with the notion of guardianship as this is usually understood in everyday life, and with the intentions of social policy to enhance the life opportunities of residents. In evaluating social policy, therefore, it is important to consider both the declared aims of policy and of the service institutions, and also the professional and administrative procedures adopted to implement those aims.

AN HISTORICAL FOOTNOTE

It has been suggested in this chapter that it is not possible to consider the work of the social services in isolation from a broad context of political, social and economic institutions and values. The recognition of this association is largely, however, a twentieth century phenomenon. Previously, works of social benevolence, as distinct from the operation of social control, were regarded as essentially an area for voluntary effort and individual philanthropic responsibility. Our present social services represent a somewhat uneasy marriage of control and benevolence.

The advocacy of a statutory commitment to this broader conception of social welfare found its earliest expression in health services (particularly for mothers and young children and for the blind), in education (with the development, for example, of school meals), in the introduction of social insurance, and in services to assist the unemployed (Forder, 1975). But for some years, the emphasis in statutory welfare provision was upon services capable of uniform administration, rather than on those in which provisions could be adapted to the expression of individual *differences* of need; with the exception of work in probation and in hospitals and clinics, social work services remained outside the statutory sector of provision until 1948.

Furthermore, as has been implied in the earlier comment about the variety of service structures, services were not associated with the formulation of consistent policies about public welfare as a whole. They developed piecemeal, often as a reflection of the specific interests of notable politicians. The broad social issues which lie at the heart of all welfare provisions were defined in administrative rather than political terms. Neville Chamberlain expressed a Conservative view in the 1930s when he described unemployment as 'above politics'; within the Labour Party until the Second World War, there seems to have been no general reformist policy upon which a coherent and comprehensive system of social services might be based.

When we consider the development of the personal social services, therefore, we shall need to have in mind that their work has only recently been considered in a broad context of social policy and political debate. The boundaries between administrative and political responsibilities, and the nature of accountability in the day-to-day provision of the personal services, remain uncertain.

PART I

The Personal Social Services
and the Concept of Welfare

1 Introduction

Personal social services are those concerned with needs and difficulties which inhibit the individual's maximum social functioning, his freedom to develop his personality and to achieve his aspirations through relationships with others; needs which have traditionally been dealt with by personal or family action ('The state's principal duty is to assist the family in carrying out its proper functions', Ingleby Committee 1960); needs for which we usually ascribe some individual responsibility; and needs which call for a high level of adaptability in the helping process, rather than a uniformity of provision. If one thinks of them in terms of doing justice to others, the personal services are concerned with the kind of justice which treats different people differently rather than the kind which treats people equally. Resources are tailored to individual or group differences rather than to the similarities between people. The personal social services seek a balance, therefore, between highlighting the shared needs of particular groups (for example, children deprived of a normal home life, the elderly) and emphasizing the individual needs and rights of one particular member of any group (this particular child, or this particular old person).

Personal social services are usually associated with the practice of social work. In Scotland, for example, the local authority personal social services are organized through departments of social work. But it is inappropriate to link personal service and social work too closely: some personal services, like the home help services, are highly individualized but are not staffed by social workers; while, on the other hand, social workers are increasingly concerned with levels of activity, such as working with neighbourhood groups, where the concept of individualization is of uncertain application.

The personal social services are concerned with the individualization of services, and with adjusting the use of certain resources by individuals, families or groups, according to an assessment of their differential needs. Although these services form only a small sector of the total range of social services they are the services most associated in the public mind with philanthropy and welfare. Both words need some consideration bearing in mind what has already been said about the social services in more general terms and about their dual concern with both the needs of citizens and the maintenance and development of social functioning, with both benevolence and control. Statutory personal social services may indeed represent philanthropic intervention, but it is philanthropy tempered by an awareness of the risks to society as a whole if individual and group distress and alienation go unchecked. The services are not *simply* ways of supporting people whose personal resources have broken down or have proved to be inadequate in the face of distress; they are also part of a wider programme geared to the maintenance of our present social life. They fulfil their part by emphasis on differential rights and responsibilities and on certain qualities and values in social relationships.

Similarly, the word 'welfare' in this context includes not only the attempt to offer partial compensation for physical, material or emotional handicap, but also an element of social protection. The statutory care of a child deprived of a normal home life is partly (some would argue, essentially) for his own personal benefit, but partly also to ensure if possible that he should grow up as a good (i.e. responsible, well adjusted and productive) citizen. These two functions are not, of course, necessarily incompatible; the quality of a service may be judged by the degree of compatibility it achieves. A probation officer's responsibility for an offender similarly contains these two components. Carrier & Kendall (1973) have drawn attention to the possible tension between these elements of service by questioning whose definitions of social reality are actually embodied in social welfare legislation: legislation is not formulated in direct relationship to the realities experienced by the citizens whom it is intended to help; it is rather the outcome of political, administrative and professional opinions, and from these emerge a definition of what is 'best' for those in need. This is not intended to imply an attack on the personal social services or the legislation they implement: it is hard to see how social legislation could embody the multiplicity of different 'realities' which lie within the experiences of service recipients. It is, however, significant how little research has been undertaken in this country to discover how the users of service feel about the personal relevance of the services they receive. It is, moreover, a matter for debate how far the users' definitions of a satisfactory service are of relevance to the evaluation of the service (see Part IV). In personal social services, therefore—as in the broader range of social provision—the concept of welfare has to be seen in terms of economic, political and cultural imperatives as well as of individual needs.

Nonetheless, welfare, as Titmuss has shown, must always imply a process of individualization: one cannot talk of the welfare of citizens without some regard for their own personal definitions of their welfare, and current social work practice is rooted in this idea. This inevitably calls into question whether one can have 'welfare specialists'. To some extent one can: it is possible for a social worker or other public servant to develop a specialized knowledge of available resources and relevant legislation; similarly, it may be possible for him to develop skills in communicating with others and in understanding what they are trying to express (certain handicaps, e.g. physical and emotional, make the self-expression of needs and feelings difficult). Yet it is doubtful whether citizens welcome specialists who tell them how they *ought* to live their lives, how they *ought* to behave towards their families, how they *ought* to behave at work, how much they *ought* to save from their incomes. Moreover, however skilled one may be in communicating with another, one can never wholly (if at all) know the reality of his life as he perceives it. A professional commitment to the welfare of others is thus a complex business: it involves the social service employee both in the development of specialist skills and knowledge, and also in the recognition of his need to learn, at best inadequately, from those he seeks to help what 'welfare' means to them, and how in *their* view they can make the best of their lives in the face of their current difficulties and disabilities.

2 The Growth of the Personal Social Services

The growth of private charities during the last century demonstrated not only a commitment to philanthropy but also that the money was available to promote individual welfare. By 1861 in London alone, there were 640 private charities of which 144 had been founded within the previous 10 years. With their total aggregate income of £2½ m a year, they exceeded by about £1 m the annual budget of the metropolitan Poor Law. The operations of the Poor Law were geared to the philosophy of a free economic market—those citizens who sought help from the Poor Law were treated (both in amount and quality) at a lower level than obtained for the lowest paid worker, irrespective of the circumstances giving rise to their needs. Private charity, on the other hand, removed some processes of help from the natural operation of the free market (see Seed, 1973) and removed them also from statutory responsibility.

In contrast to this situation, Titmuss (1950) wrote that 'By the end of the Second World War the Government had . . . assumed and developed a measure of direct concern with the health and well-being of the population which, by contrast with the role of Government in the nineteen-thirties, was very little short of remarkable. No longer did concern rest on the belief that . . . it was proper to intervene only to assist the poor and those who were unable to pay for services . . . Instead, it was increasingly regarded as a proper function or even obligation of Government to ward off distress and strain among . . . almost all classes of society.'

It is not appropriate here to trace the stages by which this transformation occurred. Reference should be made to Marshall (1965), Bruce (1961) and Seed (1973). But this change is associated with certain ideas which are fundamental to an understanding of the personal social services and of their current achievements and dilemmas: first, the philanthropic element in the personal services and in social work has its roots in voluntary effort rather than in statutory policy. The implications for this will be discussed in later chapters on the nature of social work and its professionalization. Second, change is associated with the complex social movements which we sum up in the phrase 'Welfare State'. Third, it is associated with the emergence of some consistency in statutory social policies, replacing the *ad hoc* provisions associated with private charities and with reform movements.

3 The Welfare State

This concept is directly associated with the assumption by Government of responsibility to protect minimum standards for *all* citizens in respect of income, nutrition, health, housing and education. Out of this universality of concern inevitably grows a demand for higher standards and improved quality of service. Services which are designed for a minority group of poor and powerless citizens are likely to be run 'on the cheap' and to be stigmatizing in influence: but those available to all citizens become democratically accountable for the quality of their provisions and for the quality of their staffs. Moreover, they tend towards social egalitarianism. Titmuss (1950) quotes a *Times* leading article (1 July 1940) which illustrates this movement: "If we speak of democracy, we do not mean a democracy which maintains the right to vote but forgets the right to work and the right to live. If we speak of freedom, we do not mean a rigid individualism which excludes social organisation and economic planning. If we speak of equality, we do not mean a political equality nullified by social and economic privilege."

The personal social services have been part of this movement towards higher standards, wider availability, more democratic accountability and more egalitarianism. The scope of their operation has increased as the extent and multiplicity of unmet needs have been detected; higher standards have called for more and better trained staff; more egalitarianism has meant the need for more time to be spent in sharing decisions with their users, in preference to the application of ready-made solutions and the wholesale distribution of 'good advice'. Developments of this kind, however, tend to emphasize two problems. First, that the Welfare State is not an end-product which has been or can be finally achieved: as late as the 1950s some social workers saw their work as residual, assuming that if they worked effectively a time would arrive when they would no longer be needed. On the contrary, it now seems apparent that the more sensitively they detect unmet needs the more needs are presented to them; the higher the acceptable standard of living, the greater the likelihood that more people rather than fewer will seek help; the more accessible the services become (both geographically and emotionally), the more they will be used. There is, therefore, a problem of morale within the social services: recent expansions in the size of services and in the numbers of social workers have boosted morale, but this is offset by the apparently never-ending nature of the work ahead, and at the present time by economic constraints on further expansion. For both reasons, the personal services and their employees sometimes feel they have bitten off more than they can chew. Furthermore, the greater the size of the organization needed to cope with increasing work responsibilities, the more difficult it becomes to keep it responsive to demands for greater public accountability, for more democratic involvement and for greater adaptability to individual needs. From the standpoint of the personal social services, therefore, the Welfare State is, at best, an ideal which guides their development but is essentially unachievable. In particular there are five dilemmas which obstruct the achievement or near-achievement of an ideal social situation:

(1) the problem of defining 'need' and of putting boundaries round the definition;

(2) the problem of defining a 'social problem' and of establishing which problems fall within the scope of the personal services and which should, more appropriately, be dealt with by other kinds of social action;

(3) the problem of defining the beneficiaries: whose needs are being served, and to what ends;

(4) the problem of establishing priorities for action when needs are apparently unlimited and cannot by their nature be compared (consider, for example, the need for a pre-school play group compared with the need for additional home help staff for the elderly, if there is insufficient money to provide both); and linked to this;

(5) the problem of judging the effectiveness of service.

These problems will be briefly considered in turn.

4 Problems of Definition

NEED

The use of the concept of 'need' as a basis for the delivery of social services always implies a complex of pre-existing values. To describe oneself as being in need is to imply that one's life in certain respects is worse than it ought to be. But two people in similar circumstances may differ in whether they apply the concept to themselves, or in the extent to which their experience of need leads them to express it and to expect help with it. Personal judgments about both the presence and the severity of need will depend on the reference groups with whose values one identifies—that is to say, on the values held by the social group to which one belongs, to which one aspires, or with which one wishes to be associated in the eyes of other people. One may relate to a variety of reference groups for different aspects of one's life-situation and as the means of defining one's own social class, one's social status or one's perceptions of one's actual or desired power (Runciman, 1966, 1972). The onlooker also tends to relate his use of 'need' to his own personal standards of social satisfaction and deprivation. Here again, the onlooker's personal view may be tempered by the views held, as a consensus, by his professional group or by the organization by which he is employed.

In the personal social services, needs achieve recognition through administrative, political and professional processes; policies for meeting needs are not therefore necessarily related to the direct experience of suffering. In political and administrative terms, needs may often be defined as serious or less serious according to the actual or potential availability of the resources to meet them. If, for example, one considers total social expenditure as a percentage of public expenditure during the period 1938–1970, one finds that this has risen from 11.3 to 23.7 (Borland, 1974). Clearly, this does not reflect the presence of greater personal suffering so much as the political viability of change in the allocation of public resources to permit more needs to be met. Political change may be attributed to an increased public awareness of unmet needs, to the influence of pressure groups, and to changes in the policies of political parties.

The word 'need', therefore, may relate to a variety of values and experiences: it may be the experience of suffering, the demand of the individual for attention to his circumstances; its perceived intensity may be related to community values of various kinds, to the professional opinion of the expert, to the administrator's allocation of resources, to the influence of a power-group within society, and to political viability.

Field workers in the personal social services tend to define and evaluate needs from an essentially individualistic stance, either identifying with the consumer's formulation of need or with their own professional expertise, both of which may be at variance with the policy formulations of the service. In ideal practice, a social service worker should be concerned with the reference values of his client, his agency and himself in defining the presence of unmet need, with the extent of their mutual compatibility, and with the personal and social values embodied in the various alternative means available to him for meeting needs. But this is a counsel of perfection. In reality, the user of a service has no guarantee that he will receive help in a form which is congruent with his own perceptions of need.

In short, therefore, the word 'need' involves an interrelationship of facts and values so complex as to limit its utility as a universal criterion for the planning, organizing and delivery of services.

A SOCIAL PROBLEM

Those 'social problems' dealt with by the personal social services have characteristics related both to the individual and to society at large. Delinquency represents an affront to society but is also (at least to the extent that he is caught) a problem for the individual. If an elderly neighbour suffers from hypothermia this is an affront to ideals of social justice and welfare as well as a problem to the neighbour himself. The social situations of individual citizens, however severe and unjust, are designated as social problems only if both conditions are seen to apply. The personal social services attempt to deal with social problems in this sense; yet here again the concept of the 'social problem' is of limited value in trying to establish the parameters of their work. To begin with, the 'social affront' characteristic of a social problem comes into existence only when public opinion is alerted to it in some way; yet most (perhaps all) social workers would wish to intervene in certain conditions of individual distress, irrespective of a wider social awareness of and concern for these conditions. Take, for example, the situation of women who are severely ill-treated by their husbands; this would not at the present time fulfil the conditions of a social problem, and would be approached by the social worker using the criterion of need rather than problem as justification for his intervention. In time, public awareness of this kind of distress may be enlarged to the point where it is designated as a social problem and the social worker's basis for intervention will then subtly change. One may see this occurring at present in the case of the physical abuse of children by their parents. This phenomenon helps to account for the apparent increase in social problems: social life may not have worsened, but many of the adverse conditions experienced by citizens have been sufficiently measured and advertised to give them the status of problems.

Again, some social conditions are redesignated as problems when, through measurement and advertisement, a feeling is generated among the public that society is seriously unprotected against a threat to its stability or values. This may take various forms: for example maternity and child welfare provisions advanced considerably in the first decade of this century, less because infant health had suddenly declined than because of public concern about the physical unfitness of volunteers in the Boer War and the implicit threat to national security. The rapid growth of the probation and after-care service in recent years has had less to do with increased public sympathy with the needs of offenders (though social policies have sometimes implied this) than with increasing public awareness and concern about the statistical increase in criminal behaviour. By a reverse process, the perceived social threat of male homosexual behaviour in the 1950s, which led to the spurious protection afforded by rigorous prosecutions and harsh sentences, has now abated; adult male homosexuality, if a problem at all, is now defined as an individual rather than a social problem. The actual nature and extent of human needs associated with these social conditions do not change in the way that problem-designation and de-designation might seem to suggest.

It is, therefore, a fundamental issue for the personal social services how far the form and quality of their intervention should be adapted in accordance with the contemporary definition of social problems. Should the social worker act as 'society's conscience' and adapt the focus and manner of his work in accordance with whatever happens to be regarded publicly as a problem at any particular time? Should he instead look for the relative importance of problems in the expressed views and experiences of those who seek his help? Should he formulate his own standpoint on which social conditions matter and how much they matter irrespective of pressures from public opinion? If the last, then his intervention will be based on some kind of professional identity which may promote priorities of intervention incongruent with current social demands and possibly with the policies of his employers. For example, it is doubtful whether most activities of probation officers are directly related to the goal of reducing crime.

A further dilemma exists in defining the appropriate responsiveness of the personal social services to social problems. It has been suggested that a social problem has both individual and social characteristics; the alleviation of problems has traditionally been seen as involving change in the individual user of services rather than in society. In the last century this was true of problems like poverty and unemployment, which we now regard as more properly dealt with by social and economic planning than by a one-by-one moral shift in the attitudes of the poor. At the present time, delinquency, vandalism, sexual promiscuity and to some extent homelessness are usually seen as representing a failure of individual moral responsibility. If a child steals, public opinion will usually find someone or something to blame other than the child; but if he steals as an adult, blame will usually be focussed upon himself. Yet it is at least arguable that social and economic factors may be major contributors to these problems. If so, then the individual caring approach of the personal social services may be at best insufficient and at worst irrelevant. One of the problems for the personal social services at the present time is therefore that of assessing the nature and aetiology of problematic social conditions, to determine how far the traditional personal service approach is appropriate, and to recognize those situations where—with the best will in the world—they may be papering over the cracks of a social problem (and perhaps colluding with the moral stigmatization of an individual) rather than drawing attention to its true nature.

BENEFICIARIES

This has already been touched upon in the broad context of social services, and mention has been made of extensions since the last war in the potential range of beneficiaries, in terms both of expressed need and social class, within the operation of the personal social services. The advantages of being a beneficiary, however, have to be seen in the context of the ways in which social problems are defined. I have suggested that sometimes an inappropriate degree of social responsibility is placed upon the individual recipient of service; it may be argued that one of the costs of being a beneficiary of service is that one accepts high *personal* responsibility for one's way of life. The probation and after-care service provides an example of the uncertainty of beneficiary: its statutory operation (that is to say, omitting the people who seek help informally) is concerned with those whose personal behaviour is seen to be in need of change. As probation orders require the consent of the offender, he is required to consent to an unpredictable process of personal change, irrespective of his own views about the nature of his needs and problems. The task of the probation officer in respect of his clients is to achieve some measure of congruence between individual needs (however these are to be defined) and more general social requirements of good behaviour as identified by the courts and by his own service. This is often not so difficult as it sounds, but it makes the definition of beneficiary a complex one.

While probation is a welfare service imposed by law, some other personal services wait to be approached. Child Guidance Clinics, for example, customarily rely on self-referral (supported usually by the advice of schools);

with the shortage of available staff, however, some parents who wish for help cannot be offered the extent of service they seek, while others may be virtually compelled (by the attitude of a head-teacher) to seek help irrespective of their wish for it. In the latter situation, it might be argued that the head-teacher is the primary beneficiary.

In respect of some services (for example, school clothing grants), beneficiaries may be defined by a means test, and in others (for example, entry into an old people's home) by their position on a waiting list.

In short, therefore, the personal social services define and select their beneficiaries by reference to a range of concepts of right, entitlement, demand, need and responsibility which may not be mutually compatible nor compatible with the user's perception of the intensity of his need or with public perceptions of the seriousness of particular social problems. In recent years, some social workers have attempted to resolve the philosophical untidiness of defining the beneficiaries of services by a total commitment to the client's definition of his needs and to advocating the client's rights and entitlements; for them, the client is the only beneficiary that matters. This may be naive, particularly when it leads to the adoption of a 'my-client,-right-or-wrong' stance. But one can sympathize with the wish for a greater clarity of operational intention. Where one stands in this debate is related to how far one considers that social services should be purely supportive and how far they should be normative: how far associated with the preservation of freedoms and how far with the rights (as well as the obligation) of the State to intervene in individual behaviour. Most social workers adopt a compromise position in which the rights and freedoms of the client and the rights of intervention by the community are given varying weight according to the particular circumstances of the case and the worker's individual philosophy and discretion. In situations of personal violence, or of the ill-treatment of children or handicapped people, the rights of intervention by the community irrespective of the views and needs of the 'offender' are not in dispute, though the social worker would hope to have in mind the offender's needs and an obligation to meet them as far as was compatible with the protection of others. The concept of ambivalence in motivation is important in this context; it is rare to find anyone who wholeheartedly and at all times wishes to do harm to others. Acts of violence to a child may be interspersed by periods of caring in which the needs of the 'offender' and the needs of others in his environment (including the victim) are compatible; one task for the social worker is to promote the extension of this compatibility. It is often inappropriate therefore to assume that clients and society are in competition with each other as beneficiaries. Furthermore, some people seek help from the personal social services precisely because they wish to experience some kind of personal change—to sort out their ideas about what to do in a particular set of circumstances, or to resolve feelings of anxiety or depression.

There are, however, times when the issue of defining the beneficiary and the appropriate area of change is difficult to resolve. For example, where an elderly person wishes to live with his children who feel unable to cope with the responsibility: here, the decision whether to persuade the old person that he should leave or to persuade his children, against their own judgment, to look after him may depend on the availability of residential services rather than on an assessment of the clients' rights and responsibilities. In such a case, one of the clients will feel that he has been successful and the other unsuccessful in the decision that is finally made; but if the decision is based primarily on the availability of a place in an old people's home, then neither client can truly be regarded as the primary beneficiary of service. Social workers sometimes find that their work is used to substitute for the lack of another kind of social resource: in such a case, it may not be appropriate to equate 'client' and 'beneficiary', even though the client may feel that he has in some measure benefited from the intervention of the social worker.

PRIORITIES AND EVALUATION

If we accept, as Parker (1967) suggests, that needs are potentially infinite while resources are always limited, then, however efficiently organized and provided, the personal social services are bound (if related to the idea of meeting needs) to appear to be inadequate. In recent years this potential inadequacy has been partially masked by a steady increase in resources (of cash and manpower). It was masked, furthermore, by the functional divisions between services which permitted some unmet needs to be ignored as lying outside the responsibilities of any service. Since 1970, both local authority and probation services have been given new responsibilities and expected to achieve higher standards of comprehensive care, with the result that complaints of inadequacy of services have increased in spite of their greater resources. It now seems certain (1976) that resources will not increase at the same rate for some years. The problem of establishing priorities of statutory intervention is therefore an urgent one if service morale is not to decline.

The process of rationing has been helpfully studied by Parker (1967) and Hall (1975). Both have emphasized the importance of devising systems of rationing which are explicit, based on agreed principles and understood by the general public, in preference to a manipulation of the scope of service by the presentation of deterrent attitudes, by selectivity of clients based on the personal preferences of social workers, by inaccessibility, by the incomprehension of the general public, or by the dilution of standards of work.

Rationing of statutory help by the establishing of priorities of intervention need not however mean that certain people in need will receive no help of any kind. It implies, rather, that alternatives to *statutory* service may be necessary and possibly that some techniques of helping may need to be adapted. Greater emphasis may be required on alternative forms of community care (for example, by domiciliary rather than residential provision), on the use of volunteers and voluntary groups, and on techniques of group-help in preference to individual assistance. If alternative systems of help are to be encouraged, however, the problem remains of establishing the appropriate scope of intervention by the statutory services; which work should they retain and which should be delegated to other individuals or groups? And in what way should they adapt their services, bearing in mind that they are labour-intensive and therefore expensive in manpower terms?

Questions of this kind are partly administrative and partly political. On the one hand, there is the administrative problem associated with an increase in work, partly through new legislation and partly through a real increase in the expression of needs—an increase estimated to be running at the rate of 25–30% a year in some areas. On the other hand, there is the political issue surrounding the extent to which statutory services should be obliged to intervene in response to the expression of needs. Three operational concepts have been developed in recent years which in different ways attempt to meet these dilemmas, by offering alternatives to the need for indefinite expansion in the statutory sector of service while at the same time emphasizing the rights and responsibilities of citizens in the face of a welfare system dominated by large-scale statutory powers and organizations. These are community care; preventive work; citizen participation in policy formulation and the provision of services. These operational concepts will be considered in later chapters in the context of the provisions of services and their administration.

Clearly, one of the difficulties involved in establishing priorities of statutory intervention and how best to intervene is the present uncertainty surrounding the effectiveness of different kinds of help—and, indeed, by what criteria effectiveness can be assessed. Criteria of effectiveness may vary according to one's assessment of the accountability and responsibility of services: for example, the use of foster-care for homeless or deprived children in preference to institutional care may be judged by its effect on children's present feelings, by its influence on their future behaviour, or by the relative costs of the two kinds of service. Similarly, in caring for the elderly or handicapped, the choice between domiciliary services (such as 'home help'), day care centres, sheltered workshops and social work services may be related to measures of relative effectiveness judged by the satisfactions of the service-users, the extent to which the services enable the user to make a reciprocal contribution to the welfare of others in the community, or by economic considerations related to the containment of the problems of age and handicap. The choice of services is therefore in part related to the values one wishes to express in action, particularly as we lack reliable measures of effectiveness in behavioural terms. An additional complication is that, in some circumstances, the more effective a service is in reducing the level of felt need in one particular user, the more it is likely to be sought for by other users. The demand for services tends to expand if they achieve a good reputation. Similarly, a satisfied user who feels comfortable in his association with a service may express unmet needs which, if he were dissatisfied, he would keep to himself. Effectiveness may therefore, in different circumstances, be measured both by reductions and by increases in demand.

Within the day-to-day operation of a particular service-provision, however (for example, in considering the different ways in which a 'home help' can undertake her tasks or a social worker may select his techniques of intervention) certain evidence is now becoming more readily available to serve as criteria for effectiveness in the use of manpower. As this evidence is directly linked to methods of social work practice, it will be considered in a later chapter.

5 Social Policy and the Personal Social Services

Hitherto in this section we have been looking at some of the dilemmas which arise for the personal social services from the uncertain definition of key words related to the promotion of welfare. It was said earlier that one of the reasons why the personal social services have expanded rapidly since the Second World War is the emergence of a relatively consistent social policy in place of *ad hoc* measures to solve specific social problems. One can say no more than 'relatively consistent': personal social services vary in the ways they define beneficiaries, and in the extent to which they emphasize individual rights or community benefits. Furthermore, in so far as they allow for individual discretion among members of staff, they cannot all operate in the same ways. As Titmuss (1974) has suggested, the services do not add up to a single system with a single objective, but represent a variety of systems and objectives, which are not necessarily harmonious. Nonetheless, some degree of consistency of policy exists between the services, and this is exemplified by the fact that it has been possible and acceptable to train the social work employees of services in generic courses (rather than administratively specialized ones) since 1954. Firstly, all personal services would subscribe to the view that individual welfare is central to their work—that is to say, they share a policy of attempting to promote a high degree of congruence between the aspirations and needs of the individual client, the needs of others in his environment, and the nature of the resources available to him. Secondly, they would agree that certain kinds of individual suffering are intolerable, partly on humanitarian grounds and partly in respect of values associated with the maintenance of social order and the health of the community. Thirdly, they would support the view that social legislation should emphasize welfare rather than economic utility; Bruce (1961) has suggested that the major shift in legislation between the 19th and 20th centuries can be defined in these terms. No doubt one could find other areas of general agreement among policy makers and workers in the personal social services. This is certainly the case if one discusses policy in high-level ideological terms. At a lower level of debate, as we have seen, the definition of policy objectives encounters dilemmas of choice, not only in what we wish to achieve but also in selecting the means to achieve it. One cannot, therefore, speak of social policy as representing a fixed programme based on consensus: 'To understand policy, to distinguish between ends . . . and means, we have to understand it in the context of a particular set of circumstances, a given society and culture, and a more or less specified period of historical time' (Titmuss, 1974). Social policy is concerned with changing choices between variously formulated political, administrative and professional goals and between the various possible means of achieving them. In the personal social services, however, and indeed in any other services, there are evident disadvantages if the debate about ends and means constantly leads to changes of direction. Speed (1972) has described one of the duties of a Director of Social Services as to 'choose wisely, choose well, and choose once'. Neither the public nor the employees know where they stand if—as appears to be the case with housing—policies change with governments. Thus, policies relating to the personal social services go through phases of relative stability, when change is incremental and marginal, followed by phases when major rethinking takes place, and a new temporary stability is achieved between political movements, shifting definitions of welfare and the experience gained from earlier practices. It will be the purpose of Part II to trace some of these phases in the recent development of particular services.

Policies are essentially guidelines, rather than blueprints, for action. In the personal social services they are directly concerned with affecting the quality of life (for families, individuals and groups) and with defining acceptable social relationships, by allocating resources which meet expressed needs and which influence the role, behaviour and status of an individual or a group in accordance with dominant social values. If dominant values are competitive, then policies will tend to endorse inequalities by favouring those who are best able to make socially acceptable use of the resources made available to them. Though 'deserving' and 'undeserving' are not acceptable words in social policy at the present time, it is likely that some such judgment is sometimes made in assessing the kinds of help (and the attitudes expressed in helping) made available to the users of services. If egalitarian, then policies will tend to favour the powerless, and those whom Goffman has described as 'the socially dead', the 'human junk'. Between policy and action, however, lies a range of administrative decisions and interpretations and an accumulation of traditions of practice; at any one time, therefore, within the personal social services one must expect to find some degree of disjunction between policy and practice. One of the tasks of managers, professional groups and pressure groups alike is to keep the gap as small as possible, either by adjusting practice to policy (a managerial task) or sometimes by adjusting policy to practice (principally the task of the professions). The role of the pressure groups is critically to examine the manoeuvres of both.

In this matter the role of social workers is particularly complex; it is an issue for debate whether they should take some part in the development of agency policies or should uncritically implement the policies as defined elsewhere.

When we come to consider in the next section the provisions of the personal social services, particularly those of the local authority social services departments, we shall discover that social policy has been embodied within a massive piecemeal accumulation of legislation. This legislation has been concerned with specific client-groups without regard for the comparative needs of other groups; it has invested varying degrees of power in the services and in the roles of employees; it has made it difficult for services to regulate their provisions equitably and to earmark their resources on the basis of a coherent vision of local welfare. Furthermore, legislative concern for specific client-groups has until recently focussed attention on the needs of certain kinds of individuals rather than on the support of the family as a unit of concern and intervention; concern for the promotion of the welfare of whole local communities has been entirely lacking from personal social service legislation except in Scotland, even though it is now widely recognized that much individual need, suffering and maladjustment may be traced, partly at least, to community values and patterns of living.

The role of social workers and other employees in the personal social services is, therefore, complex and unsatisfactory at the present time; according to the legislative basis of work, the role may, with different clients, be therapeutic, custodial, controlling, protecting, supporting; it may involve the channelling of material resource at one moment and attempting to prevent emotional disorder at the next. There is at present not only the lack of adequate definition of these functions individually, but also the lack of a conceptual framework which would unite them within a single role. Each duty and function, moreover, while good in itself, may imply work which in certain cases loses sight of those causes of need and distress which lie outside the dynamics of individual and family life, and loses sight also of the common experiences of local living shared by people in legislatively different client-groups.

The appointment by social services of generalist social workers (who would deal with all client-groups rather than exclusively with particular groups) provides one possible base upon which one might begin to define a unitary approach to welfare provisions and a unitary role for the social worker. But any such attempts tend to be offset by the profusion of legislative responsibilities, and to be limited by legislation to a restricted client-service model of intervention.

PART II

The Provisions of the Personal Social Services

1 Introduction

Personal social services are those 'outside health and education which are adjusted to the particular needs of individuals, families or groups and which require personal contact between provider and recipient' (Parker 1967).

This definition emphasizes two characteristics of major importance when one considers the provisions of the services and the methods employed in their operation.

(1) *The adjustment of services to differences between people's needs* A service which embodies the intention of individual adaptability will tend to become increasingly flexible as the needs of recipients are more accurately understood. Although duties are laid down in legislation and in administrative directives, the tasks undertaken by workers directly engaged in the provision of services are likely to become wider and of greater variety than their statutory duties demand because of their recognition of the complexity of their clients' needs. Similarly, by the same process of work-extension, it becomes difficult to say with precision what the functions of the service are at any particular time, for to some extent these functions are reformulated in response to the needs presented by the different users of the service. In the personal social services, therefore, the 'front-line' worker is more than merely the implementer of policy and legislation: he assumes personal responsibility for the form in which the service is delivered; he exercises discretion in choosing between different qualities of service, and in deciding how best to use his time and his authority; and he becomes responsible to his client and to the employing agency for his acquisition and development of those skills necessary to make the services directly relevant to the needs of the client—for example, skills in communication, in marshalling various kinds of resources and in channelling them in ways which are appropriate to the client's needs.

(2) *The giving of service is associated with personal contact* This intensifies the tendency noted above; 'front-line' workers see far more of the users of services than do the policy-makers, and adaptations to the services

offered are made within this personal contact. It is likely, therefore, that identification takes place between worker and client in which the needs of the client sometimes assume primacy over the legislated duty or the intentions of the policy-maker.

These factors need to be taken into account when considering the growth of professionalism among social workers. In this country it is rare for social workers to practise outside the personal social services; the services are therefore the base for social work and the context within which professionalization has taken place. In the probation service, the whole service is now constructed on the values and techniques of professional social work, though this was not always so and it would be rash to assume that it need always remain so. Within the local authority social services departments, social workers form a key professional group, but the service is not exclusively a social work service, and professional social workers constitute only part of the total work-force. The relationship between social work and the personal social services is, therefore, a complex one.

Social work is not the rationale for the existence of the personal social services; personal services could exist without social workers. But what has emerged in recent years is a growing compatibility between the objectives of the services and the values and techniques of social work. It has been in the interests of the services to employ increasing numbers of social workers and in the interests of social workers to pursue that form of employment. The result is that it is now all too easy to assume that services and social work are identical, that a good social worker can be identified by his acceptability as an employee and that what is good for the services is good for social work. A later section will be concerned with social work and with social workers as a professional group. For the purposes of the present chapter the words 'social work' will be used as a way of referring to a particular range of skills, techniques and values, used by certain employees in the personal social services, which relate to, but are not wholly contained within, the formal definition of the duties of the agencies. 'Social work' offers a frame of reference for clarifying certain of the responsibilities of the employee, a frame of reference which is usually complementary to official statements of his duty.

Not all personal service workers would describe themselves as social workers. Some identify themselves primarily by reference to their administrative responsibilities rather than to the operational methods which they share with colleagues in other services. Probation and After-care Officers in England and Wales (but not in Scotland) use the title not only to describe their administrative duties and allegiances but also to define themselves as a professional group. The National Association of Probation Officers retained its identity rather than merge with the other professional social work associations at the formation of the British Association of Social Workers in 1968. Somewhat similarly, there are employees in other social services who use techniques of work which in many respects are identical with those of social work, but who would not at present regard themselves as social workers: for example, Education Welfare Officers and Youth Employment Officers in the Education Departments, Disablement Resettlement Officers in the Department of Employment.

Social work is, then, closely related to the provision of personal social services. Social workers offer advice, legal protection and care as prescribed within the legislative duties of services; they help people to participate more fully in the life of their local communities. But at the same time they define their responsibilities more widely than their duties sometimes require, particularly in helping people through the formation of close, supportive and therapeutic relationships. In this respect, therefore, social work may extend beyond agency function. But the personal social services also offer kinds of help which require skills other than those of the social worker: for example, help through sheltered employment, help with housework, the provision of accommodation and meals. These other services are in no way secondary to social work practice; nor are the skills they require of a lower order than the skills of social work. It is unfortunate that, because of the status of social work, non-social work employees are sometimes regarded as performing a secondary role in the work of the services. The development of training for home help organizers, day care centre staff, and residential care assistants may in time change this situation and help to clarify the place of social work as only one component in the work of the personal social services. Hitherto, however, the development of services has been closely linked with the employment of social workers, and the social work component of services will inevitably be uppermost in the following brief review of provisions.

2 The Main Local Authority Personal Social Services

CHILD CARE

Up to the Second Word War services for children in need of care or protection developed piecemeal and in association with the recognition of specific areas of difficulty rather than in response to the formulation of a comprehensive policy about the needs of children. Legislation and services have traditionally focussed on four areas of concern:

(*a*) the care of orphaned children or those permanently deprived of normal home life;

(*b*) linked with this, the adoption of children;

(*c*) children in need of temporary care and the development of foster-care;

(*d*) children subject to cruelty, danger or neglect within the home;

(*e*) children who have committed criminal offences.

For children permanently deprived of home life and whose parents were unable to make provision, responsibility rested initially with the Boards of Guardians for the administration of the Poor Law and from 1929 with the Public Assistance Committees of Local Authorities. Parents who had neglected their children could be prosecuted by the Boards of Guardians by an Act of 1868 and this protection was extended to children still living at home by the formation of the NSPCC in the 1880s and by the Prevention of Cruelty and Protection of Children Act 1889 which gave statutory powers to the Society for the prosecution of parents guilty of cruelty or exploitation.

Nineteenth century alternatives to Poor Law care lay in the voluntary sector, notably in the work of the Waifs and Strays Society (subsequently the Church of England Children's Society), the National Children's Homes of the Methodist Church, and Dr Barnardo's. But in addition parents might make private paid arrangements for adoption or fostering. Protection for these children became available through the Infant Life Protection Act 1872 and was developed further through legislation in 1896, 1908 and 1933.

The Boards of Guardians also made some use of fostering arrangements. This facility, though given impetus by the Public Assistance Order in 1930, was little used, and most children in statutory care remained in large institutions. Formal procedures for legal adoption became available by the Adoption Act 1926. Other legislation was developed piecemeal to protect children from seduction, frequenting brothels, begging, the purchase of alcohol and cigarettes, unprotected fires and inappropriate hours of employment.

In respect of delinquent children, juvenile courts were established in 1908 and their work extended to offer protection to non-delinquent children by the Children and Young Persons Act 1933.

It will be apparent from this brief statement that some form of co-ordination of responsibility for the care of children, and indeed some focus for developing a unified child care policy, was essential. Child care until 1948 fell within the responsibilities of Public Assistance Committees, Local Authority Health Committees and the Local Education Authority. Following some public disquiet about the public care of children during the war and the establishment of a Department (Curtis) Committee of the Home Office in 1945 (Cmnd 6922 HMSO 1946), the Children Act 1948 was passed to unify responsibility for the care and protection of all children.

Children Act 1948 This Act required each local authority to appoint a Children's Officer and adequate staff to assist him in the exercise of his functions. The functions of the new Children's Departments were, in brief:

(*a*) to receive into care any orphaned or abandoned child or any child whose parents were for any reason unable to provide adequately for him, and where deemed appropriate by a court to assume parental rights up to the 18th birthday;

(*b*) to care for the child in accordance with his individual needs and best interests; emphasis was placed on foster care rather than institutional accommodation, and reception centres were established to permit the assessment of individual needs;

(*c*) to provide after-care up to the age of 21 for young people who had been in the care of the local authority;

(*d*) to assume duties under existing legislation concerned with child protection, adoption, the care of children before the courts and their subsequent disposal.

Subsequent developments in child care are as follows.

The protection of children in their own homes The Act of 1948 made a major contribution to the public care of children following the onset of difficulty or breakdown in family life, but offered little in legislative terms to prevent family disruption. A circular published jointly by the Home Office and Ministries of Education and Health in 1950 promoted the establishment of local co-ordinating committees to which representatives of services could refer families thought to be in difficulties, and at which an agreed policy of preventive work could be formulated. In some local authorities, this work was grafted on to existing joint committees, chaired by the medical officer of health, concerned with the management of children's homes and the boarding out of children in the care of the authority. Some children's departments appointed social workers specifically to assist families with multiple problems in an attempt to prevent the need to receive children into care. But difficulties arose in both of these developments: in the activities of the co-ordinating committees the needs of families were sometimes secondary to the administrative convenience of the participating services—they offered an opportunity to off-load responsibility rather than to share it; and the preventive intervention of specially designated social workers inevitably took second place in the bid for resources against the urgent crisis work of their colleagues engaged in implementing statutory responsibilities.

The extension of legislation to cover preventive work was achieved by the Children and Young Persons Act 1963, which empowered local authorities to offer advice and assistance (including financial help) to families in which children were thought to be at some risk of deprivation. In particular, by Section 1 of this Act [Section 12 of the Social Work (Scotland) Act], grants and loans can be made to prevent undue hardship arising from financial mismanagement, unexpected financial difficulties, and the non-payment of rent or other bills. Studies of this power of financial assistance have been made by Heywood & Allen (1971) and Jackson (1974). While there can be no doubt that financial help at a point of crisis has been of considerable help to many families and, no doubt, to many social workers who had hitherto felt unable to offer wholly relevant assistance to some of their clients, this power carries with it certain dilemmas both in administration and in policy. For example, no local authority can divert to this purpose all the money that might be appropriately expended in the views of some staff, especially at a time when prices are rising and the incidence of unemployment is increasing; the more money made available for this purpose, the less remains for other kinds of work. Jackson (1974) has shown that the net expenditure under Section 1 payments has increased from £66,000 in 1965/66 to £2,426,000 in 1973/74. Local authorities usually allocate a fixed sum annually to this purpose, within which difficult decisions have to be made concerning the relative priorities of needs between different applicants for help. The tendency seems to be to relate payments to a family's perceived suitability for longer-term casework help; but this is an arbitrary criterion based on a very uncertain quality of assessment. Furthermore, unlike the provision of social security payments, there is no clear procedure for a family to appeal against the local authority's decision; and the unlimited discretion of local authorities in respect of these payments has led to inequitable variations in practice in different geographical areas. It may be argued also that the availability of this power offers an encouragement to other services to refer families inappropriately: some social workers are of the opinion that Section 1 payments are used in cases where an emergency Supplementary

Benefit payment would be more appropriate, and that (although this is not supported by statements of policy) emergency help from social security offices is less easily obtained than in the past, particularly at weekends. Similarly, where social services departments have helped families with rent arrears payable for local authority housing, this represents in effect a transfer of resources from one local authority department to another which is, arguably, inappropriate.

The development of preventive work in respect of the care of children has, therefore, led to an increasing involvement in the needs of families as a whole and to an extension of the kinds of resources used by local authorities. The process has drawn attention to the relationships between services, and to the extent to which different services employ different criteria of intervention and different attitudes to those in need. It raises in a stark way the question whether or not local authorities should be engaged in making discretionary financial payments, for what purposes and with what safeguards.

Adoption procedures have been modified by Acts of 1958, 1960, 1964 and by the Children Act 1975. By the Act of 1958, which consolidated earlier legislation, certain clear principles were formulated: adoption was possible for unmarried children between the ages of 6 weeks and 18 years; adoption orders could be made by juvenile courts, county courts and higher courts, guided by the enquiries and reports of a *guardian ad litem* (usually a local authority social worker or a probation officer); and adoptors must be the child's parents (as, for example, when the mother marries after the child's birth), relatives over the age of 21, or unrelated married couples where the husband is at least 25 years of age and the wife at least 21.

By the 1975 Act, local authorities were required to establish adoption agencies integrated with the work of the social services departments. The period of probationary care (under the supervision of the *guardian ad litem*) was increased from 3 to 12 months. And, by Sections 33 to 46, an alternative to adoption was established, namely 'custodianship', whereby custodians might be given powers over the person of the child without the assumption of full parenthood; this power is intended to safeguard the interests of children living with long-term foster parents who might otherwise be arbitrarily re-claimed by their natural parents.

The 1975 Act emphasizes that the welfare of the child is the paramount consideration. This has two effects in respect of the status of the natural parents and that of long-term foster parents. First, the consent of the natural parents to their child's adoption can be set aside when the child is abandoned or persistently ill-treated or where, in the view of a court, their consent is unreasonably withheld. (The father of an illegitimate child must be informed of his child's adoption, but his consent is no longer required unless he has previously applied for the child's custody under the Guardianship of Minors Act, 1971.) The Act introduces also the concept of 'freeing for adoption'; that is to say, the natural parents may formally release their child for adoption to an adoption agency, and all parental rights then rest with the agency. The further intention of the 1975 Act is to safeguard the child's rights by ensuring his adequate representation when the court reaches a decision.

Secondly, the Act (particularly in respect of the provision for custodianship) re-emphasizes the importance of foster-care and the status of foster parents. In terms of policy, this appears to represent a return to the intentions of the report of the Curtis Committee and to the professional ideology of the early Children's Departments after 1948, when it was held that substitute home-life was virtually always preferable to institutional care—a belief that has been modified recently, but is now, in legislative terms, to some extent re-affirmed. Freeman (1976) has pointed out that one of the effects of custodianship orders may be to emphasize a form of foster-care which wholly excludes the influence of the natural parents on the child's life and upbringing. This raises an important issue in social policy in respect of the care of the children, namely how far their parents should be involved in their care following placement with foster parents. Emphasis on the child's rights and the rights of foster parents, and the accompanying reduction in parental rights, may be morally sound; but Freeman cites evidence to suggest that emotional harm for the children may sometimes arise from the exclusion of natural parents from the care given by foster parents. Furthermore, natural parents may fear the loss of their rights and become reluctant to apply for their children's admission to care when this would be in the children's best interests.

No doubt these are issues which will become clearer over time. There seems little doubt at this stage that the Act of 1975 will improve the quality of adoption services and will offer greater safeguards than have existed hitherto for the welfare of the child considered for adoption or placed in long-term foster care (see additional notes in Chapter 8).

The protection of children placed privately with foster parents has been extended by the Children Act 1958 and the Children and Young Persons Act 1969 by which people acting as foster parents for more than 6 days to children not personally related to them are subject to inspection by the local authority.

The day care of children below school age is available through day nurseries and nursery schools (National Health Service Act 1946, Section 22). This facility was developed during the war to enable mothers to go out to work. Since then, there have been mixed views about encouraging the employment of mothers of young children, and priority is therefore given by local authorities to the children of single parents and parents whose health or living conditions are seriously adverse. At the same time, there has been an increase in privately provided day care, and people offering these facilities are subject to inspection and registration by the Nurseries and Child Minders Regulations Act 1948 and by amendments in the Health Services and Public Health Act 1968 (Section 60).

The Local Authority, Police and NSPCC have power to remove children and young persons from their homes up to the age of 17 and to bring them before Courts for *Care Proceedings* (Children and Young Persons Acts 1933 and 1969). The problem involved in this process is one of balancing the rights of both parents and child with the opinions of the authorities concerning the child's best welfare.* The court must be satisfied (1969), first, that the child or young person is in need of care or control which he is unlikely to receive unless an order is made, and, second, that one of the following conditions apply in his case:

(1) that his present upbringing is preventing his proper development;
(2) that he lives in a household where another child has suffered neglect;
(3) that he is in moral danger or beyond control;
(4) that he is not receiving adequate full-time education;
(5) that he has committed an offence.

By this last condition, juvenile offenders may now be dealt with by the juvenile courts in the same way as non-offenders. The 1969 Act is of particular importance in seeking to blur the distinction hitherto drawn between offenders and other children, thus Remand Homes and Approved Schools have ceased to have separate identities and have become part of a general and comprehensive system of Community Homes, organized on a regional basis and managed by local authorities and voluntary organizations in co-operation.

A child or young person brought before the Juvenile Court may be made the subject of *either* a Supervision Order (to which, since 1973, an order for Intermediate Treatment may be added, i.e. the provision of recreational or training activities devised by specially constituted Regional Planning Committees) *or* a Care Order which transfers the legal custody of the child to the local authority.

Care and supervision orders may be made also in situations *where the parents have legally separated or divorced* under the Matrimonial Proceedings (Magistrates Courts) Act 1960 and the Matrimonial Causes Act 1965 respectively.

Local authority's 'parental rights' under a care order extend until the young person's 18th birthday (19th in some instances), but these may be revoked by a Court on the application of a parent, the young person or the local authority. Parental contributions towards the maintenance of children subject to care orders are obligatory.

Part I of the Children and Young Persons Act 1969 emphasizes, however, the importance of keeping children out of the Courts as far as possible. At present only about 25% of all children cared for by the local authorities are subject to care orders. Packman (1968) has shown, however,

* By the Children Act, 1975, primary consideration will in future be given to the welfare of the child. (See additional notes in Chapter 8.)

the difficulties of defining both the best welfare of the child and how best to meet his needs. Difficulties are especially apparent in two respects within current provisions: first, the relative emphasis to be placed on the rights of natural parents and on the protection of the child; and second, knowing when and how to intervene to prevent the need for a child to be taken into care. The number of children now in the care of local authorities has risen steadily since 1948 and at March 1974 stood at 95,867. In the year 1973–74, 52,680 children were received into care, 13,794 because of the short-term illness of parents, and 7088 because of homelessness or inadequate housing (White Paper, HMSO, 1974). Many social workers question the adequacy of a social work service for children, divorced from wider policies governing housing provisions. On the matter of preventing family breakdown, the DHSS jointly with the Social Science Research Council has made available £500,000 for a 7-year period from 1974 for research into the transmission of deprivation between generations of families; and a further £112,000 has been granted to the NSPCC to establish treatment units for families in which child-battering takes place.

About 40% of children in the care of local authorities are now boarded out with foster parents. This method of care was emphasized in the Children Act 1948 and the proportion rose from 25% in 1946 to its present level in 1955 when the Boarding Out Regulations stipulated the frequency of social workers' visits to these children, the keeping of records, and the 'form of undertaking' to be required of foster parents.

Increasingly an attempt is being made by local authorities to use foster homes as a less expensive alternative to residential care, particularly for children whose behaviour is difficult or unruly. In Kent an experiment has been established whereby 20 foster homes are designated as specialized in this kind of work: the foster parents receive a payment of £42 a week for each child and are regarded by social workers as, in effect, professional colleagues rather than as unqualified well-meaning child-minders.

George (1970) and Adamson (1972) have drawn attention to wide variation in the practice of social workers in their assessment of foster parents and the child for suitability and matching. Broadly speaking, assessment is based on the material conditions and emotional climate of the foster home and the understanding of foster parents of the role expected of them. Since the Children and Young Persons Act 1969, boarding out has ceased to be a duty in all practicable cases, as it has been recognized that this is not always the best kind of substitute care for all children. There are at present 40,600 places in local authority 'community homes'.

TOWARDS A FAMILY SERVICE

Two themes have run through the legislation and duties outlined in this section: the gradual strengthening of concern for the rights and well-being of the individual child relative to the rights of parents; and the raising of standards and expectations of family care in recognition of the importance of the family as the primary socializing agent in our society. Wilmott & Young (1957) have written for example of "a new kind of companionship between man and woman reflecting the rise in status of the young wife and children". The Children and Young Persons Acts 1933 and 1969 imply an increasingly long list of parental responsibilities which can be enforced by law.

It is important to set against this idealization of the family group, an awareness of the million children living in single parent families and to recognize the special difficulties of these parents (Wynn, 1968; Finer Committee, 1974). Recognition of the importance of joint consideration of the needs of children and of the needs and difficulties of their parents was first embodied in a joint Circular (1950) published by the Home Office and the Ministries of Education and Health which encouraged the establishment of Co-ordinating Committees between local agencies concerned with the needs of children. Subsequently the Report of the Ingleby Committee (Cmnd 1191 HMSO 1960) envisaged a local authority family service as the most effective means of dealing with child neglect and juvenile delinquency, and this was endorsed in the White Paper, The Child, the Family and the Young Offender (Cmnd 2742 1975).

On the basis of a recommendation in paragraph 7 of this White Paper, the Committee on the Local Authority and Allied Personal Social Services was set up (the Seebohm Committee). The Committee reported (Cmnd 3703) in 1968, and in 1970 the Local Authority Social Services Act provided for the replacement of the Children's Department and other Local Authority social work services by Social Services Departments. At central government level, the Local Authority Social Services Division was established within the DHSS, which assumed child care responsibilities (other than the work of the Courts) from the Home Office.*

The re-organization of local authority services has made possible a more coherent planning of provision for families as a whole. Publicity given recently, however, to the extent of non-accidental injury among children and to the deaths of young children in the care of their parents has highlighted certain weaknesses in services: particularly the inadequacy of co-operation and the lack of co-ordinated action between social workers, health visitors, doctors and teachers. Area Review Committees have been set up since 1974 specifically to unite provision in respect of non-accidental injury to children. By July 1975, 83 of the 105 local authorities which had set up Review Committees had devised registers of children thought to be at risk of injury. The establishing of structures of this kind, however, does not guarantee the level of personal co-operation upon which effective preventive services depend. The work of Committees will be strengthened by the implementation of the Children Act 1975, which regulates further the way in which children in the

---

* These developments apply in this form only in England and Wales. Equivalent developments in Scotland are dealt with in a later section.

care of the local authority should be supervised, and provides for their regular medical examination. But the Act does not increase the protection of children in the care of their own parents, for whom the skills of detection possessed by the various professional personnel involved with the family are the only safeguard.

THE CONTRIBUTION OF SOCIAL WORK TO THE CARE OF CHILDREN

This brief review of policies and legislative duties has indicated the complexity of provision in services for families where the care of children is, or may become, inadequate in some way. In general terms, the duty of the social worker is to individualize situations so that his intervention is specifically related to the present and future needs of the child and, where possible, of all members of the family both individually and as a group. Thus, within the same family, he may at various times and with various members act as a protector, an 'authority', a friend, and an agent for change, development and growth. For example, he will be expected to advise adopting parents on the processes of adoption, to support them and the child during the waiting period, and to assist in such matters as when and how to inform the child that he is adopted, and how to cope with unexpected behavioural responses or physical disorders. Irrespective of the social worker's age and life experience, he will often be regarded by his clients as a specialist both in the care of children and in the processes of the law, as well as, in some sense, a friend.

Though friendly, however, he has powers which may be difficult to understand and which may seem to some clients to be arbitrarily (even unjustly) used. The social worker is required to assess the suitability of people who wish to adopt or foster children, and he sometimes has to convey the rejection of an application. This is inevitably an emotionally distressing experience, however much he may attempt to minimize its potential destructiveness to self-esteem.

When a child is taken into care by order of a court, the social worker contributes to decisions about his placement, (for example, whether he should go to a foster home, to a residential home or nursery, to a voluntary home or special school), and about the quality of care and supervision appropriate to ensure the child's future welfare.

Similarly, the social worker exercises power when he receives applications, under Section 1 of the CYP Act 1963, for 'advice, guidance and assistance' to prevent the need for substitute care; he has to decide whether, especially in view of the relative shortage of local authority funds for this purpose, he should offer material or financial help, should undertake intensive interviews to promote change in the patterns of communication, feelings or management within the family, or should negotiate and coordinate the provision of help from a wide range of community resources.

When clients are asked about the performance of their social workers, it is not unusual for them to be described as 'a sort of psychologist'. (In a recent research interview, I was told by one client that his social worker was 'as good as a psychoanalyst': this was meant as high praise, though it was probably not a description the social worker would have welcomed.) Children may be placed temporarily in care by their parents because of domestic difficulties, (for example, marital difficulties or the hospitalization of a parent) and, in such cases, arrangements for the physical well-being of the child will often be associated with helping him through the distress both of separation and of anxiety about the future, and with working towards other goals (for example, to promote marital reconciliation or to plan for the parent's convalescence). Similarly, in the context of a supervision order there are no aspects of family functioning in which a social worker may not become involved from time to time. In working with one-parent families (with unmarried mothers, or with a parent following divorce, separation or widowhood), the social worker may encounter extremes of emotional distress; the remaining parent may react to his situation with resentment or apathy; he may be cynical or bitter; there may be problems of loneliness and sexual frustration. Both parent and children may look to material possessions as some sort of compensation for emotional loss and deprivation, irrespective of the money available to pay for them. In disturbed family relationships, emotional attitudes and responses may become entrenched and difficult to change; and in considering the needs of the child the social worker's concern will be directed not only to present distress but to its possible reverberations in the child's adaptations in later life, for example, to his own marriage and to parenthood.

The social worker is required also to be concerned with the needs, behavioural difficulties and emotional problems of teenagers. He may become involved with young people whose attitudes to their parents, teachers and other 'authorities' (of which the social worker is one) are hostile, ambivalent or muddled. He may have to work through a period of rejection by the teenager while at the same time coping with the dissatisfactions of parents or teachers who may have hoped for some supplementation of their own power. Both the nature of desirable change and the appropriate speed of its achievement may be differently defined by all the people in the situation. He needs to be alert to the possibility that a young person's disturbed or anti-social behaviour is symptomatic of stress within other members of the family or in their relationships.

If the child or teenager appears before a court, the social worker will be asked for a report for which he has not only to determine the relevance of all the material available to him, but to express an opinion concerning future care. This opinion is expected to be founded on a substantial and (where possible) verifiable body of information relating to: behavioural and emotional patterns; the quality of family relationships; the attitudes and intentions of parents and child, and their likely reactions and responses to various kinds of intervention.

An important aspect of the duties of the social worker is to provide support and guidance to others responsible for the care of children, and to negotiate a working partnership with them, irrespective of different styles of work or training. Foster parents have an anomalous relationship with the social services department: initially they are applicants whose suitability for fostering has to be assessed; if accepted, they become indispensable colleagues in the welfare of children, and their colleague-role needs to be preserved even though they may from time to time lean heavily on the support and advice of the social worker regarding the care of a child, or may require help with their own personal problems. Similarly, the social worker is available to support the staff of residential homes: to recognize the strains of round-the-clock care, and to ensure that field and residential services together promote a coherent pattern of assistance for each child and family concerned. The social worker may be required to work in partnership with child-minders, play groups and nurseries, all of which have to be registered with the local authority and are entitled to seek advice and help, both in general terms and in relation to the needs of a particular child.

Finally, alongside colleagues in the voluntary child care services, notably the NSPCC, the social worker has to learn to cope with his own anxieties and distress when confronted by situations of considerable hardship, suffering, or uncertainty: for example, how to deal with families where marital disharmony creates constant fear in the lives of the children, but where the parents are, for practical or emotional reasons, unable to separate; or how to achieve understanding and a sense of direction when children are physically abused or subjected to gross cruelty. In order to cope with one's own feelings of anxiety, inadequacy or even revulsion, it is essential to acquire some understanding of how these situations arise: to recognize, for example, that when a parent loses emotional and physical control he cannot simply be categorized in terms of immorality and depravity, but may be reacting to a physical or emotional disability, to stresses in some other part of his life, or to a weight of responsibilities which he is emotionally unable to sustain. The lasting importance of early childhood relationships is now widely recognized, and cruel parents are frequently found to have suffered in their early years in ways similar to the sufferings they now impose on their own children. Even when the social worker recognizes the signs of transmitted emotional deprivation, however, the problems of dealing with the present situation are not lessened. He may understand and sympathize with the parents as well as the child, but he has still to decide whether, in spite of injury or neglect, to continue to work with the whole family or to remove the child. He still has to ascertain whether an injury is accidental or not, and to decide whether to report it to the police, and, if the child is removed from home by a 'place of safety order' (for a period of 28 days), the social worker still needs to decide what to do during and after that time. These are situations which require not simply intellectual competence, professional technique and skill; they involve the social worker's own emotional responses and reactions to extremes of human suffering, and they require the exercise of considerable moral and emotional strength.

Underlying this work, there are two fundamental issues: what (generally and specifically) constitutes a degree of deprivation or risk which will warrant intervention, and how extensive this intervention should be. And, secondly, how can statutory intervention and the facilities of care be used in such a way as to prevent the heightening of clients' experiences of deprivation, unreasonable interference or personal inadequacy and failure?

Given these responsibilities and dilemmas, the social worker can never achieve perfect work; his organization, his clients and the community he serves are fortunate if his work appears to them to be generally adequate. It needs to be borne in mind that the local authority social worker is, in addition to his work with children, expected to achieve competence in work with other client-groups; and that, because of the recent demands of administration and management, many highly experienced social workers are no longer in touch with the agency's clients. Much social work skill at the present time is locked up in administrative duties, while the complex needs of clients are often left to the young, newly trained and relatively inexperienced. Furthermore, all the skills and decisions implicit in this outline of the social workers' contribution to child care depend essentially on the judgment of individual practitioners; social policies are statements of intention, not blueprints for action and in any case the skills required are too extensive to be easily formulated. Certain skills are, however, particularly relevant to the implementation of policy intentions at the present time, and need to be emphasized here.

There is, first, the skill of assessing the child's developmental needs in relation to his own wishes and the wishes of his parents. A decision may sometimes have to be reached which runs counter to the wishes of some of the people concerned. Such decisions need to be conveyed and explained in ways which demonstrate an appreciation and recognition of the complexity of feelings involved. The removal of a child from the care of his parents almost inevitably will be experienced by the parents as implying a moral condemnation of their fitness as parents. In the less dramatic situation of a supervision order, similar feelings may be present, and may find expression in hostility towards the social worker—'I've done my best for him, he's your responsibility now'—or in other forms; for example by overstating the responsibility of other people for the problems that have arisen, by dependence on the social worker for advice in aspects of living which seem to have nothing to do with the problems of the case, or by denial of the presence of any problem. Sometimes the behaviour of a parent can be understood only by reference to earlier life experiences which in various ways have impeded the formation of a satisfying relationship with his own child. Sometimes one child out of several will be made a scapegoat and considered especially bad and meriting punishment.

Secondly, there are the skills in residential services of maintaining individually appropriate levels and expressions of care for each child in the group; of maintaining links with the parents in a form which will give satisfaction rather than pain to the child; coping with the child's grief, bewilderment and resentment not only at the time of admission but at various stages of his stay in the institution when, for example, he compares his life circumstances with those of other children, or when his parents fail to visit, or when their visit has been unhappy in some way.

Thirdly, there is the need in all forms of care to recognize the importance of small things. Affectionate and satisfying relationships are established not only by pronouncements of intent and by the skilled handling of major traumatic events, but by the accumulation of indications of understanding and goodwill implicit in small acts of behaviour and in chance remarks.

Fourthly, there is the skill involved in achieving effective co-operation between field and residential staff. This is particularly critical since the 1969 Act; the decision whether or not a child shall enter a Home is now largely within the social worker's discretion after a care order is made, and the unified system of community homes, replacing the earlier single-purpose homes, will in time enlarge the range of types of accommodation to which the social worker has access. The appropriate and effective use of residential resources can be developed only if residential and field social workers are together able to clarify their goals of work and to evaluate the effectiveness of their joint efforts. At present, relationships between these two kinds of social worker are sometimes clouded by stereotypes and defensive views about relative status, which vitiate not only the achievement of effective overall planning in the use of resources but even sometimes the achievement of a coherent plan of care for a single child. Some of these difficulties are historical; when child care training was introduced in 1946, the residential care of children was not regarded as an aspect of social work. Similarly, a committee set up by the National Council of Social Service (NCSS, 1967) to enquire into the staffing of residential homes came to the conclusion that, while there were common skills in all forms of residential care, these were in important respects different from the skills of social work. The uncertain status of residential workers has been exacerbated by the lack of training facilities: at the present time only 4% of all residential staffs (for all kinds of institution) have formal training, and the current policies of the Central Council for Education and Training in Social Work are concerned both to emphasize that residential care *is* social work and also to give priority in the next few years to the training of residential staff.

The field of child care and family casework is a large and complex one and references to further reading about the skills required will be found in the final chapter of this book. It provides an interesting example of the way in which social policy in respect of the problem of deprived children (seen as a homogeneous group) and the individualistic value-orientation of social work have coalesced. Since the publication of the Curtis Committee Report (1946) policy has been concerned, as is social work, with individual need and with individual differences, and with the attempt to consider the child as a whole person rather than in relation to particular problematic attributes.

A fundamental problem confronting the Seebohm Committee was what (for the purpose of devising a family service within their terms of reference) constituted a family. Their solution was radical and far reaching, and the structural and operational implications of their solution will be considered in a later section.

JUVENILE OFFENDERS

The effect of all criminal justice legislation in respect of children and young persons since 1933 has been to establish as a central principle that, irrespective of the reason for the court appearance of the juvenile offender (and more recently offenders up to the 21st birthday), courts shall have regard for his welfare. It has already been noted that, for juvenile offenders (i.e. aged 10 to 17), the Children and Young Persons Act 1969 lays down that an offence alone should be insufficient to warrant a court appearance. The former Approved Schools and Remand Homes have been merged within a general system of Community Homes so that the care of the juvenile offender need not be automatically divorced from the care of other young people. The Home Office is now considering the closure of Detention Centres (at present available for 14 to 21 year olds) and Borstals (for 15 to 21 year olds). Similarly it is proposed to end the imprisonment of young offenders by the development of Care and Control Orders (for which new institutions will be required) and Supervision and Control Orders within the province of the probation and aftercare service. (See Home Office, 1975.)

At present, if dealing with a young offender (up to the 17th birthday) under Care Proceedings laid down in Section 2 of CYP Act 1969, a court may make one of the following orders:

(1) A supervision order (within the responsibility of the social services department or, temporarily, the probation service);

(2) A care order (which confers parental rights on the local authority until the 18th or 19th birthday);

(3) An order requiring the parent or guardian to exercise proper care and control;

(4) A Hospital order or Guardianship order (under Part V of the Mental Health Act 1959).

Alternatively a case may be brought *under criminal proceedings*; the sentences then available are:

(1) Absolute Discharge;

(2) Conditional Discharge (which permits the offence to be reconsidered

if a further offence is committed within the stated period—usually 12 months);

(3) Binding over the offender and/or his parents to keep the peace;

(4) Fine, with or without an order for compensation or restitution;

(5) Detention Centre, if over the age of 14;

(6) Borstal, if over the age of 15;

(7) Attendance Centre, (available for 10 to 20 year olds, run by the police, and providing training for a stated number of hours during the free time of the offender).

Courts may add a requirement of 'intermediate treatment', within the context of a supervision order. Intermediate treatment was defined in the White Paper, *Children in Trouble*, 1968 (Cmnd 3601) as a new form of treatment 'intermediate between supervision at home and committal to care'. In practice it may involve:

(*a*) residence in a local authority home or a training/recreational course for up to 90 days in the *first* year of a supervision order, or

(*b*) temporary residence or group participation for periods up to 30 days in *any* year of the supervision order.

It is intended that, in time, intermediate treatment facilities will replace Attendance Centres (BASW, 1973). The scope and facilities for intermediate treatment rest with the Children's Regional Planning Committees set up by Sections 12, 18 and 19 of the CYP Act 1969. In addition to drawing up a list of local provisions, each Committee is responsible for assessing the need for and the development of new facilities. The appointment of special staff in social services departments to undertake the development of schemes, and consultation with the magistracy, are important prerequisites for the effective development of this new approach to treatment.

An important aim of intermediate treatment is to offer help to delinquent children by shared activities with other children who have not been in trouble. An essential skill in the use of this kind of facility is, therefore, the ability to assess which kinds of activity will best suit the individual child and to which settings he will most readily adapt. Intermediate treatment depends for its effectiveness, therefore, on the quality of relationship between the child and his supervisor, so that this assessment can be accurately made and the activity introduced at an appropriate time in the child's development. For these reasons, courts may not specify the particular form that intermediate treatment should take in a particular case, nor should the treatment be regarded by the child as a punitive imposition. The intention of this policy is that treatment should be willingly, co-operatively and constructively accepted by the child and his family as offering new relationships and the experience of a new environment.

Intermediate treatment facilities devised by the Regional Planning Committees are subject to approval by the Secretary of State; some pooling of ideas between areas has been made possible by a DHSS development project and by the local advisory functions of the Social Work Service Officers of the DHSS.* The costs of facilities are a direct charge on local authority funds, and, in the present economic difficulties, schemes may suffer in this respect. For example, in Birmingham in 1975, social workers undertook fund-raising in order to promote facilities which could not be afforded from the grant of £2500 made available for that year.

Since the passing of the Children and Young Persons Act 1969, two kinds of anxieties have been expressed: the first relates to resources and the second to philosophy. It is doubtful whether resources of manpower and money will for some time be sufficient to implement fully and effectively the intentions of the Act. Although one of its objectives was to keep young people out of penal institutions, the Junior Detention Centres (for 14 to 16 year olds) are still full, and in 1975 there were 1100 15 and 16 year olds in Borstal training, compared with 200 in 1969. Furthermore, in 1974, 3889 children awaiting trial and 1246 already convicted were admitted to prison establishments (principally adult remand centres, though 400 were remanded to adult prisons). Unconvicted children may therefore face conditions and regimes which are clearly unsuitable and are likely to increase the risk of their committing further offences. The situation is all the more disquieting when it realized that nearly half of those awaiting trial were subsequently found not guilty or were made the subject of court orders of a non-custodial kind.

Children may be remanded to prisons or adult remand centres under a magistrate's 'certificate of unruliness', used when it is thought that the child cannot safely be remanded to the care of the local authority. This situation may be rectified when Sections 69, 71 and 72 of the Children Act 1975 are implemented, in that the Act provides for direct government grants to local authorities to establish secure accommodation for unruly children on remand and for those in the care of the local authority who persistently commit offences. But provisions depend on the conversion of some community homes or the building of new establishments; the need has been self-evident for some time, and it is disquieting that Government and local authorities have so far made so little headway in meeting it: a grant of £2 m for building secure accommodation was announced jointly by the Home Office and DHSS in 1975.

This issue raises also the need for more careful definition of the role of community homes in the care of juvenile offenders. 'Certificates of unruliness' are not arbitrarily issued by courts, and the fact that the number of certificates virtually doubled between 1971 and 1974 (see a reply by Dr Summerskill, Parliamentary Under Secretary, in the House of Commons, *Hansard,* 17 February 1975) indicates either a dramatic increase in un-

---

* Examples of Intermediate Treatment schemes, and the procedures for authorization, are set out in *Intermediate Treatment* (DHSS) HMSO 1972.

ruliness or, more likely, the rejection of difficult children by local authority staff responsible for community homes. Difficult children subject to the terms of care orders, are occasionally returned to their families simply for want of adequate local authority accommodation, often against the advice of their teachers and without the knowledge of the juvenile court which made the order.

Furthermore, although one may agree with the humane intentions and fundamental purposes of the CYP Act 1969, it is appropriate to question the philosophy, or at least the theoretical basis, of some of its provisions. The Act is based largely on concepts of 'treatment' and 'care'; and on the importance of family relationships and of the individual psychology of offenders as major factors in the development of delinquent behaviour. In these respects, it follows in the family casework traditions of the CYP Act 1963, the White Papers *The Child, The Family and the Young Offender*, 1965 and *Children in Trouble*, 1968; although intermediate treatment is based on a broader perspective than family casework, the use of the word 'treatment' is indicative of a theoretical stance, and most supervision orders depend exclusively on a family casework approach. Yet juvenile offenders are at present responsible for about 40% of all burglaries and robberies; one must surely question whether increases in juvenile crime can be wholly attributed to malfunctioning family relationships and whether family casework is a sufficiently adequate method of dealing with the problem. (The same may be said of the increasing complaints, especially from teachers, of hooliganism, vandalism and violence in schools.) Problems of this order are essentially a social phenomenon, not symptomatic merely of individual deviance; yet broader sociological issues and social influences tend to be overlooked in the working of the Act, and we are still without guidance and adequate knowledge about the possible criminogenic influences of, for example, housing developments, large and impersonal schools, certain leisure pursuits and activities, poverty and unemployment.

Thorpe (*Community Care* 28 January 1976) has shown that in the period 1969–1973, although the number of prosecutions had fallen (119,928 to 117,779), the level of juvenile offences had risen to over 210,000. The number of police cautions doubled in this period; in 1973, 87,248 juveniles were cautioned. It may be an indication of the disquiet of courts about the implementation of the Act that, during this period, the use of absolute and conditional discharges and of supervision orders declined, while care orders to community homes increased from 6567 to 7602, detention centre orders from 2228 to 3694, and Borstal committals from 828 to 1448. There are, in all, 40,600 places in community homes in England and Wales. As Thorpe comments, 'the last few years have seen a return to institutional care as the preferred method of managing juvenile offenders, and this has occurred since much of the decision-making ... has passed from the judiciary and probation service to local authorities.' It is ironic that this situation has arisen since the passing of the CYP Act 1969 which advocated a more flexible approach to the problems of juvenile crime, and in spite of the rising costs of places in community homes (now as high as £3500 per annum for each place) and other institutions, and increasing doubts about their effectiveness.

Unfortunately, critics of the Act sometimes attribute the apparently worsening situation merely to the softness and incompetence of social workers and magistrates. The National Association of Head Teachers, in evidence to the House of Commons Expenditure Commmittee's Sub-Committee on the Social Services, 1975, commented that some young people 'deserve to be punished, especially to discourage the regular offender from whom society needs protection'. Even if one accepts this view, recourse to individual discipline of this kind is not, in isolation, likely to solve the problem; parents of delinquent children frequently complain of the pernicious influences of local schools and they may be right, although Head-Teachers are never called upon to answer this point before the courts.

The CYP Act 1969 has suffered, therefore, both from a lack of resources and from a too narrow view of the sources of criminal behaviour. The Act was made the subject of enquiry by a House of Commons Sub-Committee in 1975 which recommended that juvenile courts should have the power to make 'secure care orders', that greater use should be made of Attendance Centres, and that intermediate treatment facilities should be extended.

Subsequently a White Paper has been published (HMSO May 1976) which considers further the recommendations of the Sub-Committee. The White Paper supports the intentions of the Act as a humane contribution to the problem of juvenile crime, and supports also the present role of the local authority; it recognizes, however, the particular problem created by the persistent offender, and the unsatisfactory results achieved so far by custodial sentences. The recommendations of the White Paper are:

(1) to phase out remand to prison establishments;

(2) to strengthen the powers of the courts: courts would be able to require parents to ensure the payment of a child's fine, and would have powers to recommend the placement of a child in secure accommodation and to require periodic reports from the local authority on the progress of the child;

(3) to extend, strengthen and improve intermediate treatment facilities, supervision orders, attendance centres and fostering facilities;

(4) to establish a National Advisory Council to improve consultation between agencies and institutions concerned with juvenile crime.

The White Paper rejects, however, the earlier recommendation of the Sub-Committee that courts should have powers to make 'secure Care Orders', on the grounds that this would unnecessarily blur the lines of responsibility between court and local authority.

The proposals look, therefore, rather like 'more of the same'; the White Paper recognizes that legislation can provide only one element in dealing with the problems of juvenile delinquency, and the effectiveness of the recommendations may depend considerably on the composition and terms of reference of the National Advisory Council.

The treatment of juvenile offenders in Scotland follows a different pattern from that outlined above and in the earlier section on child care legislation. The Social Work (Scotland) Act 1968 preceded the passing of the Children and Young Persons Act, 1969; it established a structure and a process which has not been superseded by the later Act, but is not in fundamental disagreement with it.

In Scotland, Children's Panels and Hearings have replaced juvenile courts for young people up to the 16th birthday. Like juvenile courts, they have powers to deal both with offenders and with other children in need of care and control. The key administrator for local children's hearings is the Reporter, appointed by the local authority, who receives notices from the police and from the Social Work Department in respect of the commission of offences or the presence of need; he negotiates with social workers and teachers for the submission of social enquiry reports, and reaches the decision whether a child should be brought to a Hearing.

A child may be referred to the Reporter for one or more of the following reasons: that he is in moral danger or beyond control; that he is the victim of serious neglect in his own home or of an offence; that he is a member of a family in which incest has taken place; that he fails to attend school; or that he has committed an offence. It will be noted that the commission of an offence is itself a sufficient ground for referral. The Reporter may decide, on the information before him, to take no action, or to refer the case to the School Work Department for informal help, or to bring the child before the children's panel because of the possible need for compulsory provision. (A child cannot be prosecuted as a criminal offender except on the instructions of the Lord Advocate.)

The purpose of the Panel is to ensure that help is made available to children in need of it: 'to discuss in a concerned and informal way the difficulties of children and to provide the most appropriate measures of care and treatment for those who need them.' (Social Work Services Group, Scotland). Each panel consists of three members (both sexes must be represented) who are required to have an interest and aptitude in dealing with children and to undertake some training for the work. In these respects, therefore, they are not unlike juvenile court magistrates in England and Wales.

Information about the child and his family, and about the reasons for his appearance before the Panel, is presented by the Reporter. If the child and his parents agree with this presentation, a discussion follows between the panel members, the parents and the child about what should be done in general terms. If there is dispute about the facts, the case goes to the Sheriff for arbitration but returns to the Panel for discussion and for decisions on treatment. Appeals against the decisions of the Panel may be made to the Sheriff. Legal aid is available for proceedings before the Sheriff but not at hearings by the Panel.

The powers of the Panel are similar but not identical to those of the juvenile courts. The Panel may make a requirement of supervision (by the Social Work Department or another suitable person); the supervision requirement may be augmented by a requirement of residence, with a relative or foster parent or in a Children's Home, or by other conditions designed to change a child's negative behaviour into constructive behaviour (for example, by the provision of special educational and social experiences). The Panel may refer the child to the education authority for 'ascertainment' for special schooling, or to a mental health specialist in the Social Work Department with a view to admission to hospital care or to the making of a guardianship order under the Mental Health (Scotland) Act 1960.

A child subject to a requirement of supervision is effectively in the care of the local authority: the authority may, if necessary, assume parental rights as under a care order in England and Wales. Supervision requirements must, however, be reviewed at least annually by the Panel and should not continue beyond the needs of the child.

As in England and Wales, there are, however, increasing problems of juvenile crime which threaten to overload both the Panels and the staff of the Social Work Departments. At present, about 15,000 children come before the Panels each year, and the number of new supervision requirements increases faster than the rate of their discharge.* Neither has it been easy to maintain the ideal in practice of informal discussions between Panel members, parents and children. Difficulties have been found in attracting working class recruits to the Panels (see *The Guardian* 11 February 1976); only one in five of the present 1500 Panel members are manual workers (see Martin, *New Society* 12 February 1976). And although every effort is made to achieve informality of discussion at the Hearings—every care is taken, for example, to hold Hearings at times convenient to parents it is difficult to avoid the impression of a punitive intention. As in the work of the juvenile courts, the philosophy of the Hearings is one of individual treatment, largely divorced both from 'common sense' views of justice, deserts and punishment, and from effective recognition and action in respect of wider, and possibly more fundamental, causes of delinquent behaviour in the social environment.

* In the period 1972–74, offences by children up to the age of 16 rose from 29,790 to 38,993. In respect of these, police cautions rose from 9766 to 11,474; referrals to the Reporters rose from 17,470 to 24,619; about 3000 a year are dealt with by the Sheriffs' Courts.

3 Mental Health and Mental Disorder

Earlier legislation governing the disposal both of the mentally ill and of the mentally handicapped was consolidated in the Lunacy Act, 1890, which remained in force, amended by subsequent legislation, until the Mental Health Act 1959 and the Mental Health (Scotland) Act 1960. The effect of legislation in the first half of this century was to separate the care of the ill and the care of the handicapped. Thus, by the Mental Deficiency Act, 1913, local authorities were empowered to provide institutional care and training centres for the mentally defective (at the present time about 5000 mentally handicapped adults are resident in local authority homes), while the care of the mentally ill (in particular, to provide for voluntary admission to hospital in addition to admission by certification) was regulated by the Mental Treatment Act, 1930. Following the Report of the Royal Commission on Mental Illness and Mental Deficiency (1954–57), the Acts of 1959 and 1960 again re-united consideration of the treatment of illness and handicap within the concept of 'mental disorder'.

The shift in opinion between 1890 and 1959 was considerable. Nineteenth century legislation was primarily concerned with the dangers of wrongful detention in lunatic asylums, with safeguarding the property rights of patients, and with public protection from dangerous behaviour. The Acts of 1959 and 1960 reflected instead the optimistic view that medical treatment would become increasingly effective in respect of mental disorder: most of the mentally ill were to be placed on the same footing as the physically ill; certification was abolished and most patients became 'informal patients', save for those unable to recognize their need for care and treatment; treatment was to be offered in general as well as mental hospitals; and emphasis was placed on the care of the disordered in the community rather than in institutions. The role of the local authority was therefore considerably increased to match the movement towards informality of treatment and community care. Local authorities were required to provide residential accommodation and domiciliary services for the disordered, and centres for the training and occupation of those unable to work; mental welfare officers were appointed to offer a wide range of social work services; the local authorities undertook guardianship responsibilities for those mentally disordered people who could not be supported by their families; and were empowered to provide any additional services appropriate to the needs of all citizens covered by the Acts. The role of the local authorities was further emphasized, implicitly or explicitly, by Circular 25 (1961) from the Ministry of Health, which forecast a reduction in the number of hospital beds from 150,000 to 80,000 in the following 16 years; by the same Ministry's Hospital Plan in 1962 which emphasized that hospitals should be concerned with treatment rather than with long-term custodial care; and by the Community Care Plan, 1963.

These policies have not, however, been adequately implemented so far. A survey undertaken by MIND in 1971 showed that 40% of local authorities had no hostel provision and 70% offered no day care centres; 24 hospitals still had in excess of 1500 beds; and only about 6% of all financial resources for the mentally disordered was available for local authority services.

The problems of shifting the emphasis from hospital care to care within the community have been very considerable for three reasons. First, for a century or more, we have come to think of mental disorder as a medical rather than a social condition; therapy is traditionally based on a clinical rather than a social model and few social workers have the skills necessary to devise social treatments which are conceptually different from those of medicine. [Significantly, of the 300 trained psychiatric social workers available in the early 1950s, only 8 were employed by local authorities. The local authority officers (Duly Authorized Officers) appointed in implementation of the Mental Treatment Act 1930 were drawn from employees of the Public Assistance Committees and were responsible for facilitating the administrative procedures for the admission and discharge of patients rather than for their treatment in the community.]

Secondly, and related to this, the diagnosis of mental disorder has traditionally been related to the behavioural abnormalities and inadequacies of the patient rather than to the assessment of his potential for normal community living.

Thirdly, the institutions themselves, that is asylums and hospitals, inevitably developed a life of their own, often geographically and socially remote from the life of the communities they served. This goes some way towards explaining the occasional scandals (for example, that at Ely Hospital in 1967) particularly associated with the institutional care of the mentally handicapped, which have led to the appointment of the Health Service Commissioner (from 1973) 'to re-inforce the rights of those who use the Health Service'.

Difficulties of a more specific kind, however, relate to the detailed provisions of the 1959 and 1960 Acts and their implementation, and in order to consider these difficulties it is necessary first to review the provisions.

Mental Disorder is defined [Section 4(1) 1959] as comprising three kinds of condition:

(1) *Mental illness.* This is a somewhat vague term about which there are increasingly divergent views among psychiatrists, particularly in respect of aetiology. Some would argue that mental illnesses are genuinely illnesses, caused by the onset of physical malfunctioning in the brain; others consider that 'illness' is merely a convenient term to describe behaviour which is an inevitable response to intolerable stresses generated by the patient's family or social environment. Thus, some practitioners emphasize the importance of an accurate individual diagnosis (of, for example, schizophrenia or manic depression) as a guide to physical or psychotherapeutic treatments; others focus their diagnostic assertions on the functioning of the family, and emphasize the importance of family therapy; others again would define mental illness as retreatism from constructive action, and would incline to use coercive rather than therapeutic techniques. All we can be sure of at this stage of psychiatric knowledge is that mental illness is probably a phenomenon without a single simple cause, and that the diagnostic categories currently used are convenient labels rather than precise prescriptions for particular styles of intervention.

(2) *Arrested or incomplete development of mind.* This is subdivided into subnormality, which is deemed to be susceptible to medical treatment or other kinds of special care and training, and severe subnormality, in which the patient is incapable of independent living [Section 4(3)]. Difficulties may arise, however, in making a distinction of this kind: capacity for independent living depends to some extent on the patient's social environment, and a medical diagnosis is at best rough-and-ready which does not distinguish, say, between life in a bedsitter in Brixton and life in a large family group on a remote farm.

(3) *Psychopathic disorder.* 'A persistent disorder or disability of mind ... which results in abnormally aggressive or seriously irresponsible conduct ... and requires or is susceptible to medical treatment' [Section 4(4)]. At the same time, sexual promiscuity or immoral conduct taken in isolation from other behaviour is not regarded as psychopathic [4(5)]. Here again, the diagnostic problem is considerable, as much depends on the moral views of the individual psychiatrist, and on the general or specific cultural background of the patient.

Diagnostic difficulties of these kinds are particularly important when admissions to hospital are compulsory rather than informal. Compulsory treatment in England and Wales is based on medical opinion rather than a more legalistic kind of evidence. The issue of susceptibility to treatment may lead some psychiatrists to accept patients and others to reject them, irrespective of their need for help of some kind: this may be of critical importance in respect of the disposal of defendants before the criminal courts when the choice between hospitalization or imprisonment is an uncertain one. Similarly, the question of discharge from hospital or continuing treatment is to a large extent conceived in medical terms, and may overlook the social influences which have helped to precipitate breakdown or which may be awaiting the patient when he leaves hospital. To meet some of these difficulties, a system of Mental Health Review Tribunals exists, made up of legally qualified, medically qualified and lay members, to which some patients under compulsory order may appeal against the continuation of treatment. Tribunals are appointed to Regional Health Authorities by the Lord Chancellor, in consultation with the Department of Health and Social Security, under Section 11 of the National Health Service Act. The Act of 1960 relating to Scotland devised an alternative appeal system by the establishment of the Mental Welfare Commission. The procedures for appeal are discussed later in this section.

Compulsory admission to mental treatment may take the following forms in England and Wales:

(1) A patient may be admitted for observation for 28 days under Section 25 of the 1959 Act, if recommended by two doctors and either the nearest relative or the Mental Welfare Officer of the local authority.

(2) An admission for treatment following diagnosis, under Section 26, may be made on the same recommendations, but only if treatment is essential to the health or safety of the patient or for the protection of others. If the nearest relative objects, a treatment order can be made only by order of a court.

(3) An emergency order for observation for a period of 3 days may be made under Section 29 on the recommendation of one doctor and a mental welfare officer or any relative; but if the order is to be extended, a further medical opinion must be sought.

(4) A patient may be made the subject of a guardianship order (Sections 33, 34) to the local authority or a named individual.

(5) Criminal Courts may order the admission of offenders to specified hospitals or to guardianship (under Section 60), following the recommendations of two doctors, one of whom must be a psychiatrist. Higher Courts may place restrictions on the discharge of such patients (Section 65).

(6) Under Section 136, the police may take a mentally disordered person, found in a public place, to a place of safety, to be detained for up to 72 hours while medical examinations are arranged. Related to this, a mental welfare officer may obtain a warrant for the entry of the police to a place where a mentally disordered person may be in need of treatment (Section 135). Mental welfare officers have powers (Section 22) to inspect premises where a patient is living.

In Scotland, the 1960 Act provides (under Section 23) for detention orders when, on the recommendation of the nearest relative or a doctor, supported by a further medical recommendation and the approval of the Sheriff, a patient is deemed to be incapable of independent living, or has a mental illness leading to abnormal aggression or irresponsibility, or is a danger to himself or others. A detention order is valid for one year. In addition, emergency orders not requiring the agreement of the Sheriff are available for observation or treatment for up to 7 days.

Patients admitted under Section 26 of the 1959 Act may appeal to a mental health review tribunal within 6 months of admission. When the diagnosis of the patient's mental condition is changed, he or his nearest relative may apply for discharge within 28 days of receiving information about the rediagnosis. Patients admitted under Section 60 may apply to a tribunal for discharge at the end of each of the first 2 years. Similarly in Scotland, patients admitted under Section 23 of the 1960 Act may appeal to the Mental Welfare Commission against their detention within 28 days of admission.

The work of the tribunals has recently been adversely criticized by a working party of MIND (Gostin 1976). Under Section 123 of the 1959 Act, a tribunal may order the discharge of a patient if he is deemed to be suffering from a disorder or if further detention in hospital is unnecessary; but tribunals have no power to substitute an alternative form of care, or to impose conditions on the discharge of a patient. Furthermore, their powers relate only to patients admitted under Sections 26 and 60, and, thus, in 1971 92% of patients compulsorily admitted to hospitals had no right to apply to a tribunal. The MIND working party has suggested that about 60% of compulsory admissions are made under the emergency powers of Section 29, and that this section is probably excessively used. Similarly, there are wide regional variations in the use of the emergency powers of the police under Section 136. The working party therefore recommends that the requirements relating to compulsory admissions should be narrowed to the single criterion of personal or public danger, that the powers of tribunals should be extended to cover Sections 25, 29, 135, and 136, and that greater help should be given to patients and their relatives in understanding their rights of application to tribunals and in presenting their case. Alternatively, a system of automatic review of all patients under compulsory orders might help to offset the difficulties of patients who are afraid of the authority (real or imaginary) of the tribunals, who are depressed, or who are unable, for whatever reason, to carry the responsibility of making a formal application.

The position of the informal patient—i.e. a patient admitted by the joint consent of himself or his guardian and the hospital authorities—seems on the face of it to be less contentious. In 1971, 84% of all admissions (151,784 patients) were informal, and informal patients constitute over 90% of the resident population of the mental hospitals at any one time. The MIND working party, however, suggests that here too some process of review should be instituted, bearing in mind the possibility that some informal admissions result from the threat of the use of compulsory powers, and that Section 30 of the 1959 Act allows for the transfer of patients from informal to compulsory status.

In short, MIND argues for greater opportunities for ensuring the patient's consent to his situation, a readier procedure for the redress of grievances, greater confidentiality for the patient's correspondence (which at present can be held back if it is thought by the hospital authorities to be harmful to his interests), and for more advocacy of the patient's rights (including access to the courts). Furthermore, there is need for greater clarity about the role of the social worker who, in compulsory admissions, carries considerable power.

While endorsing these views, it is important to bear in mind that adequate care of the disordered cannot be achieved simply by reforms within hospital procedures and the processes for admitting patients. Whether or not a patient needs to be admitted to hospital will frequently depend on the kind of support available to him in the community, and, as we have seen, the optimism embodied in legislation has not been fulfilled in practice; in spite of the powers given to local authorities in the National Health Service Act and Section 6 of the 1959 Act, and the emphasis on community care in Circular 22 (1959) and Section 12 of the Health Services and Public Health Act 1968, community care remains a hit-or-miss process at the present time. In particular, more use needs to be made of community based facilities (residential and non-residential) which offer immediate crisis help, which combine support with opportunities for social education (see, for example, the recommendations in respect of mentally abnormal offenders made by the King's Fund Centre: *Lost Souls*, 1975), and which unite the resources of a range of professional experts. Furthermore, in order to help families to cope with the onset of disorder, greater resources are necessary to provide information about treatment and about practical help to combat the loss of morale and to offset the emotional damage caused by the sudden loss of the patient on admission to hospital. But more important, perhaps, than increasing resources in absolute terms is our ability to use what we already have in more imaginative ways than hitherto.

RECENT TRENDS

The care of the mentally handicapped was made the subject of a White Paper *Better Services for the Mentally Handicapped* (Cmnd 4683) in 1971. This recommended that the 59,000 hospital beds available for the handicapped should be used for treatment rather than simply for custodial care, that hospitals should develop more extensive day-patient and outpatient facilities in preference to in-patient care, and that—by more effective co-operation between hospital and local authority services—patients who could not be cared for in their own homes should be accommodated in small homely units or, where possible, placed in foster-care or flatlets with the support of social workers.

It was estimated in 1971 that the cost of this re-organization of care over a period of 15 to 20 years would be £120 million: in-patient beds would be reduced by about half (from 52,100 in 1969 to 27,000), day-patient facilities increased ten-fold (from 700 to 7800 patient-places), local authority accommodation would be increased from 6100 to 34,300 places, and foster-care (arranged and supported by social workers) from 650 to 8400 places. The outcome of these recommendations clearly depends on the availability of resources (of cash, homes and social workers) and on effective co-operation between hospitals and local authority social services departments, to permit the phased reduction of one kind of care in accordance with the availability of resources to promote care in the community.

Recent formulations of policy for the care of the mentally ill have followed a similar pattern. The availability of new forms of therapy, notably the psychotropic drugs in the 1950s and 60s, has led to the possibility of reducing confinement in hospital in favour of greater care in the community; the 1962 Hospital Plan and the 1963 and 1966 Health and Welfare Plans of the Ministry for Health envisaged a reduction of in-patient mental hospital beds to 1.8 per 1000 population (cf. 1.3 : 1000 for the mentally handicapped), the greater use of beds in general hospitals, and the extension of day treatment and other forms of residential and day care provided by local authorities. The feasibility of these projections has been analysed by Maynard & Tingle (1975) particularly in terms of the resources available to the local authorities.

The White Paper *Better Services for the Mentally Ill* (Cmnd 6233) was published in 1975. This again endorsed the long-term expansion of Local Authority hostels, day care centres, foster-care, clubs, home helps and other facilities which would permit the mentally ill to live in their own homes or at least in their local communities. In the words of a proposal from MIND, patients should always be placed in the least restrictive setting. The White Paper estimated that at present 5 million patients a year consult their general practitioners about mental health problems, and of these 600,000 are referred to specialists.

To some extent the aims of the White Paper are already embodied in practice: the current annual attendances at out-patient and day-patient psychiatric departments of hospitals now number $1\frac{1}{2}$ million and 2 million respectively and in-patient care is normally of short duration. But 75,923 of the available 104,638 in-patient beds in 1971 were occupied by patients who had been in hospital for 20 or more years. The extent of the problem of resettling the chronically mentally ill is therefore considerable.

THE ROLE OF SOCIAL WORK

As we have seen, at present only 16% of psychiatric hospital admissions are made on a formal, compulsory basis, but nonetheless the procedures involved give rise to certain anxieties. Social workers express mixed views about their powers to implement compulsory admission 'for the patient's own good'; it is sometimes argued that, as social policy has become wider in application and increasingly concerned with the regulation of personal problems and personal relationships, the rights of the individual citizen to influence the decisions made on his behalf have been eroded. This is an area, therefore, where debate about the adequacy of the social worker's expertise and training and about the relationship between his professional and employee roles is particularly important. There are several inter-linked issues involved in the expression of this kind of anxiety.

First, there is the problem for many social workers of inadequate expertise in mental health work. The re-organization of the local authority services by the Local Authority Social Services Act 1970 has required all field social workers to develop a working knowledge both of the provisions of the Mental Health Act and of the types of behaviour and disorder to which the Act refers. Former mental welfare officers, appointed as social workers in the new departments, brought a specialist expertise with them and serve as a resource at field and consultancy levels. But the amount of re-training needed by other staff is considerable, and for those at present in social work training courses the breadth of their studies prevents adequate concentration and specialization in this particular aspect of the work. Some of the skills already mentioned in respect of field social work for the care of children are transferable in broad outline: notably the skills of assessment; of conveying decisions which run counter to the wishes of the patient or his family; of managing the complexity of responses in the family following the patient's removal; or alternatively of coping with the anger and disappointment which may arise in a family when it is decided not to admit a patient. But in addition there are other more specific skills: for example, allaying the anxiety of the patient's family that his disorder is inheritable or 'catching'. It may be necessary to support the family in their attempts to understand the onset of the disorder and to cope with the fear that bizarre behaviour generates. If the social worker considers that the source of the disorder lies in a particular set or constellation of family relationships, then the work he needs to do with the family during the absence of the patient and following his return may be extensive; families do not change their patterns of relationship overnight in response to good advice. Skill is required also in understanding the logic of behaviour and of thought-processes that lies behind the apparent irrationalities of the patient, and in offering help to the patient which is comprehensible to him. Implicit in these comments is the view that responsibilities for mental health care require administrative and professional expertise which many social workers lack. This lack may itself provide one reason to fear that the interests of patients are not adequately safeguarded by their social workers.

Secondly, inter-professional relationships between doctors and social workers have worsened in many areas, especially in relation to mental health care. Psychiatrists and the former mental welfare officers had established close and informal relationships based on a high degree of specialization and common concern on both sides. The size of social services departments (compared with the mental health section of the former public health departments) and the recent rapid movement of local authority social workers, both hierarchically and between geographical areas, have militated against a rapid redevelopment of personal relationships at field level. Letters from individual doctors to *The Times* since 1971 reflect a body of opinion in the medical profession (it is impossible to estimate its size) which regrets both the loss of personal contact with social workers and the decision to remove social work services concerned with health from the control of the former Medical Officer of Health. The most serious aspects of this situation, from the point of view of the patient, concern the loss of colleague-relationships; mutual respect between the two professions is a factor not only in the provision of a coherent and comprehensive service but in safeguarding the rights of the patient, in that colleagues of equal status can disagree and influence each other, while those of unequal status (in each other's eyes, at least) move from disagreement to entrenchment.

Among social workers also, there are anti-professional and 'anti-casework' movements which reject any association between the professionalization of social work and the professional model of the doctors. It is often hard to tell whether the rejection of psychiatric diagnosis and methods of treatment among some social workers is based on the politics of this kind of anti-professionalism, or on the theoretical rejection of psychiatry, or on a wish to protect patients from what is sometimes regarded as an excessively powerful professional oligarchy. (See the analysis of current trends in 'radical' social work thinking in G. Pearson: *The Deviant Imagination*, Macmillan, 1975.) The problem thrown up by this pattern of attitudes is that it worsens relationships between social workers and one of the sources of potential help to clients and families known to them. (It could be argued that there are other potential resources in the community which remain untapped because of ideological divergences.) Furthermore, there is a likelihood that, in the present ideological climate, some mental health needs are not recognized as such. To take an extreme example, a woman may present re-iterated complaints of persecution by her neighbours, and may be advised by a social worker about rehousing, irrespective of whether the examples she gives of her neighbours' behaviour are based on verifiable factual information. In more general terms, clients may present their problems in ways which appear to them to fit in with the expectations of the social workers they meet. Thus, there are equal risks that environmental problems may be presented in terms of personal feelings, and that problems of feelings and attitudes may be presented in environmental terms.

When considering work with the mentally disordered, and their families, therefore, the principal need is for the re-establishment of some kind of teamwork between the professions involved: the same is also true of other client-groups. As the underlying policy involved in these services is to effect a transition from benevolent care (seen in terms of the patient's passivity, and his exclusive need for medical treatment), to more active forms of rehabilitation and social education, so its successful implementation depends on the formation of interdisciplinary teams (teachers, doctors, nurses and social workers) and the acceptance by all participants of a team-model as essential to satisfactory practice. The National Health Service Reorganisation Act, 1973 (section 10) imposes a duty on health authorities and local authorities to co-operate together 'to secure and advance the health and welfare of the people of England and Wales'. Advice on collaboration at a local level is the responsibility of Joint Consultative Committees with members representing the two groups of services. The degree of effectiveness of this collaboration will no doubt become apparent as one observes the future development of day care facilities within the local authority and allied services.

A further need in the development of effective mental health care is the promotion of community support to patients and their families following discharge from hospitals. The onset of mental illness is associated with costs to the National Health Service and the local authority, and with heavy emotional burdens on the families concerned. While it is difficult to see how this first onset can be prevented—for the problems involved in detecting those at risk of breakdown are considerable—a somewhat more manageable task (and one which has hitherto received inadequate attention) is to prevent the recurrence of illness among those who have been discharged from hospital. Discharge is itself a difficult hurdle for many patients; they cannot be certain how they will be received by their families, neighbours and friends or by the after-care services; many patients return to situations of loneliness and social isolation which may have been influential in the original development of their illnesses; the experience of hospitalization may have re-inforced the illness as part of a life-style which is difficult to change. (See P. McCowan and J. Wilder: *The Life Style of 100 Psychiatric Patients*, Psychiatric Rehabilitation Association, London, 1975 and T. J. Scheff: *On Being Mentally Ill*, Weidenfeld and Nicolson, 1964.) The treatment of mental illness and the aftercare associated with it are based more on the presence of symptoms of disorder than on the mode of living which generates the illness and encourages its recurrence. It can be argued that the present funding of mental health care encourages this tendency: in financial terms it is frequently advantageous to a local authority to shift the responsibility of care to the National Health Service when symptoms of disorder are detected; and, similarly, it is advantageous to the Health Service to discharge the patient when his symptoms are reduced, irrespective of the quality of social life to which he will return. The effective prevention of a recurrence of illness requires a concerted effort to integrate the patient into 'healthy' social living among friends and neighbours and at work. Social work support, divorced from a concern for the whole way of life of the patients, is likely only to delay further breakdown rather than to prevent it.

4 Services for the Physically Handicapped and Disabled

There are at present about 3 million physically disabled people in Great Britain (Harris, HMSO, 1971). It would, however, be inappropriate to describe them all as handicapped; the distinction lies in whether or not they are able to lead a full life, to maintain themselves in employment and to play an active role within their own families (Topliss, 1975). In 1971, there were 96,000 registered blind persons, 40,000 registered deaf and 234,000 in other registered categories.

Statutory provision for sheltered employment and for employment of the disabled in the community was established within the Ministry of Labour (now the Department of Employment) in 1944. The National Assistance Act, 1948, section 29, continued and promoted the welfare of handicapped persons through local authority provisions initiated within the Poor Law.

A comprehensive definition of the social needs of the handicapped was first made in the White Paper on Health and Welfare, 1963, when local authorities were recommended to offer guidance and help on adjustment to handicap, domiciliary services (including physical adaptations to the home), hostels, sheltered employment, recreational facilities and, where necessary, holidays and special transport to permit the full use of these other facilities. More recently, the Chronically Sick and Disabled Persons Act 1970 has extended the scope of services to cover all the *disabled* rather than those who are demonstrably *handicapped*. By this Act, local authorities maintain a register of all disabled persons and ensure that comprehensive information about services is available to them. Practical assistance in the home may now extend to the provision of television, mobile library facilities and telephones. By the requirement to draw up a register of the disabled, the onus to promote the welfare of the individual disabled person has been shifted from himself and his family to the authority. Welfare provisions are not associated in this Act with economic considerations of the productive potential of the handicapped person.

Here again, however, the resources required for the full implementation of the Act would be considerable, and it is possible (though this has not been precisely demonstrated) that unrealistic public expectations have been aroused.*

The broad aims of social work with the disabled person are to assist his independence within the limitations of his disability, to help him to come to terms emotionally with his disability, to enrich his social relationships, and to assist his family to cope with their own feelings of inadequacy in the face of pain and frustration. How far it is feasible for social workers to undertake these responsibilities adequately is a matter for debate. Bayley (1973) has drawn attention to the day-to-day hardships and difficulties of these families and has advocated the development of more effective *informal* local caring as of more relevance to the needs actually experienced by the families than the occasional supportive visits of social workers. Such development would, however, depend on skill in community organization which at present few social workers possess, and on the quality of co-operation achieved between the local authority services and formal and informal voluntary groups. We shall need to consider this matter further when we examine the concept of 'community care', which in respect of work with the handicapped has somewhat equivocal connotations. When one considers the 'community care' of the mentally ill, for example, (if we may assume that the disorder is a temporary phenomenon) the aim is fairly clearly to provide services as a means to the achievement of full independence in the life of the patient. The community care of the permanently disabled may embody a similar aim or it may instead aim to generate a sense of group-belonging as a permanent way of life. The definition of purpose will of course vary between groups and between individuals, but needs to be clarified (preferably in consultation with those who use the services) if problems are to be avoided of divergent aims and values between those who are offering help.

If the aim of local authority services is to offer comprehensive community caring as a permanent aspect of life for the disabled, then this raises certain issues about the relationship between services and these particular clients. Traditionally, social workers in the statutory social services have tended to deal with crisis situations; it has been assumed that at non-crisis times the disabled will conduct their own lives without the intervention of social workers. Comprehensive life-time support would imply both a greater degree of partnership between the providers and users of services and also the deeper involvement of the services in the day-to-day lives of disabled people and their families. These implications have yet to be fully explored: for example, we have yet to find ways of directly representing the interests of disabled people on policy-making bodies concerned with their welfare—should every Social Services Committee have at least one disabled person on it? Secondly, concern for the whole life-style of the disabled will require

* Topliss (1975, p. 113) argues that so much local authority finance is used on income substitution measures that there is insufficient left to provide the *special* personal services required by the disabled.

some rethinking about the physical conditions which constitute disablement. Disablement means different things to different people, depending on their personal attitudes and on the requirements of their daily lives; more attention would need to be given by social workers to the emotional and physical problems associated with disablement in marital and family relationships in, for example, feelings of guilt, of martyrdom, of sexual frustration, of physical revulsion.

The 1970 Act was a humane and idealistic piece of legislation; the social services and social workers have yet to learn to live with it. It is no doubt unrealistic to expect local authorities to provide comprehensive care; and effective help to the disabled will therefore depend on the development of partnership between services and a wide range of informal resources, and a public recognition of the limitations of statutory intervention.

5 Services for the Elderly

In this section, most of the services described relate to groups of people who have always been regarded as, in one sense or another, posing a problem to society either by their behaviour, their vulnerability or their dependency. We do not traditionally regard the elderly in this way. All of us are inescapably involved in the ageing process; if we live long enough we shall all join the ranks of the elderly, whereas relatively few of us belong, or will belong, to the other groups for whom provisions are described here.

Because old age is not in itself the source of a social problem, the care of the elderly has occupied an ambiguous position in the policies and attitudes of the social services. Men over the age of 65 and women over 60 now constitute 16% of the population, yet in medical schools there are only 7 Chairs of geriatric medicine. The care of the elderly now accounts for nearly half the expenditure of the personal social services (Klein *et al* 1974); yet it was not until 1968 that comprehensive legislative provision was made for their care; and, by most social workers, work with old people is regarded as peripheral to their professional interests.

Until recently, then, the needs of the elderly have been given little attention: that they are now beginning to be regarded as a problem is the result of demographic and medical changes. Before the First World War, the elderly represented 6.7% of the population; they were traditionally cared for by their families; they were expected to die soon. Their increasing numbers as a proportion of the total population, the mobility of their families and their longevity together present a new social challenge. The proportion of old people living alone has doubled in the last 20 years; the 1971 census showed that 8 million old people (95% of the total population of the elderly) live in private households; of these, 25% live alone and 25% only with husband or wife. Of those in residential care, 75% are now over the age of 75, and the trend in admissions is towards the care of the very old (the over-85s). Advanced old age is associated with an increasing incidence of psycho-geriatric disorders and immobility; 10% of the old are housebound, and this proportion may increase as the elderly infirm live longer.

These figures offer some indication of the extent of need among the elderly which the personal social services have only recently begun to meet systematically. They have done so by a virtual reversal of earlier policies: the National Assistance Act 1948 Part III (Section 21) set out the responsibility of the local authority to provide accommodation for those in need of care and attention, and by 1960 some 37,000 old people were accommodated in converted Poor Law institutions and a similar number in other local authority homes. The increasing costs of residential care and the sharp rise in cases for which, in the terms of the 1948 Act, such care would be appropriate have led to the belated development of an alternative policy of providing domiciliary services to support the infirm in their own homes and to prevent the need for admission into local authority accommodation. The National Assistance (Amendment) Act 1962 empowered local authorities to provide meals and recreational facilities (hitherto undertaken by voluntary organizations) and to support voluntary organizations in meeting these needs. But domiciliary care and long-stay residential care remained in functional terms wholly separate; few provisions existed, save in the voluntary services, for short-stay residential care as a supporting service to domiciliary care, and it was not until the Health Services and Public Health Act 1968 and the formation of comprehensive social services departments in 1971 that local authorities assumed and implemented their present powers to provide comprehensively for the general welfare of the elderly.

The Act of 1968 promoted day care centres, short-stay residential care and chiropody services, and emphasized the importance of planned co-operative effort with the voluntary organizations active in this field. Since 1974, similar co-operation has been encouraged, through inter-disciplinary Health Care Planning Teams, with the National Health Service, particularly to determine the complementary uses of local authority homes and nursing homes.

By March 1973, local authority homes were available to 106,361 old people. Home help services now reach about 500,000 households, most of them containing old people, and it is estimated that about 1 in 16 of the elderly receive this kind of domestic help. Meals-on-Wheels services at present rarely offer more than 2 cooked meals a week. Local authorities exercise also certain emergency powers under the 1948 Act, notably, when empowered by a Court, to permit the forcible removal from home for up to 3 months of an old person living in insanitary conditions, and to safeguard property and to arrange burial in the absence of relatives or friends (Sections 47, 48 and 50).

Variations in the quality of local authority care are, however, considerable. Baugh (1973, 1975) records that in 1970 one old people's home spent only £1.33 a week on food for each resident. A working party report for the Personal Social Services Council (1975) found it necessary to recommend the establishment of national minimum guidelines for physical conditions and standards of professional care in residential homes, for complaints procedures to be made available to residents, and for 'a clearly worded contract to assure rights of tenure and to remove the fear of summary eviction' (*Community Care*, November 1975). A review of services for the elderly undertaken by the Social Work Service of DHSS (*Social Work Service,* DHSS December 1973) in 1972 commented, 'the impression was that only a very few social service authorities could yet be said to have defined policies for the elderly in precise terms' (*Community Care*, November 1975).

More positively, however, although effective working partnerships between local authority and hospital services are difficult to achieve, some authorities have made joint social work appointments for geriatric care; joint planning with housing authorities has led to increased provision of dwellings with a street warden service; some local authorities have appointed specialist field work advisors to assist social workers in their work with the elderly; and some efforts have been made to de-institutionalize residential care. The implementation of the Chronically Sick and Disabled Persons Act 1970 has ensured that most local authorities have undertaken enquiries to estimate the extent of need among old people, sometimes with the research assistance of the Local Government Operational Research Units, community development projects and universities.

One of the most important aspects of these studies has been to achieve greater precision in defining needs, and to reduce the tendency to regard the elderly as a homogeneous group. A report of *Social Work Service* has drawn attention to 8 vulnerable groups among the old: those aged 75 or more; those living alone or housebound; the very frail and mentally infirm; those newly discharged from hospital or awaiting admission to residential care; the elderly sick or disabled; the recently bereaved; those in new estates and high-rise flats; and those who have stopped attending clubs. In meeting the needs of those vulnerable groups, local authorities have adopted various strategies: the development of domiciliary services of all kinds, volunteer friendly visiting services, street warden schemes, day care linked with residential institutions, communication and alarm systems, and the development of foster-care services.

As in other aspects of the work of the local authority social services, the further development of care for the elderly is impeded by financial and staffing problems, by a widespread increase in referrals since the reorganization of 1971, and by the pressures of other work.

The care of the elderly presents particular problems of understanding for field and residential social workers. It is necessary to be aware of the changes involved in the ageing process: physical problems, for example, the onset of chronic illness, are the most apparent of these, but they are accompanied by other changes which may affect the quality of interviews and conversations with the elderly. The ability to remember information, and to organize it in useful ways, may be adversely affected; certain characteristics may become heightened, for example, a tendency to anxiety or to obsession with particular ideas. Furthermore, the old person may well have to cope with dramatic changes in his social roles and expectations such as retirement, reduced income, the transition from marriage to widowhood, restricted mobility, the loss of friends and of close relatives. The encouragement of independent living requires of the social worker an awareness of these changes and of their individual effects.

A further concern of the social worker must be to avoid regarding the elderly as a homogeneous group: 'old age' may cover a span of some 30 years, and within that period the 'life tasks' of the individual will change considerably. On retirement the concern may be the creation of a new style of living; 10 years later, there may be a period of indecision about how far to disengage from certain aspects of life (whether, for example, to continue to attend certain clubs, to continue to visit certain friends), this indecision being intensified by physical and emotional changes. Later still, disengagement may become essential if the old person is incapable of living alone and needs some form of institutional care. The problem for both social worker and client is how to make the most of a situation which may be fraught with a sense of loss, a feeling of being out of touch with the modern world, of uselessness. Social work with the elderly involves a *gradual* limitation in long-term planning and in looking ahead: the aims of the work tend to become short-term (compare, for example, work with young people) and the pace of interviews to become slower; communication may be impeded by difficulties in hearing and in self-expression, by apathy, or by mistrust. In this situation, it is all too easy to make plans 'for the good of the client' without fully taking into account (or even understanding) his own hopes and feelings. This may be particularly the case when the decision is reached that the client should go into a Home; the emotional shock of this transition, of abandoning one's neighbourhood and some of one's possessions, and of adapting to new routines and relationships, may remain unexpressed and unconsidered by others. Morris (August 1975) has suggested that the concern of some local authority homes with the provision of high standards of living (sometimes considerably higher than the old person has been used to), the frequent neglect of relationships between residents and their local community, and the unwitting encouragement of feelings of helplessness and uselessness may lead to a rapid 'system-induced' acceleration of old age; the old may be 'killed by kindness'.

The problems of residential care of the elderly offer one example of the general dilemma of residential institutions: how to promote individual choices and to cater for individual differences within a restricted environment which has to provide both shelter and comprehensive care. The need to maintain the smooth running of the institution leads, perhaps inevitably, to the denial of personal differences and to withdrawal from the influences of the outside world. Furthermore, institutional life may intensify divisions between the needs of the staff (for a quiet life) and the needs of residents, which in turn lead to the formulation of rules or to the imposition of subtle emotional and moral pressures. If, as often is the case with Old People's Homes, the institution is regarded as the 'last resort', this may have a damaging effect on the morale of both staff and residents. Institutional life may be a prison for both; the 'custodial sentence' is frequently longer for staff than for residents. These tendencies can most effectively be offset by greater association between field staff and residential staff, the provision within the same Homes of short-stay and long-stay places, and the promotion within Homes of day care and similar community-oriented facilities.

In addition to local voluntary services, which until recently have carried responsibility for most of the community care of the elderly, there are 4 national bodies which promote public awareness of their needs: The National Corporation for the Care of Old People, Age Concern, Help the Aged and the British Association for Service to the Elderly. The manifestos published by Age Concern offer reliable information not only about the services available to the old but about their attitudes to their social situation.*

In view of the numbers of old people in our society, the extent of their need, and the fact that getting old happens to everybody, the provision of services not only requires the exercise of certain priorities but needs also a social philosophy of intervention. Ageing is not in itself a social problem, and it is regrettable that this natural process has sometimes come to be seen as problematic and as a source of anxiety among statutory social workers. The process of ageing certainly is a challenge, in that it is inevitable and requires the definition of new life tasks; but ageing is not the same as feeling old. Feeling old is a subjective experience: it is related to feelings of uselessness and of being out of touch with the world; it is related to the development of small defensive strategies to make living less painful (the re-iteration of compulsive habits, the development of rigid attitudes); it is related to the fear of dying, the fear of further grief though the loss of loved ones. The task of the helper is to give help appropriate to the ageing process while attempting to combat the tendency to feel old. Goldberg (1968) has shown that, by social work intervention, it is possible to alleviate the depression involved in feeling old and to increase an old person's satisfactions with life.

The functioning of the personality of an individual is largely related to his having a sense of his social value. Services for the elderly need therefore to be concerned not only with meeting individual needs in material, emotional and environmental terms, but also with establishing and sustaining where possible a sense of social worth and status; to be *only* the recipient of services can be demoralizing experience which encourages the feeling of being old. Those who live alone are the chief users of the personal services and are also those who express most needs of all kinds (Brockington & Lempert,

---

* See particularly Age Concern: *On the place of the retired and the elderly in modern society* 1975 and *Attitudes of the Retired and Elderly* 1975.

1966; Tunstall, 1966); significantly their problems are not only material (about 40% of old people live at or below the level of supplementary benefit, and many have problems with housework and shopping); they are also those who suffer most from loneliness, social isolation and feelings of uselessness. Effective help consists of meeting both kinds of needs, by mobilizing direct individual services and by the development of informal patterns of local involvement such as good neighbouring, volunteer visiting, recreational and work opportunities.

Group activities offer a way of off-setting isolation and loneliness, as is shown in the development of old people's clubs attached to many churches and voluntary organizations. But group activities can work in two ways: on the one hand, they may tend to reinforce feelings of being old, of being part of a socially marginal group; or alternatively they may act as a stimulus for change in the life of the individual. If a member is encouraged to relate to others and to learn about their needs and ideas, he may find himself not only making a direct contribution to their welfare but also achieving a greater sense of his own identity and worth.

Basically, therefore, those wishing to offer service to the elderly have two main problems to solve: first, how to determine when intervention is essential and at what point, if at all, eccentricity of behaviour and response should be defined as a serious risk; and second, how to mobilize formal and informal resources in ways which increase the social contribution and social status of the elderly as well as meeting their needs.

DAY CARE SERVICES

The provision of Day Care centres has developed piecemeal in the last 50 years. The Blind Persons Act 1920 made local authority centres mandatory for the blind, the National Assistance Act 1948 for the physically handicapped, the Mental Health Act 1959 for the mentally disordered, and the Health Services and Public Health Act 1968 for the elderly and those in need of psycho-geriatric care. By 1972, there were 562 day care centres, mostly for the elderly and physically handicapped, and 383 adult training centres for the mentally handicapped (*Report of the Working Group on the Training Needs of Staff in Day Centres*, Training council for Teachers of the Mentally Handicapped, 1972). Since then, there has been a rapid growth of day care facilities variously sponsored by local authorities and voluntary agencies and by joint action between the two sectors. In addition to catering for the needs of the client-groups listed above, day services are now available in some areas for people addicted to drink and drugs, for those without a settled way of life, and for pre-school children; and in this aspect of social service there are now many experimental centres where co-operation exists between a wide range of statutory services and voluntary groups, and where volunteer help is regarded as a major resource. Furthermore, outside the personal social services, some housing departments have set up day centres for the homeless. The reception centres for vagrants provided under the National Assistance Act 1948, which originally offered up to 3 nights' temporary lodging, have been translated, under the auspices of the Supplementary Benefits Commission, into centres for resettlement. The development of day training centres within the probation and after-care service is a further indication of widespread commitment in the social services to a policy of day care in preference to institutional care on the one hand or neglect of needs on the other.

In recent years, however, the size and quality of provisions have not kept pace with changing policy. In 1972, only between 2 and 3% of all handicapped people attended day centres; of 1150 staff employed in direct work with clients in the 562 local authority centres for the handicapped, only 364 held any kind of professional qualification, of whom 15 were social workers; only about half the qualified staff were employed full-time. This gap between policy and provisions indicates primarily a lack of resources, rather than a failure of intent. But in addition there have been 3 dilemmas associated with the concept of day care which have inhibited its translation into practice. First, what is its main purpose? Second, what kinds of people should promote it, and how should they be trained? And third, what are the problems involved in promoting the multi-disciplinary teamwork upon which effective day care depends?

In considering the purpose of day care centres, there is a fundamental choice between attempting to enrich the lives of clients (in the broadest sense of enrichment) and concentrating more narrowly on enhancing their contribution to society. To some extent, these aims need not be divergent; for example, a young physically handicapped man may feel enriched if given an opportunity to undertake some economically productive work. But even in this case, too great a concentration on his work-potential might prevent his being offered opportunities for broader (non-vocational) education or for wider social intercourse and recreation. When one considers the situation of the elderly infirm or the severly handicapped whose work-potential is very small, a policy which relates the provision of services to their economic contribution is well-nigh irrelevant. It has been suggested earlier that, in fact, the most severely handicapped have (at least until recently) received the worse quality of services, and that the quality of social service provisions in general has been traditionally related to the productive capacity or future potential of service users, rather than to their felt needs. In respect of day care services, this dilemma is illustrated in a report published in 1967 which described their purpose as 'to provide facilities for disabled people to leave their home environment so as to engage communally in activities which will benefit them individually *and thereby improve their contribution to society*' (italics not in the original) (Ministry of Health 1967). A further report in 1968 (Ministry of Health) spoke of the centres offering 'realistic work training ... and further education and social training'. Both these comments seem to assume that individual needs can be met and social productivity enhanced within a single process of help, and that need should be defined in socially productive terms; both assumptions are debatable.* The 1972 report, to which reference was made earlier, indicates some modification in this viewpoint, though it again emphasizes the importance of 'productive occupation'. The report recognizes that unemployment may have a demoralizing effect on people, and recommends that 'centres can . . . help them preserve responses to a work situation, to maintain old skills and to learn new ones'; it suggests that social and recreational needs should be met, where possible, through social clubs rather than in the centres. At the same time, the report emphasizes that, by a team approach to individual needs, those who use the centres may be helped to adjust to their limitations and may receive 'compensatory stimulation'; and that the needs of families for help with the burdens of care should also be met. To some extent, therefore, the aims of provisions in the statutory and voluntary sectors appear to be converging, whereas hitherto voluntary societies have emphasized social needs and recreation while statutory provision has emphasized productiveness. Different user-groups clearly require different qualities of day-service, and the effectiveness of day care depends on a sensitive balance of recreational and work opportunities, geared to the needs of individuals rather than to a supposed homogeneity within handicapped groups.

This has implications for the kinds of people employed in day services and for their training. The Central Council for Education and Training in Social Work was given responsibility for the training of day centre staff in October 1974, and in a paper published in 1975 defined certain principles of staffing and training (CCETSW Paper 12). First, that all day centres (i.e. irrespective of the personal potential of their users) should replace systems of 'passive care' by planned programmes which would promote rehabilitation and social education. Second, that staff should be trained in such a way as to open for them a career structure in the broad field of social service (i.e. that day care should no longer be a dead-end job on the margin of social welfare); an estimate was made that 1800 training places a year would be necessary to meet the needs of present and future staff. Third, that training should be multi-disciplinary, in recognition of the complexity of needs among those who use the services. And finally, that some staff members should be trained as social workers, with particular skills in co-ordinating the work of day centres with the wider social needs of users and their families, in co-ordinating the understanding and skills of a wide range of professionals and other workers, in monitoring changes in the situations and needs of users and their families, and in developing and mediating the use of community resources in respect of the work of the centres.

The CCETSW paper emphasizes the importance of team-work, and the approach to training which the paper defines illustrates this emphasis. But

---

* The present low level of pay to clients in many local authority centres which offer productive work seems to imply to clients that neither their employment nor their need for self-respect is held in much regard.

team work is difficult to achieve in practice. Problems tend to arise in defining the specific orientation of the work of teams, and their appropriate professional reference point. Should the team leader or consultant be a doctor, for example, or a nurse, or a social worker? The DHSS Working Party's Report on *Social Work Support for the Health Service*, 1974 states in another context: 'We suggest that team work . . . means that all members of the team accept that each has a professional contribution to make in his own right; and that it is both the right and the responsibility of each member to make that contribution if the patient needs it. Such a responsibility derives not from the prescription of the head of the team, but from the right of the patient to have the benefits of all the team's skills as he needs them.'

LOCAL AUTHORITY RESIDENTIAL SERVICES

There are at present about 11,000 residential centres of all kinds provided by local authorities. Together they accommodate 395,000 people, cared for by 65,000 residential care staffs. As has been noted elsewhere, only about 4% of staff have received an appropriate form of training for their work; the target set by the Central Council for Education and Training in Social Work is to increase the proportion of qualified residential staff to 25% in the early 1980s. This, however, will require an establishment of 8000 training places in social work courses and the appointment of about 700 tutors.

CHARGES FOR LOCAL AUTHORITY SERVICES

At the present time, local authorities may impose charges for the following services: residence in old people's homes, provided under Part III of the National Assistance Act, 1948; the provision of residential and day care services for children, and boarding children with foster parents; Meals-on-Wheels and day centres for the elderly and handicapped; and the home help service. The scales of charges are determined by individual local authorities and thus vary considerably between areas. The purpose of levying charges is primarily to reduce the burden falling on the general ratepayer; but little is known about the effects of these charges on the consumer or potential consumer: for example, whether they have a deterrent effect on the take-up of services, and at what levels they should be set to increase revenue without causing undue hardship. It is a matter of individual opinion whether the scope of charges should be extended or reduced: some anomalies appear to exist in the present system, where, for example, an elderly person may be required to make a contribution for the services of a home help, but not for a home nurse.

The money obtained through direct charges on consumers varies as a percentage of the total expenditure on different services. Thus, charges provide 33.5% of the expenditure on homes for the elderly, but only 15.8% of the expenditure on children's homes; recipients pay 13.5% of the costs of

Meals-on-Wheels but only 5.4% of the cost of home helps; 11.2% of expenditure on the day care of young children is contributed by charges, but only between 4% and 5% of the expenditure on training centres for the handicapped and other forms of day care is met in this way (Department of the Environment, 1975).

OTHER WELFARE SERVICES PROVIDED BY THE LOCAL AUTHORITY

The care of mothers with young children

This is appropriately regarded for the most part as a medical concern. In 1936 local authorities were given responsibility for ensuring an adequate service of midwives, and from 1946 (National Health Service Act) the earlier powers to provide services for expectant mothers and children up to 5 years of age were made obligatory. Area Health Authorities are now responsible for the provision of ante-natal and post-natal care and for health visiting services for children up to school age. Increasingly, maternity and child welfare centres have been extended to serve wider purposes of community health and welfare, and in some areas the services of a local authority social worker are made available within the centres on a part-time basis. Reference has been made earlier to the provision by local authorities of day nurseries for young children whose mothers go out to work or are for other reasons unable to provide daily care within their own homes.

The care of the unmarried mother and her child, until recently principally a concern of voluntary organizations, is now generally incorporated without differentiation in the work of health and social services organizations. Local authorities and voluntary organizations both provide hostel accommodation for unmarried mothers, and in many areas voluntary provisions are grant-aided by local authorities.

It is, however, generally agreed that services for this group and for other one-parent families are insufficient to meet their needs, particularly after the birth of the child. One in 10 of all families with dependent children in 1971 were one-parent families. The majority of the 600,000 parents in this situation are women, divorced and separated, widowed or unmarried (Finer Committtee HMSO 1974). Their principal need is, of course, for financial security, and more needs to be done in co-operation between social service departments, the income maintenance service and (in the case of separated women) the courts. Few facilities are at present available to counsel women on their entitlements, to offer help in their negotiations with the courts, and to support them in their responsibilities and anxieties following separation and bereavement. Self-help action groups such as Gingerbread are at present the major source of moral support and advice.

The needs of single parents were little regarded by the local authority services before the 1970 Local Authority Social Services Act, and little headway has yet been made in respect of this group, save in terms of day nurseries and child-minding services.

Services for handicapped children

The care of all children, whether handicapped or not, is embodied in the Child Care legislation to which reference has already been made and which governs part of the work of local authority social services departments. Handicapped children receive special schooling under the Education Act 1944, and both the types of special schools and also the responsibility of education authorities to identify the children in need of special schooling were laid down in the Handicapped Pupils and Special Schools Regulations, 1959. The handicaps defined at that time were blindness, partial-sightedness, deafness and partial deafness, physical handicap, delicate health, and speech defects. By the Education Act 1970, educational responsibility for severely subnormal children who had hitherto been deemed unsuitable for schooling was transferred from the local Public Health Departments to the local education authorities; and three further special educational categories were added by the Chronically Sick and Disabled Persons Act 1970—dyslexia, autism and the multiple handicap of blindness with deafness.

The ascertainment of a child's need for special education is the responsibility of the local education authority.

In addition, there are at present about 8000 mentally and physically handicapped children in long-stay hospitals. The Council for Children's Welfare has recently reported (1975) on the lack of individual care and the degree of social deprivation sometimes suffered by these children, and this may be an area for the future development of co-operation between Health and Social Services authorities. The Council recommends that local authority social services departments should assume partial responsibility for the day-to-day care of these children. Similarly, a recent DHSS study (1975) has recommended the appointment of 'play-workers' for every 8 or 10 children in hospital.

In 1975, the Voluntary Council for Handicapped Children was established by the National Children's Bureau with funds from the Carnegie UK Trust. This was in response to the recommendation of a working party report (Younghusband, 1970) which drew attention to the lack of information available to parents, social workers and others about services for disabled children: the Council offers a comprehensive advisory and information service for all forms of disability in children. The Council serves to integrate a wide range of expertise: organizations concerned with specific handicaps, education, health visiting, social services and medical practice are represented, and 2 parents of handicapped children are members of the Council. The close link between the Council and the National Children's Bureau is particularly fortunate in providing a well-established research and information service and a tradition of publications designed for direct use by social workers, teachers and members of the general public, (for example, *Helping the Handicapped Child* in the family, at school, in day and residential care). The care of handicapped children is an area of service divided awkwardly between education, health and social services in the statutory sector and among a variety of voluntary services formed to generate concern for the needs associated with specific disabilities. Yet the experience of need in the family of a handicapped child cannot be neatly apportioned between services, nor is it specifically associated with a particular kind of disability. The Voluntary Council for Handicapped Children offers a promising opportunity to promote a better integration of understanding and care both nationally and locally.

Education welfare

Social work assistance for all schoolchildren (including the handicapped) is offered by Education Welfare Officers appointed by local education authorities. Their origins lie in the Education Act, 1870, when 'truancy officers' were appointed to deal with cases of non-attendance at school. Later changes of name (School Attendance Officer, Education Welfare Officer) have reflected their expanding duties associated with the growth and complexity of services available for schoolchildren. The Ralphs Report (1973) defined the objectives of education welfare officers as seeking to ensure that children benefit to the full from educational opportunities; their duties now relate to school attendance, the needs of handicapped school children, arranging for local education authority grants (e.g. for school clothing) and for free school meals for needy children, advising parents on educational opportunities and the educational needs of specific children, promoting constructive relationships between home and school, and any other activities which serve to facilitate a child's progress in his school work.

Because of their attachment to particular schools, officers serve as the major point of referral for head teachers when a child's school behaviour is unsatisfactory, when he shows signs in the classroom of emotional stress or listlessness, or when he is apparently in serious material need. The education welfare officer exercises, in effect, a dual role in meeting the needs of children whose education is suffering in some way, and helping children and parents to meet the educational expectations of teachers. The complexity of this work is self-evident: as Hargreaves (1967) has shown, the school child may be caught in the tension between academic and 'delinquescent' sub-cultures within the school and between incompatible value systems of teachers, parents and other pupils. The EWO becomes involved not only in meeting individual needs but in preventing the emergence of destructive stereotypes by which, for example, teachers, pupils and parents re-inforce certain patterns of behaviour and manipulate each other's compliance.

Principally because of the lack of adequate training opportunities, Education Welfare Officers lack the professional recognition which the demands of their work would seem to merit. In June 1972, there were only 2400 EWOs in England and Wales; 65% of these were in the age group 46–65, and it is apparent that, because of the lack of status and training, young and able recruits tend to leave the service. When the Ralphs Report was published, only 8% of this service held the Certificate in Education Welfare. As Davis has found in a recent survey, 'EWOs remain insecure about their major functions, unsure of their acceptance as social workers and uneasy about their professional position in relation to their teacher colleagues' (Davis, 18 February 1976).

The future of the education welfare service is uncertain at the present time; their need for some form of social work training is widely recognized and responsibility for providing this has now been assumed by the Central Council for Education and Training in Social Work. The employment of EWOs may in time be generally transferred to the local authority social services departments, by whom they would then be attached to schools in the same way that medical social workers are now appointed by the local authority rather than the National Health Service but continue to work within the hospitals. A letter from the Department of Education and Science to local education authorities and teachers' associations in 1975 has drawn attention to the increasing educational problems of truancy and violence, and has recommended the need for consultation and joint action between education and health authorities and local authority social services departments. As consultations of this kind become established, it is possible that the role of education welfare officer as a social worker of key importance will be stressed.

By the National Health Service Act 1946, *child guidance clinics* for disturbed children were established by local education authorities and in hospitals. The social work staff of these clinics is now appointed by local authority social services and social work departments, and their work is often concerned with behavioural difficulties at school and with truancy. Increasingly, clinics are extending their work beyond individual treatment and family therapy towards the provision of consultancy services to teachers.

Hitherto, in meeting the problem of truancy 3 distinct approaches have been made. The problem is sometimes seen in legal terms, as the wilful failure of child or parents to keep the laws relating to compulsory education; sometimes in social terms, as the result of adverse family or environmental influences; and sometimes in medical terms, as the outcome of emotional disturbances or pathological levels of anxiety. All 3 approaches are appropriate in certain situations, though there is some evidence to suggest that underlying all forms of truancy we may find adverse home circumstances and the personal unhappiness of the child. (See Tyerman 1968, West & Farringdon, 1973; Hersov 1960, 1972.) A principal difficulty at the present time, however, is ensuring the adequate assessment of factors which have led to truancy in particular cases. The appointment of social workers in schools, either as full members of school staff or by 'attachment' from local authority social services departments, would provide a means of obtaining more adequate assessments of individual need and more satisfactory co-operation between medical, educational and social service workers, among whom at present there are often divergent purposes and priorities. The plight of the individual truant is frequently worsened by the incompatible mixture of therapy, encouragement and punishment with which he is at present sometimes confronted.

6 Recent Structural Changes in Local Authority Provisions

In considering the functions of the personal social services, it will have become apparent that in the local authority sector a large body of legislation now applies. Until the passing of the Local Authority Social Services Act 1970 and its general implementation in 1971, services were provided by 3 local authority departments: the Public Health Department carried responsibility for mental disorder, physical disability, the care of discharged patients, home help services* and, in some areas, Meals-on-Wheels; the Children's Department, as its name implies, carried general responsibility for the child care provisions, though this was shared in respect of some legislation with probation and after-care officers and educational welfare officers; the Welfare Services Department was responsible for the welfare of the elderly, the homeless and, in some areas, had established family advice centres. Housing departments frequently offered the help of welfare officers who, while responsible principally for securing the payment of rents and for the arrangement of tenancies, sometimes undertook more general family welfare work. The structural disjunctions of services inevitably led to difficulties for consumers—clients needed to be referred from one agency to another, and some problems and needs seemed to be artificially divided between departments. Furthermore, as social legislation became increasingly wide in scope, and departments were given powers to extend their services to promote the general welfare of client-groups and the prevention of distress, so the problems of overlapping services and of the demarcation of

* Home help services before 1918 were, with few exceptions provided only by voluntary organizations (through paid helpers and volunteers), in recognition that in the poorest communities some people were at risk simply through inability to do their own housework. One of the most notable of these organizations was the Jewish Sickroom Help Society, formed in Stepney in 1895, which provided helpers to expectant mothers for two-week periods. Their duties were to undertake the housework and cooking and to care for the children. Home help services to undertake these duties were recommended to local authorities specifically for the care of expectant mothers and mothers of young children by the Maternity and Child Welfare Act, 1918. They became a universal resource by the National Health Service Act, 1948.

responsibilities increased. Services were competitors for resources, irrespective of their common concern with welfare; and frequently the aims and values which they held in common made co-operation difficult rather than easy.

The Committee on *Local Authority and Allied Personal Social Services* (the Seebohm Committee) was set up in 1966 and reported in 1968 (Cmnd 3703). Its central term of reference was 'to secure an effective family service' as suggested in paragraph 7 of the White Paper *The Child, the Family and the Young Offender* (Cmnd 2742 HMSO 1965). The problem was seen initially as one of co-ordinating related but separately administered local authority services which all impinged on family life, which in Titmuss's words were administered in conditions of 'balkanised rivalry', and which—by the nature of their responsibilities—intervened too much and too variously in the lives of some families while failing to meet the needs of others. The terms of reference of the committee were circumscribed by an assumption prevalent in social policy and social work that the family is the proper focus for social intervention in situations of need. One of the achievements of the committee was to question the universal validity of this assumption, not by direct challenge but by redefining the concept of the family. 'It would be impossible to restrict our work solely to the needs of 2 or even 3-generation families. We could only make sense of our task by considering also childless couples and individuals without any close relatives: in other words, everybody.' (Cmnd 3703 para 32).

The outcome of the Committee's recommendations was the passing of the Local Authority Social Services Act, 1970. This established, from April 1971, Local Authority Social Services Committees which replaced the Children's and Welfare Committees and assumed the personal service responsibilities of Public Health Committees. The functions of the new Committees were therefore in brief:

(1) The care of children deprived of normal home life, preventive measures to offset the deprivation of children and juvenile delinquency (measures considerably strengthened by the Children and Young Persons Act, 1969, which, as we have seen, regulated the criteria by which young offenders should be brought before the courts and their care following court appearances), and the protection of children in adoption proceedings and in foster-care.

(2) Welfare services for the physically and mentally handicapped, the welfare and accommodation of the elderly, temporary housing, day nurseries.

(3) The supervision of day care for the under-fives and of other child-minding facilities, the care of unsupported mothers, home helps, and services for the physically handicapped and mentally disordered—home visiting, day centres, clubs, adult training centres and workshops, **hostels** and homes.

With two omissions (the transfer of the education welfare service and the welfare responsibilities of housing departments), the Act endorsed the administrative changes recommended by the Seebohm Committee. Since the re-organization of the National Health Service in 1974, social work in hospitals and clinics has been added to the responsibilities of Social Services Committees.

The Act empowers the Secretary of State to designate further functions to local authorities under any other enactment, if these functions seem to him appropriate for discharge through a Social Services Committee. Furthermore, a local authority may refer to the Committee relevant matters within the authority's functions in respect of research (section 5(1)(c) of the Health Visiting and Social Work (Training) Act, 1962) and of financial assistance to voluntary organizations (section 65 of the Health Services and Public Health Act, 1968). A majority of the members of the Committee must be elected members of the local authority, and sub-committees must contain at least one elected member. Local authorities exercise their social service functions under the general guidance of the Secretary of State, and the Act limits the authority's powers of delegation of responsibility for services.

The Act was merely an administrative device; it did not embody the spirit of the Seebohm Report nor its philosophy concerning the focus and authority of personal social service. In this respect, therefore, some current practices sometimes appear to be at a philosophical distance from the recommendations of the Report which were concerned with more than structural and administrative change. In particular, the Report advocated a philosophy of service based on community socialization and responsibility in addition to a family focus, and the blurring of boundaries so far as possible between those who ostensibly provide the services and those who use them. Thus, the Report emphasized the relationship of both families and services to local community life; and the local community was envisaged as the proper setting for the provision of services in two senses. First, services were to be provided from a base within each local community (of between 50,000 and 100,000 people). Second, services were to be devised in such a way as to relate to the informal helping processes of community life. To some extent, therefore, the community would help to decide the form and direction to be taken by the local authority service; the social worker's accountability was to extend to the local community in which he worked as well as to his organization and to his clients; the authority of services and social workers was to be infused with greater emphasis on the caring capacities of local citizens, to whom professional services would offer support and encouragement rather than an elitist form of leadership.

By this approach, the Committee implied a reconciliation between the primary term of reference and more democratically conceived forms of service: earlier administrative divisions of clients into specific deprived and dependent groups had led inevitably to specialization within social work; this had been valuable in developing understanding and skills, but it had also tended towards an elitist separation from informal and voluntary forms of service. The new local authority service was to be both family oriented and community based. Concern for the whole community and an extension of the scope of social work were to be combined within a single administrative framework which would resolve, for potential clients, earlier difficulties of access, of the arbitrary divisions of responsibility, and of articulating complex needs in administrative terms.

To the extent that a broad appreciation of needs rather than a rigid adherence to administrative definition of duties was to become the major basis for the provision of services, the Seebohm Report represented the endorsement of social work as a profession in its own right rather than merely a service-adjunct to local authority administration. Social workers, encouraged by the Report and by the imminent formation of a united professional association (BASW), and organized to some extent in the Seebohm Implementation Action Group, pressed for the directorship of local authority services to be available only to men and women with direct experience and understanding of social work practice (in preference, for example, to medical officers of health or career administrators), and the Act embodies the requirement that directors should be appointed only with ministerial approval.

What of the outcome? In structural and administrative terms, the Seebohm Report and the Act have together brought advantages which should accumulate in the years ahead. The size of the new local authority departments ensures their greater ability to secure resources within local authority budgets. It makes possible also an increased influence in the work of other services: for example, the Supplementary Benefits Commission's local offices; the need to develop team work with local doctors; the need for co-ordinated policies with housing departments to combat homelessness and to establish housing advisory services; the need for resources for youth employment and other services for school leavers; the disparity between the extent of needs and the extent of provisions for children requiring special educational and medical help.* In all these situations, the size of the new local authority services offers the opportunity of weighty influence. The co-ordination of earlier services makes possible also a systematic evaluation of the cost-effectiveness of different kinds of provisions relative to each other such as residential care, domiciliary care, social work support, home helps, day-nurseries. Decisions about service priorities can now be based on a broad evaluation of social needs. The Report suggested that evaluation of this kind would help to clarify the social function of the personal social services, and that this clarification would serve to promote mutual understanding with other professional groups, particularly doctors and teachers.

These are all potentially important gains. But the recognition of such wide

---

* It was estimated that one child in ten needed special help, but that services only reached one in twenty-two.

and complex opportunities inevitably brings some dissatisfactions with the reality of what has been achieved in the short period since 1971. The principal sources of dissatisfaction are as follows:

The Report gave little attention to precise and practical ways by which the Committee's vision of local authority services might be realized. In particular, it did not sufficiently deal with the problems of making effective use of the resources and manpower actually available. A simple example of this is the calibre of people available to fill the directorships: the Institute of Local Government Studies, in a survey of the appointments made between the passing of the Act and the establishment of the new departments in 1971, reported that, of 136 appointees, only 53 were professionally qualified in social work and that 34 lacked both professional and academic qualifications. Similar difficulties have been encountered in filling other senior appointments; experienced social workers, used to the colleagueship of small separate departments, have been placed in positions of managerial responsibility in united departments of considerable size and complexity. They have been responsible for helping a wide range of staff drawn from earlier specializations and traditions of work to undertake new duties and tasks within a newly devised formulation of the nature of social service.

Similarly, traditional patterns of local authority structures and accountability are implicitly challenged by the social radicalism of the Seebohm Report; it is not easy to reconcile the philosophy of the Report with long-standing hierarchical patterns of service-organization. The re-organization of local government in 1974 has exacerbated these difficulties in some areas.

It is possible also that the comprehensiveness and size of the local authority service may tend to reduce the initiative of other services in those areas of welfare where co-operation is most essential. Small local voluntary organizations particularly may find it difficult to feel a sense of partnership, rather than relative insignificance, in negotiations with very large statutory structures.

Specialist social workers from the earlier departments have, understandably, found it difficult to widen the scope of their interests and methods of work and to undertake 'generalist' functions. The Seebohm Committee did not condemn specialization but recognized that it would need to be redefined; the Committee's concern was that specialization should not lead to a denial of service or to a blinkered view of the social worker's responsibility for meeting clients' needs. By a misuse of the word 'generic', however, a concept properly applied to the education of social workers has been inappropriately transferred to their practice; staff have been appointed as 'generic social workers' with 'generic caseloads'. What this has meant in practice is the partial loss of specialized skills and an unrealistic expectation that all social workers should be professionally competent in dealing with every kind of human problem and need. Insufficient regard has been given, particularly in the implementation of a rapid flow of social legislation, to the need to tailor the role of services to the capacities of those who execute them.*

The democratic idealism of the Seebohm Report has implications for the relationship between managers and field workers and between professional social workers and local volunteer helpers. How far is it possible to democratize management?† How far is it possible for staff who identify themselves as professional people to adopt a partnership role (even a secondary role) in the informal networks of help within local communities? Furthermore, it is difficult for social workers brought up in traditions of individual help and the primacy of certain treatment values to come to terms with wider forms of help and the relativity of value systems in welfare. To take a simple example, the care of the mentally disordered has hitherto been based on individual diagnosis and treatment and on the achievement of adjustment to certain behavioural values, for example, the importance of self-sufficiency through work. But it may need to be recognized that the diagnosis-treatment model is not always the most effective means of offering help; the patient may come from an environment where work is not a prime value, and this relativity of values may need to be recognized, understood and accepted if intervention is to be constructively used. How can we protect the valuable therapeutic work undertaken by social workers brought up in a medical tradition of practice, while at the same time utilizing the helping capacities of others (professional workers or local community helpers) whose approaches to need and difficulty may be entirely different? As the Seebohm Report suggested, social services need to be seen as large-scale experiments in helping. If the pre-Seebohm services had contained the flexibility of methods and values that this implies, their employees would have found the transition easier; but possibly the transition itself would not have been necessary.

The formal recognition of social work as a professional discipline and the centralizing of social workers within a single local authority department have made for some loss of contact with other professions, exacerbated by the loss of specialization in workloads. Doctors regret the loss of links with the former mental welfare officers and home help services; head-teachers complain of the loss of personal contact with child care specialists.

In attempting to make services comprehensive, and preventive as well as therapeutic, departments have encountered problems of assessment, prognosis and resource allocation. The assumption has sometimes been made that traditional social work practice, with peripheral modification, is the appropriate way of dealing with the needs revealed and presented. Traditional practice, as implied earlier, has been built on certain assump-

---

* See T. H. Marshall in W. A. Robson and B. Crick: *The Future of the Social Services*, Penguin, 1971; and Seebohm Report, para. 576.

† Reference should be made to the work of J. Algie in devising alternative managerial structures. See for example 'Management and Organisation in the Social Services', *British Hospital Journal and Social services Review*, 26 June 1970.

tions of individual or family malfunctioning. But it becomes increasingly apparent that malfunctioning may sometimes indicate ongoing and widespread problems of social deprivation which call for a broad reappraisal of policies, services and social processes lying well beyond the operational scope of the personal social services or the professional competence of the social worker. One social worker, for example, reported in *Community Care*, (24 September 1975) has said 'There has been a shift in attitude (among social workers) towards social policy. To hell with saying it is all based on personal relationship. It is a question of manipulating the structures of society'. If this is true, it is questionable whether local authority social workers (because of their employee-role, their small numbers, their relative powerlessness where policies are formulated, and their lack of the relevant skills) are the appropriate people to do this manipulation. As *The Times* leader for 14 August 1975 suggested, the Seebohm Report stimulated a spectacular increase in public provision for social welfare: in the 10 years 1963–1973 expenditure on the personal social services increased from £79 m to £500 m. Yet complaints about service inadequacy have also increased. In part this reflects new responsibilities imposed by legislation (notably the CYP Act 1969 and the CSDP Act 1970). But it reflects also the limitations of the services and of social work in comprehending and containing the complexity of the challenge of social needs. Parker (1969) has pointed out that service provision can no longer be based simply on additional resources and on more social workers. Rather, we need to devise new patterns of service provision based on a realistic appraisal of consumer attitudes, the quality and promotion of community involvement, the skills and aspirations of professionals and other workers, and the reduction of stigma among users; we need more effective resource planning in the light of demographic changes (e.g. the longer survival of the dependent handicapped, and longer life among dependent old people); and we need to recognize changing social and political values concerning citizens' rights, the distribution of power, the nature of 'help'.

The demands made upon services will certainly increase. Demand may also change in quality and may then require a qualitative change in how services are provided. If this is so, then not only the personal social services will be affected. As we have seen, for example, of the 95,867 children in local authority care in March 1974 (an increase of 2679 in one year), 7088 were admitted because of the lack of suitable family housing. In a situation like this, it is no longer appropriate to regard responsibility for the care of children simply as a matter for social services departments.

THE STRUCTURE OF SOCIAL SERVICES DEPARTMENTS

Following the re-organization of local government in 1974, departments are now situated in 39 non-metropolitan county councils, 34 metropolitan districts in the 6 metropolitan counties, and 33 boroughs in London. Each local authority is responsible for devising its own departmental organization and system of operation, subject only to the requirements of legislation and the endorsement by the DHSS of certain matters (the appointment of directors of social service, the provision of new services, and applications for building loans). In the promotion of community welfare, therefore, a wide range of managerial decisions are possible. Fundamentally the tasks of committees and directors are related to the solving of 3 problems. First, relationships with other services: for example, the effective implementation of child care legislation depends on co-operative relationships with schools, courts and income maintenance services; the care of the mentally disordered involves co-operation with the professions, institutions and structures of the National Health Service (see Jones, MIND 1973). Second, the setting of priorities: how much, for example, should be spent on the employment of home helps relative to the employment of other kinds of field staff; whether to appoint a community worker or a family caseworker. Third, establishing standards of service in relation to the needs of particular groups of clients (for example, the frequency and aims of visiting to a family where a child may be subject to neglect) and, related to this, the amount of control to be exercised over employees both in general and in specific situations. Brown (1975) suggests that there need be no fundamental incompatibility between administrative control and the professional freedom of professionally qualified employees. But this remains an area of dispute, depending on how far employees see their functions in terms of delegated duties and how far they define their work in terms of professional methods and tasks. Furthermore, relatively few employees are professionally qualified and have a professional orientation: the issue remains whether different kinds of control and of worker accountability should be devised in accordance with individual orientation, training and competence.

These are contentious issues. It needs to be borne in mind that the duties carried out by social services departments are essentially imposed by legislation *upon the local authorities*. These duties are delegated for their implementation to the Social Services Committees, and thence to the departments' employees (including the social workers); it is misleading to think of them as the employees' duties, in the sense of being directly imposed upon them by legislation. Thus, we cannot properly speak of the congruence or divergence of a social worker's statutory duties and professional tasks as if these were on the same level of conceptual analysis: the first represents the result of secondary delegation from the local authority; the second is a matter of the individual's personal orientation of values, loyalties and skills. The dilemma lies in whether one regards the professional orientation and performance as wholly contained within the delegated duties, or whether one believes that, in addition to the choices available to him in the performance of his delegated duties, the social worker has a professional obligation to undertake additional tasks at his own discretion.

It is a further function of the Committee and Directorate to plan ahead in the light of demographic change. Forward planning (on a 10-year basis) is now required by the DHSS (see Local Authority Social services Act 1970, section 7, and Circular 35/72) within centrally devised guidelines, so that the general implementation of social policy should be systematic rather than incremental, and so that nationally equitable standards of services should be achieved (see Brown, 1975). [Reference should be made to an article by the Director of Social Services for Wiltshire (Newton, 29 January 1975) in which readers were challenged to help him balance his budget in the light of local needs for services.]

The internal structure of a social services department is a matter for local decision.* The Director and Deputy Director are usually supported by 3 or 4 Assistant Directors responsible for specific groups of functions (for example, field services of all kinds; residential work; research, planning and staffing; administration). In many departments, there is a consultancy grade of appointments responsible for the promotion of work on behalf of a particular client-group or for the development of relationships with other services: for example, health services liaison, the care of the handicapped, mental health, intermediate treatment. Local teams of social workers are led by Area Directors with the assistance of appointees at Principal Assistant and Senior Social Worker grades. There are various patterns of relationship between local teams and the home help, residential care and day centre staff.

The quality of services offered by a department depends largely on the quality of the staff and on the ways they are deployed relative to their competence and skills. In addition, the effectiveness of services depends on the extent to which members of the local community understand the objectives and methods of the department's work and are able to offer complementary informal services; the Committee's support of staff and their commitment to the development of community understanding are an important resource.

At present, about 200,000 men and women are employed in social services departments in England and Wales, of whom 30,000 are field social workers or in more senior appointments. The total net expenditure in the year 1972–3 amounted to £324 m of which about half was spent on the needs of the elderly and a third on child care. The costs of different types of service were as follows: £52 m on field social work, £166 m on residential care and £106 m on community and day care. In total this represented about 7% of the total expenditure of local authorities, (Hulton, Imber & Mitchell 1974). Inflation has led to a situation of possible reduction in services over the next few years.

THE PARALLEL RE-ORGANIZATION OF LOCAL AUTHORITY SERVICES IN SCOTLAND

As in England and Wales, the promotion of comprehensive personal social

---

* See A. M. Hey & R. Rowbottom: *Social Services Departments,* Heinemann 1974. R. Rowbottom & A. M. Hey: *Towards an Organisation of Social Services Departments,* Local Government Chronicle and Charles Knight & Co. Ltd. 1970. R. Foren and M. Brown: *Planning for Service.*

services in Scotland arose from a concern for the treatment of delinquent children. The Kilbrandon Committee, (Cmnd 2306 HMSO 1964), established by the Secretary of State for Scotland to consider the treatment of children and young persons appearing before the courts, recommended two structures: the development of 'lay panels' to replace the juvenile courts, and the formation of a local authority 'social education department' into which would be merged the local authorities' child care responsibilities, so as to form a family service. The Committee reported in 1964, and the report was succeeded 2 years later by a White Paper, *Social Work and the Community* (Cmnd 3065 HMSO 1966) which, like the Seebohm Committee's report, advocated a more comprehensive service and laid stress on the importance of linking provisions with informal networks of community life.

Paragraphs 8 and 15 set out the reasons for, and the philosophy of, reorganization: first, the need for a more rational and effective deployment of the existing staffs of local authority services; second, a recognition of the complexity of clients' needs which defy adequate administrative separation and definition; third, the fact that social workers share certain common skills which might provide the professional basis for a unified service; and fourth, the importance of strengthening the personal and social relationships within local communities which provide valuable informal support at times of personal difficulty. The importance of a community basis for service is stated as follows: 'it would clearly be better for the individual people concerned . . . if the individual's own capacity to deal with his difficulties, supported by his friends and neighbours, could be increased' (para. 15). Similarly, recognition is given to the importance of preventive work, achieved through co-operation with other formal services, and with voluntary organizations and informal groups.

The White Paper made 3 major recommendations: the merging of local authority functions under the National Health Service (Scotland) Act 1947, National Assistance Act 1948, Children Act 1948, Mental Health (Scotland) Act 1960, Education (Scotland) Act, 1962 and the Children and Young Persons Act 1963, together with the work of the Probation and After-care Service; secondly, the extension of personal social services to provide *all* citizens with advice and guidance; and, arising from these recommendations, the formation of a new Social Work Department. Paragraph 9 of the report summarized the work of the new Department: it was to be based on a county structure; it was to assume all responsibilities for child care and school welfare, probation and aftercare (the title Probation Officer was to cease to exist), the community care and after-care of the ill and the welfare of the handicapped, old people's welfare, home help services, the care of homeless families, and residential services. The White Paper recommended also the formation of an Advisory Council on Social Work which would offer advisory services to local authorities by the appointment of staff drawn from the inspectorates for child care, approved schools and probation, and from the welfare officers of the Scottish Home and Health Department.

The White Paper, following the earlier recommendations of the Kilbrandon Committee (Cmnd 2603, 1964) recommended also the replacement of juvenile courts by a Children's Panel for each county and city (paragraph 63 *et seq.*); this recommendation is considered elsewhere.

The recommendations of the White Paper were legislated in their entirety in the Social Work (Scotland) Act, 1968, which, like the Local Authority Social Services Act, became fully operational in April 1971: The Scottish Act is a considerably more substantial document; it offers more precise guidance as to the working of the Social Work Departments and their operational philosophy, and, unlike the Local Authority Social Services Act, states that 'it shall be the duty of every local authority to promote social welfare' [Section 12 (1)] as well as to alleviate distress. In this respect, and in respect of the acquisition of responsibility for probation and after-care and for education welfare, the duties of Social Work Departments extend beyond the formal responsibilities of their counterparts in England and Wales. Significantly, all these duties are subsumed in the phrase 'social work'; in effect, personal social service *is* social work. Whether this is a desirable equation is, of course, open to debate; as has been suggested at the beginning of this section, a case can be made—certainly in respect of services in England and Wales—for maintaining a distinction between 'social service' and the profession of social work, and this will be examined further in later chapters.

The operations of the Social Work Departments and of the children's hearings fall within the province of the Secretary of State for Scotland and under the over-view of the Scottish Social Work Services Group within the Scottish Education Department.

7 The Probation and After-care Service

Voluntary social workers, attached to the Police Court Mission of the Church of England, offered help to defendants (particularly those charged with offences of drunkenness) in the last quarter of the 19th century. The probation and after-care service represents a statutory development of their work, based on two movements in social policy: first, a shift in emphasis from punishment to reform, initially for petty offenders and juveniles but since the last war extended to defendants convicted of more serious offences; second, the recognition of a need for alternatives to the use of expensive, inappropriate,* and in outcome, largely ineffective forms of custodial care. For example, four out of five 16-year old boys discharged from Borstal in 1970 were reconvicted within 2 years, most of them within 9 months of their discharge. Yet, following reconviction, half of them were sent back to Borstal. The reconviction rate for Borstal dischargees of all ages was 65.2%. Similarly, the reconviction rate of 16-year olds discharged from detention centres was 65.3% (Report, Cmnd 5814). The average cost of maintaining a young man in Borstal was, in 1973, £1840 p.a.

The Probation of Offenders Act, 1907, developed an earlier form of sentence, 'binding over to keep the peace,' to include the supervision of offenders by an officer of the court. The role of the probation officer was defined in the Act as 'to advise, assist and befriend'. This phrase was reiterated in the Criminal Justice Act, 1948, and is still in use. The appointment of probation officers remained a permissive power of the courts until 1925; since then there has been a steady increase in legislation to extend the work of the service beyond the supervision of petty offenders on probation. The Adoption Act, 1926, made it possible for officers to be appointed as guardians *ad litem*; the Children and Young Persons Act, 1933, established supervision orders for juveniles who were not charged with an offence but were considered to be in need of guidance—probation officers were

* A Home Office study in 1975 related the overcrowding of prisons to the imprisonment of petty offenders and of the 'maladjusted'.

frequently asked to supervise those known to be in moral danger or to have been the subject of sexual assault; Money Payments Supervision Orders were instituted in 1935, by which probation officers could be required by the courts to supervise the payment of a fine or debt to the court; marital counselling work, which had been undertaken voluntarily by probation officers for many years, became a statutory responsibility in 1937. The Criminal Justice Act, 1948, made provision for extending the use of probation orders to all offences which did not carry fixed penalties and strengthened the role of the probation officer as an after-care agent for those discharged from custodial sentences. The Matrimonial Proceedings Act, 1958, provided for the appointment of probation officers as welfare officers in Divorce Courts, responsible for investigating and reporting on the future needs of the children of divorced parents.

Up to this point the work of probation officers had been about equally divided between the supervision of juveniles (up to the 17th birthday) and of adults. Since then, the work of the service has been increasingly concerned with the supervision of adult offenders. (By the CYP Act 1969, juveniles are no longer placed on probation and their supervision, under care and supervision orders, is being steadily transferred from the probation service to local authority social workers.)

The Criminal Justice Acts in the last 15 years have been principally concerned with modifications and alternatives to custodial sentences for adult offenders: the treatment of the young adult offender was regulated by the Act of 1961; the 1967 Act permitted the suspension of prison sentences of up to 2 years and instituted Suspended Sentence Supervision Orders; the supervision of prisoners released on parole was instituted in 1967; and the Act of 1972 together with the Powers of the Criminal Courts Act 1973 promoted, through the probation service, a range of alternatives to imprisonment—bail-hostel accommodation is now available as an alternative to a remand in custody, probation orders for adult offenders may now include a condition of residence in a probation hostel, offenders over the age of 17 may be required to undertake social service for between 40 and 240 hours during 1 year within the terms of a community service order, and men on probation may be ordered to attend a day training centre for 60 days if they are unemployed and, in the view of the courts, in need of some form of social re-education.

By the Act of 1967, following a report of the Advisory Council on the Treatment of Offenders (Home Office, 1963), probation officers were re-titled 'probation and after-care officers'. They then assumed responsibility for all prison welfare work and for all forms of statutory and voluntary after-care in respect of offenders discharged from prisons, Borstals and detention centres. The White Paper, *The Adult Offender* (1965) had already led to a strengthening of the links between the service and voluntary bodies offering after-care hostels, and the National Association for the Care and Rehabilitation of Offenders was formed in the same year.

ORGANIZATION

Central responsibility for the service rests with the Home Office. Members of the Probation Inspectorate advise local services on the development of provisions, inspect services at intervals of about 5 years and confirm the appointment of newly appointed officers. Officers are appointed by local probation committees, made up of magistrates and co-opted members, and their work is regularly reviewed and discussed by small case-committees of the probation committee. The duties of the probation committee, as set out in the Powers of the Criminal Courts Act 1973 (Schedule 3), are: to provide for the efficient performance of the work of officers; to assign them to courts and to provide secretarial and other support; to oversee local provisions for ex-prisoners; to secure appropriate arrangements for the implementation of community service orders; and to provide and administer day training centres, bail hostels, probation hostels and homes, and other establishments appropriate to the rehabilitation of offenders. Case-committees have responsibility not only to ensure the satisfactory quality of the work of local teams of officers (equivalent to the area teams of social services departments) but also to support individual officers in any difficulties arising in the course of their day-to-day work and to advise on the amendment of orders: for example, when an officer is considering the early discharge of a probation order. The costs of probation services, now organized on a county basis, are shared between the Local Authority and the Home Office. Until 1973 this was arranged on a 50/50 basis, but Government grants towards expenditure on local services now stand at 80% for general purposes and 100% for hostels, homes and day-training centres. Each magistrates court must have the services of at least one male and one female probation officer.

Local teams of officers, organized on a geographical basis, are supervised by senior probation officers usually in a ratio of about 5:1. In addition, senior probation officers may be appointed to manage teams of officers concerned with specific functions—for example, day training centres, hostels, after-care, the training of staff and students, research. Local patterns of organization are devised at the discretion of committees and senior staff. The general management of the service for a county is undertaken by the Chief Probation Officer, supported by a deputy and a group of assistants. Unlike the social services of local authorities, the probation service has traditionally been non-hierarchical; within the last decade, some local services were organized on only 2 tiers. Recent developments in the responsibilities of probation officers, combined with the merger of local services within county structures, have led to the formation of managerial hierarchies; but responsibility for decisions in day-to-day work with the clients of the service remains with main-grade officers and their senior officer; and, through the case committees, officers have regular and informal access to members of the probation and after-care committee. The pattern of work-accountability in the probation service is therefore different from that of the local authority service; this difference is further increased by the status of the committee which, while directly responsible to the Home Office and morally responsible to the community, is not an elected body. Probation officers are servants of committees, not of central or local government. (See R. A. D. Forder: Lay Committees and Professional Workers in the English Probation Service, *Journal of Social and Economic Administration*, **3**(4) 1969.)

In 1975, there were 4728 full-time probation and after-care officers in England and Wales. In 1973, officers supervised about 31,000 probation and supervision orders, 8736 voluntary after-care cases and 14,785 statutory after-care cases (of which 10,500 were from Detention Centres and Borstals and 2500 on parole supervision). The average caseload of a main-grade officer is about 40 (Home Office, 1975).

THE WORK OF THE OFFICER

A probation and after-care officer has certain clearly defined mandatory responsibilities and, in addition, is encouraged to offer a range of other services relevant to the work of the courts. In the first group are included: the preparation and presentation of reports on the social circumstances of any person who appears before a court; the supervision of offenders placed on probation orders, money payments supervision orders and suspended sentence supervision orders; keeping in touch with the families of those under supervision; the provision of welfare services within prisons, and after-care to any person discharged from prison, Borstal or detention centre; the provision of information to the Parole Board to help in the selection of parolees, and the supervision of prisoners on parole; information to the Criminal Injuries Compensation Board; staffing local hostels for offenders and people on bail, community service programmes and day training centres; marital conciliation services, the welfare work of the divorce courts, and the duties of guardian *ad litem*; and help to women brought before the courts under the Street Offences Act, 1959. In the second category of work, officers are empowered to undertake voluntary supervision in pre-delinquency situations, to give advice to the parties involved in 'consent-to-marry' cases, and to offer help to people who are dependent on alcohol or drugs. In addition, some local services have recently undertaken the provision of day centres and group activities for people under supervision and for the wives and children of men in prison.

The service is regarded by the members essentially as a social work service, in which the professional values of social work are the dominant values. That is to say, the main grade officer has not been required to any considerable extent to undertake tasks or to promote social purposes incompatible with his professional ideology. I say 'to any considerable extent', as there are undoubtedly occasions when probation officers, individually or collectively, disagree with the decisions of a court or possibly with the intention and implementation of a particular law or statutory procedure. Thus an officer may be required to supervise a probationer who in his view should not have been placed on probation; he may have to arrange for the recall to prison of an ex-prisoner, irrespective of his views about the value of this recall. In as much as there is compatibility between professional values and statutory requirements, this is largely the result, first, of the freedom of the individual officer to set about his daily work in his own way, and, second, of the extent to which responsibility for making decisions affecting the lives of his clients has been delegated to the main-grade officer. One of the fears sometimes expressed by officers is that the development of hierarchical structures within the service may lead to a withdrawal of this individual autonomy. In addition, there is the possibility that new responsibilities may be added to the work of the service which officers consider to be at variance with their personal or professional values.

There are certain anomalies in the probation officer's work which hold potential for future crisis in the service. For example, the role of the officer is 'to advise, assist and befriend' those placed in his care, and, while it may be argued that 'befriend' is a somewhat ambigious word in the context of a statutory order which confers considerable power on the officer, probation officers in general would not wish for a reformulation of their role; broadly speaking, the phrase reflects very adequately the motivation of entrants to the service. An individual officer's work is frequently evaluated by his senior by his capacity to form the kind of relationship that the phrase implies. Yet the evaluation of the service as a whole is often based (in the work of the Home Office Research Unit, for example) not primarily on the quality of relationships, but on the extent of reconviction among those under supervision. Something of this dilemma is reflected in the Morison Report, 1962 (Cmnd 1650). 'Society must protect itself against the wrongdoer. It must show its disapproval of crime.' But the Report goes on to stress the importance of keeping to a minimum any interference with life and liberty, and regards the probation service as a means of protecting society while minimizing restrictions on offenders and offering them help. Thus the aim of the service is clearly related to the reduction of criminal behaviour and the prevention of crime. If one could assume that nobody will commit a crime who has the benefit of a concerned relationship with a representative of the courts, then no ambiguity of purpose need arise. But no such assumption is possible, for it overlooks the variety of environmental influences which may lead to crime, and which are outside the control of a probation officer, however skilful his ability to demonstrate concern and to form close relationships. If the purpose of the probation service is to be identified primarily with solving the social problem presented by criminal behaviour, then a reformulation of the role, scope and facilities of the probation service is essential; but such a reformulation might well be at variance in some respects with the motivation of officers and the professional techniques and values that they have hitherto upheld. This dilemma has been usefully explored by Davies (HMSO, 1974) who analyses the different kinds of 'causal texture' within the environment and their relationships to criminal behaviour, and comments:

> 'There are ... many individuals whose personalities cannot cope with environmental stress, but society at present is able to do no more than pick them up each time they fall and give them another chance of "proving" themselves ... If the problem of deviant behaviour or social need could be anticipated wholly or mainly in terms of the personality of the client, then it might theoretically be possible to deal with it (or respond to it) by focussing on the probationer in isolation from his environment. But if, as is now generally agreed, much deviant behaviour and social need are associated not only with personality factors but also with environmental conditions, then part of the task of social work must be to see the client and to treat him within the context of his environment.' (pp. 100–101)

Development of the social work task of the probation service may well be appropriate, but one doubts whether the service, or *any* single personal social service, can achieve the range of intervention that would be necessary to affect the level of crime; and it is uncertain how far the probation service can incorporate the necessary range of activities within the professional ideology of its members. The new provisions within the service, legislated by the Criminal Justice Act 1972, are a step in this direction; but the autonomy of individual officers could work *either* towards an increasing experimentation in intervention *or* towards the perpetuation of styles of work which, while experienced as helpful by many clients individually, have little general effect on the criminal statistics.

Furthermore, a probation officer may find he disagrees with the designation of certain kinds of behaviour as crimes. He will carry the responsibilities of supervision but may lack conviction about the social validity of his personal and professional involvement. In the past this applied to many officers when attempted suicide and all male homosexual behaviour were criminal offences. Probation officers may accept the role of 'advise, assist and befriend' while not accepting responsibility for reducing the number of 'crimes' in particular categories.

There are, therefore, areas of tension between individual motivation, professional ideology and public expectations in the work of the probation service, associated with the extent to which, in particular circumstances, the role of the officer should be not merely influential but coercive in the lives of others. Future developments in the work of the service, both through legislation and managerially, may exacerbate these tensions. Whether they do so will depend on the extent to which officers continue to work autonomously and on the manner in which their intervention is linked with social policies about the problem of criminal behaviour.

Probation officers have avoided some of the complexities of organizational and functional change which have affected the work of local authority workers since 1970, but they share with them certain professional dilemmas and uncertainties about the future. Although the Seebohm Report was not directly related to the probation service, probation officers were sensitive to the fact that, in the re-organization of personal social services in Scotland, the service had lost its identity within the work of the local authorities; and, taken in conjunction with recent legislation and White Papers, the Report had the effect of drawing the attention of officers to certain professional choices that needed to be made in their work; for example, how far were they social workers concerned primarily with meeting the needs of their clients, and how far should they become increasingly identified with the penal system and its purposes? What whould be the focus of work—the family or the individual offender? Should the work continue to be based on the assumption that criminal behaviour represents the abnormal personal response of an individual to his social responsibilities requiring individual treatment; or should greater emphasis be given than hitherto to social influences on criminal behaviour and to finding ways of intervening in the context of group needs and community malfunctioning? Obviously, these are not choices between exclusive alternatives; the choices lie in deciding upon relative emphases and the deployment of resources; the key skills are assessing when a particular emphasis is appropriate, and defining the criteria of appropriateness.

STATUTORY ORDERS

A probation order may be made by a court for 1, 2 or 3 years: it represents an undertaking by an offender to keep the peace, to lead an honest and industrious life, and to keep in touch with his probation officer as directed. Additional conditions may be added to the order: in particular, conditions of residence for not more than 1 year, a condition to attend a day training centre, or a requirement to undergo psychiatric treatment. A probationer who commits a further offence or who fails to comply with a requirement in the probation order may be dealt with either for the original offence for which he was placed on probation, by a fine, or by the making of a further order.

After-care services following discharge from penal institutions are now for the most part a voluntary matter from the offender's point of view; but after-care is compulsory for all offenders who were under the age of 21 at the time of the sentence and for prisoners released on parole, from extended sentences and from life sentences.

Community service orders were first proposed by the Wootton Committee on Non-Custodial and Semi-Custodial Penalties (HMSO Advisory Council on the Penal System) 1970, in the context of a rising prison population (41,000 in 1970).* The recommendation was incorporated in the

* This number was reduced in 1972 and 1973 to 36,774 but rose again in 1974.

Criminal Justice Act 1972 (Sections 15 to 19); experimental programmes were instituted in 6 areas and were made generally available in 1975, though there are, in February 1976, seven areas still without this provision. A CSO requires the consent of the offender, who must be at least 17 years of age.

The aim of the CSO is to regard the offender as a social resource rather than as a social burden, by involving him in social service of a kind that he will himself regard as worthwhile and which is linked to the life of his own local community. Offenders on CSOs are required to work for between 40 and 240 hours within 1 year; they may be attached to youth clubs and to a wide range of services for the handicapped, and the tasks of the senior probation officer responsible for the scheme in local areas are to match the offender to the work available, to ensure that he undertakes the work required, and to develop suitable settings for attachment. CSOs have been described by the British Association of Social Workers as 'one of the most promising innovations in penal policy in recent years'.* The philosophy behind them relates closely to the concern of the Seebohm Committee, noted earlier, to blur the distinction between the givers and receivers of help, and to develop a community orientation of service. The order represents a combining of punishment and therapy: on the one hand, it deprives the offender of some freedom in the use of his leisure time, but, on the other, it offers constructive activities and the opportunity for an offender to change his attitudes in respect of his responsibilities to the local community. If an offender fails to comply with the requirements of the order, he may be brought back to court (on summons or warrant); according to the circumstances of the case, the order may then be extended or revoked, or an alternative sentence passed for the original offence.†

An order to attend a day training centre may form a requirement within a probation order. The original purpose was to provide a structured educational and training programme for adult offenders who seemed unable to hold down a job or through personal inadequacy to manage their own social affairs. It has been found in the 4 experimental centres where this facility is being monitored that a less formal training programme is preferable which gives freedom to the participants to raise and discuss their individual problems; discussions tend to be concerned with feelings of anxiety and social conflict and with difficulties in personal relationships. The emphasis of the experimental centres has moved, therefore, away from formal teaching in favour of individual and group psychotherapy.

This change in emphasis is in line with the general movement within the probation service towards the development of group work supplementary to individual treatment. Many local offices offer recreational and hobby groups for probationers and ex-prisoners, discussion groups for the wives of

* Letter from Assistant General Secretary, BASW, Home Office, reported in *The Times* 6 February 1976.

† Sections 16 and 17 of the Powers of the Criminal Courts Act, 1973; and Home Office Circulars 74/1976 and 75/1976.

prisoners, and support groups for offenders with shared problems—for example, for alcoholics, drug users, men convicted of indecent exposure. The contribution of volunteer helpers and ancillary workers to these groups is now considerable (see Davies, 1971); in some areas, hobbies facilities are made available to men and women other than offenders, and in some offices, a community centre atmosphere has been created. In probation hostels, group activities are used as an aid to the personal development of individual members; some groups, led by psychiatrists, have an overtly psychotherapeutic purpose; others have no formal therapeutic intention, but are concerned to generate informality in relationships between offenders and officers and to ease the integration of the hostel into the life of the local community by the involvement of residents' families and neighbours. On a similar basis the Inner London Probation Service has set up a Differential Treatment Unit with facilities similar to those of a social club, where officers may work in informal ways based on friendly association as well as by the employment of professional interviewing skills. In situations of this kind, the dilemma between 2 roles (as friend or as agent of coercion) can become particularly acute, and will then require a deliberate choice by the officers directly concerned. In the London DTU, officers see themselves as 'social workers first, probation officers second'. A report on the work of the Unit (Davies, *Community Care* 29 October 1975) notes the anxiety of the officers concerning the proposals of the Younger Committee (1974) to extend the correctional role of the probation service.

Clearly, in work of this kind, however friendly the intentions of the officers, they cannot achieve an atmosphere of complete equality. Where the intention is therapeutic, this implies differences in status and, indeed, some elements of control. The difference between this kind of intervention and the more formal approach to probation supervision lies in the extent to which the function of the agency is directly related to the needs and interests of individual clients or to more general public expectations that offenders should be punished or 'treated'. Similar work, within the Home Office's experimental project 'Impact', is undertaken in 4 other areas, where a variety of forms of intervention and association are made available for selected clients and their families, and where volunteer helpers play an important role. In 'Impact,' the emphasis is on intensive work within the life situation of the individual offender by the use of as wide a range of techniques as can be devised by the participating officers and their clients. Clients relate to a team of officers rather than exclusively to an individual, and this has brought a new challenge to the traditional professional practice on which the work of service has hitherto been based.

These developments are a far cry from the work of probation officers working as welfare officers in the prisons. Here a more fundamental dilemma is apparent: how to provide a reformative and therapeutic form of service in a situation which is overtly punitive, where relationships are rigidly hierarchical, and where institutional pressures of routine and conformity are adverse to the individualizing of help. These difficulties have been explored by Pratt (1975) who suggests that prison welfare officers have yet to establish a clear sense of their own role, in preference to making spontaneous responses which are wholly conformist or rebellious to the institution or which involve an emotional retreat from the challenge which the institution presents to professional values and practice.

The Advisory Council on the Penal System (HMSO, 1974), has proposed the abolition of Detention Centres and Borstals, and of the use of prison sentences for offenders between the ages of 17 and 21, and has recommended the institution of a 'Custody and Control Order' in a new kind of residential establishment and of a 'Supervision and Control Order', to be supervised by probation officers. This would constitute a major change in the quality of relationships hitherto developed between probation officers and their clients: in particular, the proposal would give officers authority to arrange a 72-hour period of detention without recourse to a court. Such a development may give rise to tensions within the probation service which, in some aspects of its work, is developing patterns of relationships with clients where the controlling aspect is secondary to the expression of friendliness and concern (see comment in *BASW News*, 27th June 1974).

THE SKILLS REQUIRED IN PROBATION AND AFTER-CARE WORK

The extending scope of the probation officer's work, briefly outlined here, offers some indication of the range of skills he requires. With some offenders, work may properly be at a simple level such as helping the client to claim his statutory benefits, or to find work or suitable lodgings and the employment of ancillary staff has frequently been related to improving the efficiency of this kind of work. But in many situations the officer's work is closely linked with the dynamics of family relationships, with the expression of fear or resentment about the police and the courts, and with the attempt to achieve a common base of social values between the offender and the systems of law and authority which the officer represents in the perceptions of his clients. The man who has 'done his time' may resent the demands of after-care and may be suspicious both of the officer's role and of his intentions. By contrast, a first offender, anxious about his court appearance and ashamed of his offence, may require considerable and sensitive support and encouragement. Some offenders regard the service as a benevolent (and for that reason especially dangerous) arm of the police; others see it as equivalent to a 'counsel for the defence'. A dilemma concerning the confidentiality of information frequently arises in day-to-day work, and may have adverse effects on relationships between officers and police; it may affect the officer's decision in giving or withholding information in social inquiry reports, and may intensify problems of accountability. The quality of support from senior officers and case-committee members is critical in helping officers to cope with the range and conflicts of their work.

Skill is required also in the preparation of reports to the courts in criminal cases. Since 1950, the number of reports prepared by the service in respect of adult criminals has risen from 40,000 to 200,000 *per annum*. Each report attempts to provide information on the offender's family history and relationships, his attitudes to the offence, his work record and personal history, an assessment of his personality and of his likely response to the various decisions which the court may make.* The effect of these reports is to sway the Bench towards considerations either of treatment or of punishment; but officers are keenly aware of the inevitable limitations of their reports in this respect. Furthermore, we cannot be sure that the social history of an offender is a valid indicator of the likelihood of further criminal behaviour; nor can we be sure, if a period of supervision is recommended, how far, in the individual case, it will be possible on the basis of a social history to strike the right balance between therapeutic help and discipline which will lead to the social rehabilitation of the offender (see Preliminary Report of the Probation Research Project, HMSO, 1966).

* See the (Streatfeild) Report of the *Interdepartmental Committee on the Business of the Criminal Courts*, HMSO, 1962, Cmnd 1289.

8 Medical and Psychiatric Social Workers

Medical Social Work (formerly Almoning) began with the appointment in 1895 of a Branch Secretary of the Charity Organization Society in London to work in the Royal Free Hospital. Her task was to assess the ability of patients to contribute financially to their treatment and their need for charitable help. There was no obligation on hospitals to appoint almoners, but their administrative usefulness encouraged their appointment, and by 1949 there were 1120 in post.

The removal of their financial responsibilities by the National Health Service Act 1946 has permitted medical social workers to concentrate more on family difficulties associated with illness and hospitalization and on the practical and emotional problems of patients; they have increasingly defined their role as members of clinical therapeutic teams.

As in the case of the probation officers, their allegiance and accountability remained uncertain: were they essentially auxiliaries to the profession of medicine, or was their work allied to the professional concerns and objectives of social workers in other fields of practice? The development of local authority social services departments represented a crisis in this respect, and medical social workers remained employees of the National Health Service until 1974 when they were transferred as members of the local authority. They are now, therefore, an important resource for the development of co-operation between local authorities and the National Health Service. The NHS Re-organization Act 1973 laid down a general requirement of collaboration between the services and the formation of joint consultative committees at Area Health Authority level.

As an extension of medical social work, some local authorities have now established the post of Health Services Liaison Officer with responsibility for promoting co-operation between the services and between hospital-based social workers and those in Area Teams. A further extension of medical social work has been the attachment by local authorities of social workers to General Practices (See Collins 1965); but most medical social workers continue to work within the hospitals.

In 1971 there were 1850 social workers in hospitals in England and Wales, of whom 881 were specifically qualified in this form of social work practice (Health and Personal Social Services Statistics HMSO, 1972). There are no longer courses of training exclusively concerned with medical social work, but most generic social work courses offer elective studies in medical information and in the skills required for social work practice in hospitals.

Psychiatric social workers work principally in mental hospitals and the child guidance clinics or school psychological services provided by local education authorities. Like all other social workers their origins lie in the voluntary charitable efforts of the last century, in this case in the work of the Mental After-care Association formed in 1879 and of the voluntary visitors to in-patients of lunatic asylums.

Specific training in psychiatric social work began in Britain in 1929 at LSE and within a few years at the Universities of Manchester and Edinburgh. Unlike medical social workers, psychiatric social workers have from the outset been accepted by their medical colleagues as fellow members of therapeutic teams. and although their numbers have never been large they have been influential in the general development of social work theory and practice. This has been partly because their training was unmatched in quality until the last 20 years, and partly because they offered an alternative philosophy of social work practice, based on psychodynamic explanations of human behaviour (particularly from psychoanalysis) rather than on socio-moral judgments and on assessments of the character and strength of will of their clients.

This alternative philosophy was essentially a liberating one, although it has recently been widely attacked. Its emphasis was on the understanding of feelings rather than on the judgment of behaviour. It led, however, to a philosophical division among social workers, which has only recently been bridged, between those who defined their skills as exclusively professional and divorced both from informal modes of help and from financial assistance, and those whose allegiance was to the administration of services and who saw a place for co-operation with volunteer helpers and good neighbours [described by one author, ironically, as 'the romantic nostalgia and unrealistic norms of citizen participation (Lubove, 1965)]. As noted earlier in the section on mental disorder, few psychiatric social workers sought employment in local authority services up to 1959, and this is no doubt indicative of the nature of their professional allegiance.

In recent years it has become fashionable to criticize psychodynamic casework (that is, work with individuals and families based on the exploration of feelings and the resolution of inner emotional conflict) on several grounds: that it is elitist and, in theoretical terms, incomprehensible to the client; that it supports the maintenance of professional power over the lives of others; that it is averse to citizen participation in service-provision; and that there is no proof that 'it works'. Some, though not all, of these criticisms derive from sociological and political theories rather than from direct study of what actually happens in the transactions between caseworkers and their clients. We shall need to explore the present philosophies and functions of social work at a later stage in this book, and it would be inappropriate to consider these issues in detail at this stage. It may, however, be suggested that, by their search for a model of practice alternative to the earlier moralistic basis of social work, by which a distinction was drawn between deserving and undeserving and service was offered or denied on moral grounds, those associated with the psychiatric social work movement opened up a debate about the nature of social work which has enabled more recent ideals of service to take root within the profession.

In 1971 (Health and Personal Social Services Statistics, HMSO 1972) there were 341 professionally qualified PSWs in England and Wales. Specific training exclusively in this form of social work is no longer available, but many generic social work courses offer elective studies of the techniques and skills necessary to employment in psychiatric settings, based upon the pioneering work of psychiatric social workers.*

* For recent statements of the philosophy and skills associated with the psychiatric social work movement, see F. Hollis: *Casework—a psycho-social therapy*, Random House, 1964, and the chapter by F. Hollis in Roberts and Nee: *Theories for Social Casework*, 1970.

9 The Voluntary Sector in the Personal Social Services

Any attempt to write briefly about the voluntary sector of personal social service runs several risks. The greatest of these is the risk of omission. In 1970 there were 76,648 charitable organizations registered with the Charities Commissioners, of which 10,000 had been formed within the previous 10 years. It would be a major task even to list the extensive range of voluntary agencies which offer services locally, regionally or nationally. Then there is the difficulty of defining which organizations one should include: while there can be no doubt about including such organizations as the Family Service Units or the Personal Service Society at Liverpool or the NSPCC, which exist exclusively for the provision of personal social services, should one include also those which serve other purposes but which sometimes offer considerable support to the care of others? For example, the Rotary Clubs, which in some areas provide transport facilities for the handicapped and summer camping schemes for children in inner city areas as well as considerable sums of money to local voluntary groups.

Other organizations, again, are essentially self-help groups (Tenants Associations, for example, or People Not Psychiatry) and are concerned only with services to their own members; but if their membership is open then they too may be regarded as personal social services available in response to the expression of needs.

Some voluntary organizations offer personal service as only a small part of their activities in the welfare field: MIND and Age Concern, for example, are public information and pressure-group organizations and it would be inappropriate to regard them primarily as personal social services. But direct personal service to the mentally disordered and the elderly would be considerably poorer in quality and in the understanding of needs without the work of these organizations.

Other voluntary organizations, for example, the National Council of Social Service, offer advisory services to organizations and to Government rather than to individuals, but play an important sustaining role in the functioning of many local organizations and groups which provide services for individuals.

There are, therefore, problems of definition and boundaries in talking of the voluntary sector of personal social services. But even more incalculable than the formal voluntary organizations are the innumerable groups of 'good neighbours', sometimes attached to formal services, sometimes promoted by part-time leadership in a loose association with each other, sometimes working in wholly voluntary, unstructured and informal ways: for example, the local Leagues of Hospital Friends, the voluntary helpers in day centres and old people's clubs, voluntary local youth club helpers, street groups, the individual whose does the weekly shopping for disabled or elderly neighbours.

In broad terms, voluntary organizations concerned with personal social service fall into 7 categories according to their functions:

(1) Services concerned to promote the interests of citizens suffering from specific disabilities; for example, the Society for Mentally Handicapped Children, the Clubs established for Physically Handicapped and Able Bodied (PHAB), Age Concern, the British Epilepsy Association, the Muscular Distrophy Groups, Disablement Income Group;

(2) Trust funds set up to offer financial help to specific groups; for example, the Soldiers, Sailors and Airmen's Families Association, and the Family Fund which, financed by Government, is administered by the Rowntree Trust on behalf of the families of congenitally handicapped children;

(3) Services concerned with the needs of socially deprived people; for example, the National Council for One Parent Families, and the local Gingerbread groups which promote the interests of single parents;

(4) Services concerned with the care of children; for example, the NSPCC, Dr Barnardo's, the National Children's Bureau, a wide range of voluntary youth organizations and clubs;

(5) Services concerned with the general needs of families; for example, Family Service Units, the Red Cross, the WRVS, Community Service Volunteers, Samaritans, Marriage Guidance Councils;

(6) Self-help groups based either on geographical location—for example, old people's clubs, tenants associations, young wives groups, or on the needs of people who are in some sense regarded as socially deviant—for example, Alcoholics Anonymous, Gamblers Anonymous, Campaign for Homosexual Equality;

(7) Organizations concerned with the mobilizing and co-ordination of voluntary effort; for example, the National Council of Social Service, local Councils of Voluntary Service.

When approaching the voluntary sector, therefore, the best one can achieve is to look for broad trends of development in which these varying activities can be located even though they cannot all be specifically mentioned. These broad trends can be summarized under the following headings: the general principle of statutory-voluntary partnership in the provision of services, the work of the major voluntary organizations, formal enterprises to promote co-operation between statutory and voluntary services, and the use of volunteers.

THE PRINCIPLE OF STATUTORY-VOLUNTARY PARTNERSHIP

In the last century the restriction and harshness of statutory provision, wholly contained within the Poor Law, left ample room for the development of voluntary effort, and this in turn was supported by the country's growing economic prosperity. Reference has already been made, for example, to voluntary work in child care and to the Police Court Mission as a precursor of the Probation Service. Charitable work offered a philosophical balance between Christian belief in the importance of good works, a concern to maintain the social order at a time of growing economic disparity between rich and poor, and (particularly exemplified by the work of the Charity Organization Society, established in 1869) the desire to apply a scientific approach to problems of individual inadequacy in social functioning. The rapid growth of charities is demonstrated by the mid-century situation in London: there were 640 charities in 1861 with an aggregate annual income of £2½ m. (compared with an annual Metropolitan Poor Rate of £1,400,000); the growth rate at that time was about 10% a year, and the need for co-ordination found expression in the work of the COS which was concerned both to organize and deliver payments in ways which would contribute to individual self-help rather than to idleness, and to co-ordinate the work of the private charities with the implementation of the Poor Law. The achievement of both aims was seen as lying in a scientific approach to almsgiving and to the combating of pauperism by a painstaking assessment of the character of the recipient, his needs, and the ways in which he would be likely to use the help he received. Those who, it was thought, would misuse help were to be relegated to the rigours of the Poor Law; those who would use help to achieve greater self-sufficiency would be assisted by the private charities. The impact of this philosophical position on recipients of help is described in the couplet:

'The organized charity, scrimped and iced
In the name of a cautious, statistical Christ.'

It emphasized the primacy of character over social conditions as the source of social failure. But, seen more positively, it helped to promote objectivity in the study of social problems and skills in collecting information, and it emphasized the importance of combining concern to offer service to others with an interest in the outcome of that help.

Thus, in the development of association between statutory and voluntary service, there was an early division between mass undifferentiated provisions and the attempt to understand needs in the context of individual differences.

While there were similarities in the underlying philosophy of both, there were important distinctions in purpose and techniques.

The increasing concern of the statutory services with individualizing provisions, particularly since the Second World War, led therefore to uncertainty about the roles both of the voluntary organizations and of the volunteer on whom many voluntary organizations have traditionally depended. The Aves Report (1969) spoke of a post-war movement away from the use of volunteer helpers and of increased reliance on trained staff. The voluntary societies tacitly recognized the loss of their role as the major providers of individualistic social work help, and instead stressed the advantages of their organizational structures rather than the quality of their individual services. It was often argued, for example, that they were best able to pioneer new forms of service where the extent of need, the attitudes of the public, or the ways in which services would be used were uncertain: voluntary action assumed the lead for a time, for example, in such fields as community work and family planning. Or again it was argued that voluntary organizations could more readily experiment with forms of service which might not attract public support if offered through statutory provision: for example, in the establishment of hostels for unmarried mothers or for ex-prisoners, and of advice and support centres for young drug addicts. But for the most part, voluntary personal service and volunteer helpers came to be seen as secondary to statutory provision: as a means of supplementing the work of the local authorities by offering identical services in situations where the authority's resources were only temporarily inadequate, for example, Homes and day care, Meals-on-Wheels, chiropody services; or as a means of complementing statutory provisions at a sub-professional level of service, by friendly visiting, for example; or as a means of filling gaps in statutory service such as youth counselling provisions, Marriage Guidance Councils, Samaritan services. In short, the partnership between statutory and voluntary provisions was frequently based after the Second World War on the assumption that their values and goals were identical and that it was a matter of indifference, other than in economic terms, which sector provided particular services. The only exception to this were services which essentially depended for their success on organizational differences: in that, for example, a voluntary service is accountable to its own governing body rather than to the general public, and is funded by donations rather than through taxation.

In recent years, however, the role of the voluntary sector in social service has been the subject of rethinking. The Seebohm Report, while advocating more comprehensive provision in the statutory services, looked to the voluntary organizations not as a residual and secondary support but as the source of a different quality of help, 'in developing citizen participation, in revealing new needs and in exposing shortcomings in the services'. Similarly, in respect of volunteers, although the Report envisaged that social services departments would provide a focal point for those individuals who wished to offer voluntary service, it implied that the volunteer helper should be seen more as a colleague than as a secondary assistant, especially bearing in mind that volunteers are not necessarily untrained and unskilled people. 'We are not suggesting that volunteers can replace professional workers, but that they can assume, within the framework of the services and with some preparation, many of the duties which need not be carried out by a qualified social worker and which volunteers may even be better fitted to perform'.

The Seebohm Report reflects and represents, therefore, a turning-point in defining the partnership and respective roles of statutory and voluntary service. The steady increase in recent years both in the setting up of voluntary services and in the encouragement of individual voluntary help have been related primarily to the recognition of the importance of both in offering a quality of help which cannot always be provided statutorily and which will not therefore be superseded by expansion in the statutory sector. The partnership is based, at least in part, on the recognition of difference rather than on the assumption of similarity.

The partnership is, however, made more complex by current economic difficulties. Voluntary services, often dependent on local authority grants and on the Government's programmes for urban aid, are at present facing the need to restrict their work at a time when they have been encouraged to regard it as an essential rather than a residual aspect of social welfare. Local authority and probation services are inevitably coming to consider the increased use of volunteers as a way of augmenting the work of professional staff rather than as the potential source of a different quality of service.

Thus it remains difficult to define a clear principle of relationship between statutory and voluntary provisions of service. The maintenance of the voluntary sector and the promotion of voluntary work may in different situations be justified by a variety of reasons which are not compatible with each other: to compensate for manpower shortages in the statutory services; to offer a complementary or alternative form of service; to increase citizens' awareness of and involvement in services; to promote critical debate of service organization and provision; to promote new ideals of service. Examples of some of these various modes of voluntary service are given below. Meanwhile, some indication of the importance attached by central government to the work of the voluntary organizations is indicated by the extent of central financial support: this amounted to £16 m in 1974–5, and is expected to rise to £20 m in 1975–6.

THE VOLUNTARY SERVICES

The piecemeal growth of the voluntary services has for many years made for difficulties in co-ordinating their concerns, particularly as at no time has there been a single central government department responsible in general terms for social welfare and able to provide a framework for the co-ordination and development of voluntary effort. Some voluntary services have therefore been established, often at the instigation of government, specifically to promote co-operation among local agencies concerned with the needs of particular client groups: the formation of the Central Association for the Care of the Mentally Defective in 1913 is an early example of the promotion by government of voluntary co-operation in response to a change in policy by which the mentally defective were to be considered as a discrete client group. For similar reasons, the Central Council for Infant and Child Welfare was established in 1919. On the other hand, the formation of central co-ordinating organizations has also been initiated by pressure from local groups. For example, the National Council of Social Service was established with financial support by Government in 1918 to serve two main purposes: to provide an information link between local groups which had developed piecemeal in the early years of the century, to co-ordinate the work of volunteers and to promote local welfare programmes; and to advise government departments on the views of the voluntary societies in welfare matters. The NCSS offers a good example of the reciprocal processes of service-promotion which can take place when a central agency serves as a link between isolated local groups: since its inception, the Council has encouraged the formation of local Councils of Social Service and, more recently, Councils for Voluntary Service as ways of developing co-operation between statutory and voluntary services, and these in turn have encouraged an expansion of the services provided centrally by the NCSS. The development of the National Association for Mental Health in 1946 has followed a similar pattern: it has promoted the work of local voluntary groups, and at the same time has been encouraged by these groups to extend its own work. Among its other services, it developed programmes for the training of teachers intending to work with the mentally handicapped in both the statutory and voluntary services. Frequently, therefore, the promotion of a central co-ordinating voluntary organization, though not providing direct personal service to consumers, enables the development of direct services at local level in ways which benefit both statutory and voluntary interests. The Women's Voluntary Service (now the WRVS) and the Citizens Advice Bureaux were set up respectively by Government and by the NCSS in 1938. Each offers local services upon which central and local government place considerable reliance, and which make important and unique contributions to welfare, largely through the strength of their central co-ordination and their responsiveness both to the policies of central government and to the need of local groups.

An experimental form of centrally co-ordinated service, by which Government sponsored a critical approach to national and local policies, was the establishment by the Home Office of the Community Development Projects in 1969; these set out to develop local voluntary action groups which would co-operate with the statutory services to achieve change in the delivery of services and to improve relationships between local people and the statutory authorities. The assumptions which formed the basis of the CDPs were:

(*a*) that families suffering chronic poverty tend to be found in areas of urban or industrial decay;

(*b*) that they will not be helped merely by the provision of more services in their present form;

(*c*) that there are untapped resources of help in local communities which, if used, could reduce dependence on the social services;

(*d*) that there is a gap, caused by inadequate communication, between the actual needs of the community and the needs which find expression through reception at the social services; and

(*e*) that the most effective ways of improving standards of living in poor communities are not known.

Thus, the CDPs were committed to research, community development and to an assumption that the statutory services were not wholly effective (see CDP Information and Intelligence Unit: *The National Community Development Project*, 1974). It has been argued that the institution of the CDPs represented a delay in making improvements, for which the need was already apparent, in the quality of income maintenance services. (See, for example, R. Holman: *Socially Deprived Families in Britain*, NCSS 1970.) Nonetheless, they provided a unique experiment in the co-ordination of statutory and voluntary effort to promote a radical programme of social change. The projects consisted of teams of workers (150 people in all) in 12 small areas (with populations of 10,000 to 20,000). Difficulties began to arise, however, shortly after their inception. In 1973 the local staff of the projects reached the opinion that many of the problems of local areas lay not exclusively within the areas themselves but in national economic policies and policies affecting income distribution; some local councillors and local services felt threatened by the increasing political involvement of the projects' staff and by their demands for resources which could not be met. The Home Office ordered a review of the projects in 1974 which recommended more central control of their work; this was rejected by local staff as incompatible with the local focus and authority of their work, and in 1975, the Project was allowed to lapse.

Perhaps the failure of the CDPs was inevitable. By their nature, they constituted a lively local criticism of the established practices of existing services, yet they lacked the resources to demonstrate an effective and viable alternative method of provision. Their geographical boundaries did not match the boundaries of other services. Their loyalties had somehow to reconcile the policies of the central Home Office team and the concerns of small rival groups within neighbourhoods. They were expected to achieve both the detachment of research and the involvement of community action. Furthermore, they raised the broad issue of how community action can be dovetailed with the management of statutory services. Chapter XVI of the Seebohm Report sought to reconcile three objectives: the co-ordination of services, the development of mutual aid through spontaneous neighbourhood action, and the participation of service consumers in policy formulation. All three objectives can be justified, but the experience of the CDPs indicates how difficult they are to reconcile.

Both the formation and demise of the CDP illustrated that no agreement could be reached on appropriate action to resolve the human problems of urban living; clearly the intention of authorities to sponsor voluntary action which would challenge both their traditions of work and the accountability of their elected representatives offered too many tensions to achieve success. At the end of 1975, the Government announced the Comprehensive Community Programmes, whose work will focus, not on small neighbourhood areas of special deprivation, but on areas coterminous with local authority districts; their purpose will be to identify larger patterns of deprivation, and to help local authorities to channel their services effectively, and if necessary to divert them, towards client-groups in particular hardship.

The success of this new scheme is likely, however, to be seriously hampered by lack of funds. At 1975 prices, community services provided by the Home Office received £12.1 m; this fell to £8.2 m in 1973–4; the *White Paper on Public Expenditure*, 1976, indicates that this will be reduced further to £1 m in 1979–80. Mr Roy Jenkins (1972) argued that £120 m would be necessary to develop a community programme which would 'attack the manifold squalor in areas where poverty abounds'.

It is appropriate to consider at this point some examples of those voluntary organizations which, though dependent on central or local government for financial support, have maintained their independence in the direct provision of personal social services. Some of these base their work on philosophies wholly compatible with those of the authorities in whose areas they function, but nonetheless strive to maintain separate services on the grounds that their quality cannot be matched by the local authority. This applies, for example, in the work of Marriage Guidance Councils and Samaritan organizations: both are staffed by volunteers, but these are selected and trained in ways which closely resemble the casework training of statutory social workers. Their distinctiveness lies in the voluntary nature of their work and in the freedom which the lack of legislative demands gives both to workers and to clients.

The work of the Family Service Units shares this latter characteristic but remains distinctive for a different reason. It was initially developed to express a philosophy which diverged significantly from that of the statutory services and of professional casework. This organization started in 1941 as the Pacifist Service Unit, and at first undertook responsibility for maintaining adequate living conditions among bombed-out families who by reason of their way of life could not be boarded out with families in the evacuation reception areas. The work was written up in 1945* and the FSU was formally established in 1948. Although the work of local FSUs has

* T. Stephens (Manchester PSU): *Problem Families*, Pacifist Service Units, 1945.

from the start been closely associated with phrases like 'problem families' or more recently 'multi-problem families', and although the Units have served the statutory services as an agency to which families who were the most difficult to help could be referred, their mode of work was for many years at variance in several ways to that of the referring agencies. First, they resisted the view that their families were qualitatively different from other families, in preference to the belief that the families differed only in suffering more difficulties than most. Secondly, they assumed that all people are capable of achieving reciprocally responsible relationships, and that work with families should be based on the generating of friendliness and equality in relationship rather than on the exercise of authority. Thirdly, they emphasized that the goal of their work with any family could not be based on standards of behaviour defined outside the family itself. Thus, although the Units employed paid and professionally qualified staff, much of their work was 'anti-professional' in orientation; particularly at an early stage, their activities often took a very practical form, for example, helping with home-decorating, and some Units continue to work from houses, rather than offices, where quasi-family relationships are developed into which client-families can be absorbed. Units offer group activities, holidays and play schemes, and have become increasingly concerned with community development and programmes of compensatory education. Changes in the policies of local authority services and in the nature of social work professionalism have considerably narrowed the gap in attitudes and techniques that existed between Unit workers and other social workers in earlier years; but their freedom from the demands of statutory responsibility has enabled them to remain an 'alternative' service, particularly for families whose relationships with the statutory services have become destructive in some way.

A similar history but a different outcome may be seen in the work of the Churches in social welfare. This has traditionally been associated with the Salvation Army and the Church Army, and with the Moral Welfare Workers of the Church of England, with particular responsibility respectively for the homeless and for the unmarried mother and her child. These movements started in the last century in protest against the association of Christian charity with social utilitarianism, and the use of character assessments which differentiated between 'deserving' and 'undeserving' and which regulated service on this basis. Their concern was to champion the rights of the undeserving, and they sought to rescue from the Poor Law those whom other charities would not assist, particularly drunkards, prostitutes and unmarried mothers. The Moral Welfare movement was supported by a training scheme, at the Josephine Butler Memorial House in Liverpool, which achieved a considerable reputation not only for its professional standards, but also for its unique combination of professional education with education in moral theology. Like the FSU, therefore, the social work of the Church was separated from the work of other personal social services by differences in philosophies of need and in its non-punitive approach to social problems.

While the hostels provided by the Salvation Army and Church Army are still maintained, the professional separation of the former 'moral welfare workers' is now considerably reduced, principally in response to changing policies in the local authority services, to the comprehensive proposals of the Seebohm Committee, and to the development of a united professional association in the British Association of Social Workers. The Board of Social Responsibility of the Church of England conducted a survey in 1968–9 of diocesan social work which concluded that the continued separation from the social services departments of work with unmarried parents could be maintained in only 10 or 12 dioceses. Subsequently, moral welfare work has been largely replaced by the development of diocesan social responsibility boards or councils, in which the emphasis is on the promotion of volunteer help in support of other social services and of self-help neighbourhood groups. In several parishes, community workers are now attached to clergy teams.

The WRVS, unlike these earlier agencies, offers a wide range of activities, rather than services geared to the needs of a particular and identifiable client-group. It relies entirely on voluntary help and adapts its work locally according to requests received from other services and the scope of their work. It is particularly well-equipped to help the victims of sudden emergencies (fire, flood and accident), and has adjusted its local structure to fit the boundaries of the local authorities so as to serve a supportive role in response to requests from all public services. It provides canteen services in out-patient departments of hospitals, in-patient library services, and transport and sitting-in services in cases of family illness. It offers domiciliary help, including a shopping service to patients recently discharged from hospital. It has also been a major provider of recreational facilities, clubs, meals and friendly visiting services to the elderly. In 1975 the service provided 14 million meals. At the request of the DHSS the service is currently expanding its facilities for young children and their mothers by the formation of play groups and clubs, particularly in new towns and in new housing developments. The service at present provides about 6500 holidays for children each year. This brief review inevitably makes the WRVS sound like an odd-job service; although its provisions may lack a specific focus, and are readily adaptable to the emergence of new situations of sudden or chronic need, the service retains a specific identity precisely because of its responsiveness to central and local requests for help and because of the value it ascribes to well co-ordinated though untrained voluntary service.

The work of the WRVS illustrates the adaptability of voluntary organizations. A similar illustration of adaptability to the needs of clients is provided by those services, for example the Samaritans, which permit their clients to remain anonymous. There is no clear reason why the statutory services should not permit anonymity, though the issue of public accountability may provide a partial explanation. There is, however, some evidence to suggest that certain needs are not adequately met because of this difficulty; this may be an element in the considerable use made of the Samaritans. An indication of the need for anonymous service is similarly provided by the Barnardo's counselling service on matters concerned with adoption. This is available at present only in Leeds. Enquiries are received by those who are considering placing their children for adoption, by those wishing to adopt, and by couples who are suffering emotional difficulties because of childlessness. Bearing in mind the extensive responsibility of local authorities for adoption services, the Leeds provision illustrates the value of continued voluntary intervention based not on a divergent ideology of service but on the need for alternative help linked to the special difficulties of certain clients.

Mention should again be made of the work of the NSPCC in the field of child care. The legislated powers of the Society to enter homes where there is reason to believe that a child is suffering cruelty or neglect, to bring children in need of protection before the courts, and to prosecute neglectful parents, have made this a unique voluntary organization. It is sustained by long-standing public respect and by the well-defined nature of its interests and functions. Thus, although the philosophy and ways of working of the Society's officers are closely similar to those of local authority social workers, it continues to retain a separate status and identity. The society maintains a training programme for its officers in which the study of child care and of the laws related to children is emphasized. It has recently (since 1968) developed specialist experiments and research concerned with child-protection through its National Advisory Centre for the Battered Child: five special units have been established since 1971 to co-ordinate local action to prevent non-accidental injury to children, and two further units are currently being planned (1975).* In addition, the Society has undertaken studies of the needs of children caught in the crossfire of violence associated with marital breakdown ('yo-yo children'), and officers are now being appointed to offer specialist help in these situations.

THE ROLE OF THE VOLUNTARY ORGANIZATIONS

What, in general terms, can be said about the role of voluntary organizations in the light of this brief review? Broady (1968) has suggested that they 'have a crucial role in assessing the society in which they find themselves, in defending minority interests and concerns against the bulldozing of organized power, and in providing a medium through which opinion can make itself heard on matters of civic importance'. Voluntary organizations help also to increase people's awareness of the social needs

* The NSPCC Battered Child Research Team: *At Risk*, Routledge and Kegan Paul, 1975.

and problems of particular groups of citizens, and to promote the social and personal development of their members (see Gulbenkian Foundation: *Community Work and Social Change*, Longmans, 1968). They have a loyalty both to their members and to those other people who might in future become their members; and on their behalf they mediate in the allocation of resources, and exert critical pressure on statutory provisions. It is probably unwise to talk of 'a voluntary movement' as if this implied a consensus of ideology and purpose; all have a concern for the quality of community life, but there is much variation in how they define the improvement of life and in the processes of intervention they employ. Some organizations adopt a view of social change in which is implied a unitary concept of social welfare, while others emphasize a competitive plurality of sectional interests and the adoption of strategies of conflict.

In general, the voluntary services at local level are small, while the statutory services are large. An important issue, therefore, is whether it is appropriate for local voluntary services to combine in some way in order to achieve a more symmetrical relationship in discussions of common concern between themselves and the local authorities. Where such co-ordination is attempted, the difficulties are immense in organizational terms, especially bearing in mind the presence of separate traditions of service, and of long-standing independence from each other as well as from the statutory services.

On the other hand, statutory services wishing to develop co-operative work with local voluntary organizations encounter difficulties of communication. Recently, the Home Office has made a grant of £114,000 for the three-year period 1975/6 to 1977/8 to assist local voluntary co-ordinating organizations (such as Councils for Voluntary Service) to adapt their work to match the new local government boundaries. Development Officers have been appointed by the NCSS to CVSs or similar co-ordinating bodies in the six metropolitan counties, and the scheme, which is administered by the NCSS, allows for £30,000 of the grant to be set aside to meet local expenses associated with the re-organization and co-ordination of voluntary agencies. Steering committees, representing statutory and voluntary services, have been formed at county level to support the work of Development Officers, to guide local policy, and to form a link with the representative consortium at the NCSS which will oversee the development of the project as a whole.

THE USE OF VOLUNTEERS

The Seebohm Committee sought to 'reduce the rigid distinction between the givers and the takers of social services, and the stigma which being a client has often involved in the past. The whole community 'consumes' the social services directly or indirectly, as well as paying for them. . . .' This blurring of distinctions between givers and takers is nowhere more apparent than in the use of volunteers in social welfare: in self-help groups, for example in clubs for 'the physically handicapped and able-bodied' (PHAB) where neither group is specifically giver or taker; in the activities of volunteer groups such as the Cyrenians and the Simon Community in which volunteers live with the residents they seek to help; in the activities of men on community service orders (though they are 'Hobson's Choice' volunteers initially, some continue to serve as volunteers after the completion of their order); and in the activities of organizations such as Community Service Volunteers where volunteers often offer service in their own interests (as a form of pre-professional education) as well as in the interests of the community. Increasing use is being made of volunteers by statutory and voluntary organizations of all kinds in ways which complement the work of the services while offering personal satisfactions to the volunteers themselves.

The Aves Report (1969) defined the role of the volunteer as complementary to the work of employed staff and as exemplifying the principle of citizen participation in the social services. The Report drew attention to the need to widen the sources from which voluntary workers had traditionally been drawn in order to match the characteristics of volunteers with those they wished to help, and suggested that organizations using volunteer help should appoint an organizer of voluntary helpers, and that they should have access to a local 'volunteer bureau' which would link volunteers to services and offer advice to both. In practice, the 'volunteer bureau' functions are frequently performed by a Council of Social Service, or a church-based organization or a social services department. On the recommendation of the Aves Committee, a national Volunteer Centre was established in 1973 on an experimental basis to promote discussion about the uses of volunteer help, especially in relation to current trends in the provisions of the statutory services.

In policy terms, therefore, the use of volunteer help to support the work of the formal services seems assured and welcome. But is it so in fact? This question has been considered by Giles Darvill (Volunteer Centre 1975) to whose work reference should be made. Problems in the use of volunteers arise first from uncertainty about their abilities, and about how far it is appropriate for volunteers to be selected and trained. The experience of the probation service has shown that, with selection, appropriate training and on-going support through group meetings, volunteers are able to undertake many 'professional' responsibilities in long-term work with the clients of the service. This has similarly been demonstrated in the activities of the Marriage Guidance Council where the expertise of volunteers is often considerable.

But the process of selecting and training volunteers raises a social and political argument: namely that the process may lead to volunteers' being moulded according to established preconceptions about good social service practice, and in some ways to the destruction of the spontaneity of response and the non-professional qualities of relationship which can in themselves be a valuable contribution to social welfare. In other words, voluntary action may be regarded as a 'good' *per se* which may be reduced by too close an association with the requirements of the services or with the professionalism of social workers. Related to this, if voluntary action is good in itself, then no volunteer wishing to offer service should be refused, or should be impeded from helping; selection procedures inevitably imply the rejection of some volunteers or at least their diversion into work other than that which originally interested them. Reference should be made to the work of Barr (1971) which sets out in detail the problems associated with the recruitment of volunteers, the allocation of their work and the qualities of professional support required.

Darvill's study demonstrates that, in general, professionally qualified social workers seem more imaginative in their use of voluntary help than do unqualified staff; this was borne out by a study of voluntary work undertaken by the Yorkshire Council of Social Service in the mid-1960s, but there is frequently a difficulty in specific situations in knowing when professional service should be retained in preference to voluntary help. This may be the case, for example, in the care of an old person. Work with and for the elderly has hitherto remained primarily the concern of the voluntary agencies and of volunteers, and has been relatively neglected by professional workers in the local authority services; it is often assumed that friendship and practical domiciliary services are all that are required. But the studies undertaken by Age Concern increasingly demonstrate the complexities of feelings and of decisions which sometimes confront the elderly, complexities with which, it may be argued, professional casework help is necessary. There are often, therefore, organizational and tactical problems in relating together professional help and voluntary help without at the same time implying that the former is somehow more important than the latter. The views of the client need also to be considered in this context, not only in terms of whether he likes this particular voluntary helper or this particular professional social worker, but whether in his opinion a voluntary or a paid service is appropriate and preferable: people differ in their ability to accept paid and unpaid service.

One must be wary also of assuming that the skills associated with professionalism are available only to qualified staff. Some untrained people have natural gifts of sensitivity and understanding; some qualified staff lack these gifts. Thus, to attempt to distinguish between professional and voluntary help in terms of skills in relationship is not helpful. A more appropriate division may be in terms of accountability and of the knowledge of available resources, the professional worker knowing more about agency resources and entitlements, while the voluntary helper may know more about such local informal resources as clubs, friendship groups, and good neighbours.

It is not possible to offer any general principles about how volunteers should be used. Even the process of trying to define such principles may obstruct the development of voluntary action as a welfare resource. As Darvill suggests, the general aim should be to unite voluntary and statutory workers 'in a campaign against loneliness and injustice', a campaign which involves an alliance in which 'both sides must recognise the bargains which have to be struck, the risks which have to be taken and the trust which may emerge.' The emergence of trust is not the result simply of a general acceptance in principle of the need for voluntary help. It derives largely from the way in which that help is organized and presented. A good example of the importance of organization and presentation as factors in generating the trust of paid workers may be found in the work of Community Service Volunteers, established in 1963, and concerned exclusively with voluntary work by young people. CSVs are attached to many departments and institutions, for example, Social Services and Education Departments, hospitals, Borstals, hostels. They may include young people awaiting university entrance, ex-Borstal trainees, police cadets; in short, any young person, and their work often has an in-built training component. The Islington Social Services Department, for example, offers CSVs a twelve-session course in assessment, policies and welfare rights.* An important point demonstrated by this particular CSV programme is that training programmes *need* not be of a kind which stifles enthusiasm, spontaneity or initiative. A similar programme of CSV work has recently been developed by Wakefield Social Services Department (see S. Burville: Care Cadets . . ., *Community Care,* 10 December 1975).

A full review of the current uses of volunteers in both statutory and voluntary services has been undertaken by Darvill (1975) and need not be repeated here. The ways in which voluntary action develops in the future will depend on the extent to which volunteers and voluntary services are regarded, and regard themselves, as a competitive alternative to statutory provisions or as an ally. Alliance need not and should not imply agreement in everything; an important function of the voluntary movement is to offer a critical analysis of the ways in which public services are undertaken, and to form pressure groups on behalf of the less powerful members of the community. One thinks in this context, for example, of Age Concern and the National Old People Welfare Council, Shelter, the Disablement Income Group, the Child Poverty Action Group, the Claimants Unions.

But at the same time, in addition to this critical function, there remains the need for action to deal with the *immediate* sufferings of individuals and families. Alliance should leave room for mutual criticism, but criticism based on the recognition that immediate service is essential and on a common concern for the welfare of local people.

In personal service both action and debate are necessary; the actions may be specific to the needs of the moment but the debate should be continuous, rather than spasmodic and *ad hoc* at times of crisis. There are different methods of forming alliances: by the formation of advisory committees at-

* See, L. Knight: Lady Bountiful's Successors: *Community Care,* 17 September 1975.

tached to area teams or to headquarters in social services departments; by federations of voluntary groups using the secretariat of a Council of Social Service on which the statutory services are represented; by the formation of Councils of Voluntary Service which unite several local authority services, the churches and the voluntary agencies in equal membership; or by a combination of these models. But the effectiveness of direct action will depend also on the quality of relationships developed between local people and the area teams of social workers and probation officers, and by the acceptance among paid staff of the potential uniqueness of the contribution of the volunteer: a contribution which, while related to the function of paid staff, generates new qualities of service which the staff cannot match.

Although the advocacy of voluntary work is based on ideological grounds about the nature of social relationships and 'community care', the shortage of economic resources for the further development of statutory services may prove to be the greatest influence on the implementation of this ideology. Brian Munday, addressing the British Association for the Advancement of Science in September 1975, has said 'If we wish our society to survive, the majority need to do much more for themselves and for each other instead of leaving as many things as possible to the paid experts . . . Social workers must help the (statutory) personal social services to define a role by which they are secondary to care by the community.' An important need at the present time is to re-examine the resources which we already have in the voluntary societies and among formal and informal groups of voluntary helpers, rather than to seek an indefinite extension of statutory provision.

10 Management and the Employment of Social Workers

In this section we have briefly reviewed the functions and provisions of the personal social services. It has been shown that recent legislation in both the local authority and probation services necessitated changes in the way services are organized, the techniques of their provision and the role and scope of social work. Certain issues, for example, those raised by the Report of the Seebohm Committee, extend beyond the work of the services described here; they call into question basic assumptions about the mandate and authority of social service in general and about the place of the personal services in the context of wider social and economic values and policies. Our concern here, however, lies with the functioning of the personal social services, and in this section we shall summarize the general trends apparent in recent welfare policies and their implications for the management of the services and for the employment of social workers within them. Parts III and IV will then look in greater detail at organizational issues and at the nature of social work.

DILEMMAS IN MANAGEMENT

From what we have seen of the development of welfare legislation in recent years, it will have become apparent that the committees and managers of the personal social services face two issues: how to obtain the resources necessary to implement a growing range of statutory responsibilities, and how at the same time to maintain (and, it is to be hoped, improve) the quality of services. The central problem that unites these issues is one of rationing. As Parker (1967) wrote, 'Needs are potentially infinite, and resources are limited and therefore scarce.' A threatened strike among local authority social workers in the London Borough of Tower Hamlets in August 1975 was described by the assistant general secretary of BASW as 'an indication of the frustration (of social workers) at the apparent inability of government, both central and local, to recognise the acute pressures facing the social services'. These pressures are, by the nature of 'need', inevitable, but have been made more acute by a period of rapid economic growth in the services, when new commitments were accepted, followed in 1975 by economic stringency. The dilemma was well illustrated in August 1975 when Mr Anthony Crosland announced cuts in local authority spending while Mrs Barbara Castle, Minister for the Social Services, stated (about the Chronically Sick and Disabled Persons Act) that once a need exists 'it is encumbent on (local authorities) to meet that need'. Faced both with a shortage of resources and an injunction of this kind, a tendency arises to spread provisions more thinly so that they cover the same area but at a lower quality. But this risks what a District Social Services Officer recently described as 'an abysmal standard of service at grass-roots level.' In a recent training exercise at the National Institute for Social Work, Scott (*Community Care* 13 August 1975) found that social workers accorded high priority to areas of work where the Government exercised pressure or where the problem was ostensibly severe, and low priority (i e service-dilution) to those areas of work in which social workers were individually especially interested, where emphasis was on the prevention of future needs, and where neighbouring professions (teaching, medicine) were involved. Economic stringency and pressure of work may therefore lead not only to dilution and inequity of service but to frustration among staff whose special interests are insufficiently exploited, to dissatisfaction among other professional groups with whom co-operation has been strongly advocated in recent statements of government policy, and to the perpetuation of 'casualty' work among social workers. In the following chapter, therefore, we shall need to consider the problems involved in rationing services.

A policy of universal access to services cannot mean that rationing is unnecessary, but it implies that rationing should be explicit and open to debate. It is relatively easy to ration services in underhand ways: demand for services can be reduced by making them inaccessible, incomprehensible or stigmatizing. But more acceptably rationing should be based on principles of service which can be openly discussed. Hall (1975), for example, has suggested four principles: that the rationing of services should be rational and systematic; that it should be based on group decisions (for example, by the decision of an area team) rather than on the discretion and preferences of individual members of staff; that it shall be made explicit to the general public; and that it should be subject to regular and systematic review in the light of changing social circumstances and the availability of resources.

Personal social services have developed a variety of means whereby the rationing of resources and the reduction of over-loading can be achieved in accordance with these principles. No one would pretend to have found all the answers, but the following developments indicate the direction of management policies:

(a) *The appointment of special staff concerned with resource* *management*. Research teams have been appointed within many statutory services to carry various responsibilities: to provide information about demographic and social trends, and to forecast the future extent of specific needs; to investigate the use of staff time (bearing in mind that personal social services are labour-intensive) and to pursue organizational ways of saving time and effort; to evaluate the effectiveness of different kinds of intervention, particularly in social work practice. For example, recent studies in the United States (to which fuller reference will be made in the following chapter) have suggested that, in meeting the needs of some clients, intervention planned within specific time limits is more effective in outcome and more acceptable to the clients than longer-term, relatively unstructured work. (See, for example, the work of Reid & Shyne, Reid & Epstein and Fahs Beck & Jones, noted later in Part IV.) Similar studies are now being undertaken in this country. Considerable attention has recently been given to the processes by which clients are referred to, and received at, agencies, in the hope of developing more effective, and therefore, possibly, shorter intervention at times of crisis.* Other work has been concerned with the effects of matching the needs of clients to the skills of staff, (see the Home Office Research Unit's MESPA and IMPACT experiments).

Several services have also appointed Information Officers and Welfare Rights Officers to ensure the immediate availability of information to social workers and clients about community resources in general, and thus to save time and to prevent inappropriate and protracted intervention by social workers.

(*b*) *Decentralization and community involvement*. Many services have now decentralized staff to work from small centres (sometimes converted houses or shops) in local neighbourhoods. The grounds for this development are partly ideological (see the earlier references to the recommendations of the Seebohm Committee) and partly pragmatic: decentralization saves travelling time and petrol costs for staff, and encourages the increased knowledge of local resources and informal networks of help which may be utilized in preference to the use of staff time. Some services have appointed Community Development Officers and 'detached workers' to enhance the growth of informal caring facilities, and to facilitate links between people in need and potential sources of help such as local churches, tenants' and neighbourhood associations, and self-help groups.

(*c*) *The re-emergence of specialization in social work*. This will be considered in detail elsewhere, but it is relevant to the present discussion that in some services social workers are able to remain in social work practice on extended salary scales, in preference to seeking promotion through administrative work, and to develop specialized work with particular client groups. This development may help to increase the efficiency of social work

* For example, Hall (1975); studies undertaken by staff of the NISW and Brunel University to which reference is made in the next section; N. Shone: A Study of Intake, *Social Work Service* (DHSS), December 1975.

and the morale of social workers, and to promote co-operation with other professional groups. As we have seen, since the National Health Service Reorganization in 1974, medical and psychiatric social workers have continued to work in hospitals; many of these hold senior appointments, but continue to work with patients. Similar attachments are now being made to general practice teams, health centres and schools. Together they indicate the re-emergence of specializations and the hope of greater efficiency of intervention.

(d) *Extending the scope of social work.* This is often associated not only with managerial decision but also with a new radicalism in social work, committed to achieving greater equality in relationships with client-groups. We have seen examples of this in the work of 'Impact' teams and Differential Treatment Units in probation. Of itself, this development may not directly assist the rationing of scarce resources, but it can lead to the formation of action groups and to the generating of self help (of varying degrees of militancy) in which the intervention of social service staff is less required. Jordan's work with a Claimants' Union (1974) illustrates this approach: it is seen by some social workers as a logical extension of social work and by others as an alternative to social work. (A related issue, discussed elsewhere, is whether community work is social work and whether it is a professional activity.) Either way, this form of activism may help to offset two of the dangers which arise from the shortage of resources: first, the danger of ignoring the reality of economic constraints and of assuming that shortages are merely symptomatic of inefficient management; and, second, the danger that personal social services may sometimes re-inforce, and therefore perpetuate, poverty, social malfunctioning and dependency by concentrating too much on the perceived inadequacy of the individual client or by the use of pseudo-diagnostic categories (such as 'work-shy' and 'irresponsible') which tend to undermine the self-respect of people and indirectly to encourage their continuing dependency.

(e) *Experiments in decision-making and in promoting public awareness.* As Hall (1975) has suggested, rationing should be devised by group decisions rather than based on the vagaries of individual discretion. Considerable work has been done* on the development of decision-making processes within area teams of social workers, and increasingly service managers are attempting to adapt bureaucratic forms of line-management to encourage teams of workers to make decisions and recommendations about the local use of resources, based on precise information about service demands and budgets. This may be the first stage towards the greater involvement of local people, envisaged by the Seebohm Committee, in understanding the aims and policies of services and their economic and manpower constraints. Any social development depends on a willingness for innovation. As we have seen, the personal social services have been, and are,

* See references in Chapter 4 to the work of A. Hey and R. Rowbottom and J. Algie.

in transition from individual and unco-ordinated attempts to solve problems and to meet needs towards some kind of planned and coherent provision which will not only deal with problems and needs but will also in some measure help to combat social injustice. Within social work, similarly, there has been an extension outwards from exclusive concern with individual rehabilitation, based on moral or psychological premises, to include also a commitment to social reform. In these transitions, the services and the public they serve need to achieve *both* a consensus of superordinate values *and* opportunities for the constructive divergence and expression of opinions. One of the tasks of management in coping with inadequate resources is to contain and relate together this kind of duality in service development.

SOCIAL POLICY AND SOCIAL WORK

Our review of the provisions of services has also drawn attention to certain broad trends in the relationship between social policy and social work. As we have seen, social services have, in a variety of ways, sought to reconcile their initial concern for the containment and resolution of social problems with the sensitive meeting of individual needs. This has been apparent in the field of child care, where policies concerned with the needs of the deprived child have gained supremacy over earlier policies in which orphaned and neglected children were regarded as a social problem. The uncertainty of reconciliation between policies of problem-containment and policies based on individual need was evident in our consideration of the care of juvenile offenders. It represents a dilemma also in almost every aspect of the work of the probation service. Problem-solving calls for mass provision and intervention based on the categorization of people in terms of their social behaviour; meeting needs requires concern for individual differences between people and for the recognition of their individual fears, hopes and aspirations as well as of their social behaviour. The Report of the Curtis Committee on the care of children in 1946 was remarkable for its use of references to the individual child (rather than to children) while at the same time promoting the development of a large-scale social service. Social work is traditionally concerned with individual needs and differences in need, and with the promotion of individual well-being. The increasing employment of social workers (as a generically trained professional group) rather than administrative assistants to act as agents for the provision of statutory services has been made possible only by a shift in social policy to the position where the resolution of social problems is defined in terms of meeting individual needs.

While obviously a beneficial development in many respects, it could of course be argued that this statutory concern with the individual may have tended to perpetuate earlier viewpoints which located the source of all social problems in the malfunctioning or moral failure of individuals. Those who hold this opinion tend to regard social workers as preventing social change (and the promotion of social justice) by 'papering over the cracks' of an unjust social system. On the other hand, few would deny the importance, when people are in distress, of attempting to help them as individuals (or as groups of individuals) rather than as problem categories.

But two further problems arise (which have been implicit in our review of the provision of services) from this increasing association between the orientation of social work and the orientation of social policy. One concerns the size of services, and the other concerns the self-image and public image of the social worker.

The more social policy has become oriented to meeting individual needs of all kinds and to the rejection of administrative categorizations of need, the larger and organizationally more structured the services have become, and the greater their workloads. Organizational size does not of itself deny the individuality of people (whether clients or social workers) but it does lead to difficulties in preserving the individual's sense of his own individuality. We shall need, therefore, in the next section to consider the impact of organizational size on the status of the client and on the attitudes of social workers.

Secondly, social workers, because of their association with large-scale social organizations, have become 'establishment' figures. This has had several effects. It is difficult for example, to define their professionalism; a professional maintains the right not only to criticize administrative structures and local institutions but to reject the imposition of tasks which run counter to his professional values. Yet this is difficult to combine with the role of public service employee as we have seen in relation to the development of work in the probation service. Similarly, a problem is raised concerning the nature and purpose of social work training in relation to the social worker's accountability and allegiance; how far should he be trained simply to undertake whatever tasks are given to him, and how far should he be trained to look critically at those tasks and to develop an alternative frame of reference, for looking at social needs, to that offered by his employing body? In short, there are dilemmas for social workers of accountability and allegiance; this is readily apparent in the situation of medical and psychiatric social workers, recently transferred from medical to local authority services; it is equally pertinent, though not so immediately obvious, in the position of local authority social workers and probation officers, whose earlier styles of work were related to narrowly formulated agency functions which matched their personal interests. At an earlier stage of development in the personal social services, a social worker had a choice of employers, and could apply for appointment to duties which interested him. But in both kinds of service, the range of duties has extended considerably and alternative employment opportunities have been reduced. The dependence of the social worker on his employer has been inevitably increased by the loss of alternative places of work, while at the same time there may be considerably less sense of personal allegiance to large organizations and to a growing multiplicity of tasks.

The marriage of social work to the statutory social services may have tended also to raise and to change public expectations of the social worker. Social work theories and values were developed in the voluntary sector; even now they are frequently based on the situation of a 'voluntary' client. While it is still the case that much of the work of social services departments is related to the needs of clients who, technically, are 'voluntary', the setting of the services is often far from informal. As we have seen, some social workers are now attempting to generate informality of relationships with their clients; but this is difficult to achieve in the context of the authority and power of the organization from which the social workers come.

Public expectations of the local authority social worker seem to be increasingly that he should serve an inspectorial function; the growth of consultative and co-ordinating committees, in matters concerned with health and child care particularly, may indicate that this expectation will become increasingly embodied in social policies of welfare. The role of the social worker is now always mentioned in news bulletins when an old person dies of the cold or a child dies from ill treatment or neglect, irrespective of whether the social worker or his service have hitherto been involved in the case. This development calls into question, even further, the separate identity of social workers. Further attention will be given later, therefore, to the accountability of the social worker and to the nature of his professionalism.

PART III

The Organization and Delivery of the Personal Social Services

1 Introduction

Walter Hagenbuch (1958) described as the mainspring of social policy the intention to ensure that everybody enjoys certain minimum standards of living and certain life opportunities. Few would disagree with this statement of fundamental intention, and on this basis it might appear that the major organizational issue for the personal social services was a fairly simple one: to agree what these minimum standards and life opportunities should be, and to formulate the most efficient means of achieving them. This process is not without potential for conflict: as Titmuss (1974) has remarked 'We cannot fail to become heavily involved in the issues of moral and political values.' These issues affect debate about ends and means; they are influenced by changes in the country's economic circumstances and in the values attached at particular times to particular needs and problems. In periods of economic growth these issues are unlikely to weigh heavily on the minds of local committees and the managers of local services: to some degree, potential conflict can be reduced, if not resolved, by the incremental expansion of provisions and by slow processes of social reform. Communications between central government and local services in recent years, in respect of the forward planning of the personal social services, have implied this hope. For example, the White Papers of 1963 and 1966 (Cmnd. 1973 and 3022) on the development of community care in the health and welfare services were based on the assumption of continuing growth. Local authorities were invited to submit their various plans and expectations for future development; no central guidance was offered concerning the likely size of future resources, and the assumption was one of steady growth. Even so, however great one's hopes of future expansion of services, it remains true that realistic planning can be based only on some knowledge of future resources and on some statement of overall purpose and strategy linked realistically to those resources. Realistic planning of this kind was made more possible in the local authority sector by the combining of several local services into single departments, and in central government by the formation of the Local Authority Social Services Division of the DHSS and of the Social Work Services Group in Scotland. Thus, in the 1972 circulars offering guidelines for planning for the period 1973 to 1983,* we find precise definitions of certain minimum standards of service to be achieved: for example, the number of social workers per 100,000 population was to be raised from 25 to 50 or 60; home helps from 63 to 150; meals available for the elderly were to rise from 80 to 200 per 1000. Targets of this kind were based partly on the aspiration of the local authorities themselves and partly on information made available by recent research studies of unmet need. The proposals assumed a 10% annual increase in resources.

Planning has therefore been conceived both locally and nationally in expansionist terms. In the ten years up to 1973, current expenditure by local authorities on the personal social services rose from £66 m to £425 m; as a proportion of all local government expenditure this represented a rise from 2.8% to 5.6%, and most of this expansion was achieved in the period 1968 to 1973. Growth in expenditure was accompanied, as we have seen, by a flood of social legislation, which increased the obligations of services and aroused public expectations of continuing service-growth (notably the Children and Young Persons Act 1969 and the Chronically Sick and Disabled Persons Act 1970). See, for example, Bleddyn Davies (1968; 1971).

It is all too easy in a situation of this kind to overlook the fact that, however great the resources, not all needs can be met. Rising public expectations of service, the increased demands associated with the broadening scope and accessibility of local provisions, and the unlimited nature of the concept of need combine together to ensure that there can be no final and achievable goal towards which the expansion of services leads. This somewhat pessimistic realization has particularly gained ground in 1975 in the face of a worsening economic climate. A report by the Central Policy Review Staff (August 1975) argued that the whole treatment of social issues by Government needed to be related to a broad framework of social policy in which coherent and consistent priorities were determined. 'If the structure of social expenditure is not to become increasingly arbitrary, some better basis is needed for determining priorities.' A leading article in *The Times* commented, 'In a time of scarce resources—and that is the prospect for some years to come—priorities in social policy must be decided with greater precision and the effectiveness of existing policies, all policies, not just new ones, measured with greater care.' In November 1975, the White Paper on the rate support grant settlement made clear that the personal social services were to bear a substantial part of the economies necessary to achieve 'nil growth' in the local authorities' expenditure for the year 1976–77; expenditure in money terms would increase by £35 m, but this would in fact be £5 m less than was necessary to maintain the 1975 level of services. The

* DHSS Circular 35/72, Welsh Office Circular 195/72.

Government suggested that, in this situation, priority should be given to maintaining the effectiveness of domiciliary services and to services in respect of the care of children; but in practice it will be difficult for local authorities to pursue these priorities single-mindedly because of their existing commitments in other fields. Policies based on the assumption of expansion are likely therefore to be followed by a period from 1976 of arbitrary reductions of service and by the need to grapple with moral and political issues concerning the purposes of services. A survey undertaken by the British Association of Social Workers and published in December 1975 showed that local authorities were planning to empty or to close over a hundred homes and hostels for the elderly and handicapped, to reduce the number of home helps, and to cut back on 'Meals-on-Wheels', domiciliary aids for the disabled, and assistance to voluntary organizations. In terms of expenditure, 24% of local authority social services departments expected a year of 'nil growth' and 12% were planning cuts in expenditure. The General Secretary of BASW spoke of 'disillusion and dismay among social workers forced to ration out their help', particularly at a time when inflation and unemployment were tending to increase the number of new referrals for help.

Personal social services (both the voluntary and the statutory sector) are at present confronted, therefore, with an abrupt change in policy and planning. The incremental growth of services has been replaced by the need to choose between demands which have become mutually competitive and conflicting and which in some respects are not comparable with each other.

2 Problems of Rationing and Priorities

The present economic stringencies clearly impose problems of choice on social services staff at all levels. Several approaches to these problems are possible.

At national level, it is necessary (as Townsend was arguing as early as 1970) to develop a concerted social policy embracing all social services (social security, education, health, housing and the personal services) so as 'to provide a rationale for the allocation of national resources and control of public expenditure', and to give recognition to the inter-relationship of needs. The Secretary of State, addressing a conference of local authority associations in November 1975, spoke of her intention 'to synchronise the planning cycle for local authority personal social services and for the matching health authorities' as a starting point for debate on common purposes and aims. She spoke of the need to enable financial resources to flow across the conventional administrative boundaries between services, so that, for example, the health authorities might be encouraged to contribute to the cost of community care facilities in areas where the intention was to reduce the number of patients in long-stay hospitals. Both by the traditions of the development of services and by the content of legislation, resources have tended to be earmarked to specific services—frequently as competitors with each other—rather than shared in ways which reflect the needs of citizens. While the reorganization of local authority services went some way towards overcoming these arbitrary administrative divisions, problems of unco-ordinated service still exist when people move between the roles of in-patient and out-patient, or between the responsibilities and functions of housing authorities, education authorities, income maintenance and the personal social services. A change in the policies and provisions of one department may have considerable repercussions on the resources of another without an accompanying recognition of shared responsibility for the well-being of those who use the services. Olive Stevenson (*Community Care*, 3 December 1975) has recently commented that the social worker is frequently 'left to cope as best he may with unrealistic community expectations'; because of inadequate housing services, for example, social workers may find their own resources of time and their agencies' resources of cash dissipated in the search for bed-and-breakfast accommodation for homeless families. One approach to the problem of planning lies, therefore, in the co-ordination of services across administrative boundaries.

Secondly, within local departments there is accumulating evidence that the increased flow of work* is being contained by the determination of priorities of intervention. Priority planning of this kind is necessary for four major reasons:

(1) it is the only alternative to a widespread dilution of service over the whole range of provisions;

(2) it offers a focus for uniting the efforts of social workers who might otherwise be overwhelmed by work and dismayed by the low level of their general effectiveness;

(3) it provides a stimulus for relating resources to proven effectiveness; social service is labour intensive and expensive; where dilution of service is inevitable, therefore, it should be restricted to those areas of work where effort is not matched by results or where the expensive skills of professionally qualified staff can be adequately replaced by the less expensive intervention of unqualified staff or by the activities of volunteers;

(4) finally, planning of this kind offers the only alternative, administratively and professionally acceptable, to decisions reached on the basis of demands from local political or other pressure groups, which would risk losing the partial consensus necessary to maintain general public support for the services as a whole. Without administrative and professional decision-making, needs which lack political capital might not be met. This is not meant to imply that administrators and professionals should have a monopoly of creative thinking and planning; all organizations and their personnel are to some degree resistant to challenge and change. But their lack of planning may lead to an increasing conflict between sectional and ideological interests inconsistent with the responsibilities of departments to promote the general welfare of all people and of local communities.†

As we have seen, service priorities may be advocated by Government—the needs of children are particularly strongly supported at the present time. In more specific terms, however, productive planning for the use of staff depends on recognizing, first, the different qualities of care required by particular groups in need, and, second, the extent to which, in various situations, the effectiveness of particular styles of intervention is

---

* The Nottingham Social Services Committee has estimated that in one area office the annual increase of work is at present 25%.

† This is a legislated responsibility in Scotland. In England and Wales, the recent expansion of services and the requirements of legislation (in respect of children and the handicapped, particularly) imply acceptance of moral responsibility to promote general welfare.

related to the manner and frequency of their use.

With regard to the first of these criteria, client-groups may be differentiated according to the degree of urgency in their situation. Some situations require immediate action if serious injury is to be avoided: this applies where referrals are received in which children are at risk, where there is a threat of self-injury, or where there is a sudden breakdown in health. Clearly these are situations of high priority requiring the use of skilled manpower. Secondly, there are areas of work in which the law requires action and the use of considerable expertise within a defined period of time: reports may have to be written for presentation to a court which will carry considerable influence on the future life and well-being of a defendant, or of children of divorced or separated parents; clients may need help in presenting their cases before a tribunal; children on supervision orders and adults on probation orders may require regular and frequent visiting if their situation is not to worsen. As has been suggested in a staff paper recently published (1975) by the Nottinghamshire Social Services Department, these and similar situations represent the needs of people who have already suffered in some way and in whose cases continued suffering represents a threat to themselves and others.

It would, however, be inappropriate to limit the work of qualified staff exclusively to these kinds of activities. Ways must also be found (and these may sometimes require expert intervention) to prevent the development of social situations likely to lead to future individual and family breakdown. Social action through the development of community facilities, the support of 'good neighbour' groups, and joint planning with the staffs of other services, may help to prevent the need for expensive expert service at a later stage.

With regard to the second criterion, concerning the appropriate timing and frequency of intervention, some recent studies have drawn particular attention to the importance of intervening at the point of crisis, not only in terms of cost-effectiveness (Caplan 1969) but in relation to the successful involvement of the users of services in the processes of self-help (Sainsbury 1975). Studies by Reid & Shyne (1969), Reid & Epstein (1972) and Fahs Beck & Jones (1973) have all suggested that, in many situations, social work practice gains in effectiveness if it is based upon the joint definition of tasks by clients and social workers in the early stages of a difficulty, and on a short initial period of intensive work. In establishing priorities for the use of qualified social workers' time, therefore, it may be important to allow for immediate and frequent intervention in the first few weeks following referral in the hope that longer-term work can be avoided or delegated to less expensive sources of help. This runs counter to some traditional practices in the personal social services, by which, because of staff shortages, some clients have waited for several weeks following referral before receiving their first interview, and interviews have been widely spread over long periods of time irrespective of the nature of the referral-needs and of work-effectiveness.

A recent development in many local areas has been the establishing of 'intake teams' to ensure speedy action at the time of referral and to assess which clients or families require longer-term work after the initial phase of intensive intervention.

An attendant risk in setting priorities is that certain needs will not be met. A further management task is therefore the evaluation of alternatives to traditional ways of working. The present social services have traditionally based their work on a casework model of practice; that is to say, individuals and families have been helped individually; all the work has been undertaken by one social worker, often through a long series of interviews; and the assumption has been made that all such work required, if it was possible to obtain it, a highly skilled level of interviewing significantly different in quality from the sort of help one might expect to receive from volunteer helpers, friends or through informal patterns of family support. It is not disputed that this kind of help is sometimes essential: some people approach the social services with problems with which they have already sought informal help and found it to be unsatisfactory. In marital difficulties, for example, well-meaning families, friends and neighbours may exacerbate problems rather than relieve them. Furthermore, some emotional needs can find expression and help only in the isolation and socially unusual setting of a casework interview. In short, social workers sometimes carry psychotherapeutic and social responsibilities which can be effectively exercised only by skilled interviewing techniques. What is not yet adequately understood, however, is when this model of work is essential and when it could be replaced by other forms of help without loss of effectiveness; to what extent, for example, some clients might be helped in groups with skilled leadership; the extent to which domestic help or the frequent visits of a volunteer might serve the same ends (possibly more effectively) as the less frequent interviews of a skilled social worker.

A recent development in social work thinking which may in time help to resolve the dilemma of when to use trained social workers, other staff or volunteers is the advocacy of a team model of intervention. In this model, a group of staff and volunteers (including secretarial receptionists) assumes joint responsibility for all clients; individual caseloads are replaced by team caseloads, and, by frequent discussions about new referrals and by regular reviews of the needs of current service-users, the complementary use of various trained and untrained staff can be planned and integrated. Particular team members may, by this system, develop special skills which become available to all clients known to the team.

The advantages of a team approach of this kind are readily apparent: if a client returns to the agency because of an unexpected crisis, he can be sure to find someone who knows about his situation and who can respond quickly and efficiently to his particular circumstances. Furthermore, this model of organization offers opportunities of greater mutual support between workers in cases of special difficulty. The possibilities arise both of efficient task-definition among team-members and of promoting greater egalitarianism of decision and action. In the few places where this model has been adopted, it has sometimes been possible, as an extension of this principle, to involve clients in team meetings where specific needs and tasks are defined and allocated.

On the other hand, the implementation of this model requires some major changes in the traditional patterns of service organization. Record-keeping and work-supervision become tasks for the whole team rather than for individual members; time needs to be found for regular meetings; the philosophy and strategies of intervention have to be agreed in ways which offset the autonomy of practice of the individual worker and which may run counter to the exclusiveness of relationships between individual clients and individual social workers. Furthermore, the sharing of responsibility in the ways outlined here may be ill matched to the traditional managerial structures of agencies. Rowbottom (1973) has commented that 'hierarchical organisation is indeed alive and well. It is currently living in practically every social agency in the country'. In an organizational situation where, paradoxically, social work competence is associated with the speedy loss of contact with clients through managerial promotion,* the egalitarianism of decision and action implicit in a team approach may be difficult to achieve.

Related to this, it may be appropriate in thinking about priorities of work to reconsider in more general terms the role of the personal social services in relation to less formal processes of help. Should the services be regarded as the primary resource for meeting social needs of all kinds? Are there some situations of need where they might more appropriately be regarded as a secondary resource, supporting informal processes of help, and acting only when these informal processes fail in some way? It would be necessary as part of this debate to distinguish between the role of the service as a means of solving social problems and its role in meeting individual and social needs. One cannot, of course, draw a clear distinction between these roles in many situations: some social problems imply the presence of unmet needs; some unmet needs give rise to problematic situations. For example, the rise in unemployment among young people in certain areas is a problem requiring co-ordinated action, while at the same time it contains within it a variety of experiences of unmet individual need. The unmet needs of a child may give rise to delinquent acts which will constitute both a family problem and part of a wider social problem of juvenile crime. Even so, meeting needs and dealing with social problems may involve different processes of work which, while complementary, need not be combined within a single process or under single auspices. Indeed, the confusing of these two processes has sometimes led to unrealistic assumptions of the effectiveness of certain kinds of intervention. For example, it has sometimes been assumed, without evidence, that the provision of recreational facilities for young people will

* See A. Sinfield: *Which Way for Social Work?* Fabian Society Pamphlet 1967.

reduce juvenile crime; or that the availability of assistance and advice regarding contraception will reduce the illegitimacy statistics. The close association between social work and the social services has tended to encourage the view that meeting needs and solving problems are interchangeable ideas, and that the social services should serve as the primary provision for meeting needs in a very general sense. It may be appropriate as an aspect of planning the use of service resources to question these assumptions, and to consider ways in which the responsibility for meeting certain needs can be shared with or delegated to voluntary effort of various kinds.

The determination of priorities of intervention within the statutory services, therefore, implies certain managerial and professional tasks:

(a) to assess needs and resources within a single process of planning; to have regard to the kinds of manpower and helping potential available not only within their departments but elsewhere;

(b) to identify objectives within the limits of resources, and to find a balance between providing a 'casualty' service and developing preventive work;

(c) to evaluate alternative methods for solving problems and meeting needs, and to encourage alternative auspices within the community; to evaluate which skills are needed and where they are most likely to be found in the interests of different client-groups;

(d) to monitor performance; to measure the effects of different kinds of intervention in relation to their different costs; to recognize that research and planning are integral processes in the effective delivery of services.

A comment about its own work, in the first Annual Report of the Personal Social Services Council 1975, is applicable at the present time to all personal social services: 'When obligations are great and resources ... are short, then it becomes vital that we should discuss our procedures the more carefully, scrutinize the deployment of manpower more closely, try to disseminate the more effectively knowledge of fruitful innovations or new patterns of departmental collaboration, help with the crucial task of establishing priorities, and stress the vital contribution the Social Services must make, not least in a time of rapid social change and straitened circumstances ... The concentration of resources and energies is mainly devoted to work which is remedial. But the only rational development would be the adoption of strategies that are preventive if successive generations are not to encounter identical and accumulating problems of deprivation and need.' It is imperative that the traditions implicit in social service policies in recent years should not inhibit the exploration of alternative ways of defining and meeting needs. In particular, it is necessary to challenge those values which have led to the arbitrary division of related functions both between services (health, education and personal social services, for example) and within services (field work, residential work and day care). It is necessary also, as Rein (1970) has suggested, to challenge the tendency to over-emphasize rehabilitation at the expense of preventive programmes. The realization of some values may involve the sacrifice of some others if we lack the resources to implement both.

PERSONAL SOCIAL SERVICES AS RESIDUAL OR PERMANENT

Earlier in this book, the standpoint was taken that social services form a permanent and essential part of social life. Even as recently as twenty years ago, there was some doubt whether this applied to the personal social services in the way that it applied to more basic provisions. Social workers at that time still spoke of 'working themselves out of a job', and the assumption was sometimes made that, with the further development of the basic services, the personal services would become increasingly residual. They were usually small and inadequately housed as befits a marginal and declining activity. Recently, as we have seen, personal services have expanded rapidly and assumed greater responsibilities; they have a permanent look about them. At the same time, I have argued that they should be seen in some situations as a secondary rather than primary resource in meeting needs, and this may sound like relegation to a residual position. My intention, rather, is to suggest that they have functions other than the direct meeting of needs, and that their preoccupation with social work service may have diverted attention and resources from other kinds of intervention and purpose which they are well-suited to promote. In broad terms, I suggest that they should have three functions other than social work service.

First, the provision of skilled advice to people seeking to make use of other institutions and services. To a considerable extent, advice has been available through the voluntary activities of Citizens Advice Bureaux and co-ordinating voluntary organizations such as local Councils of Social Service and the Central Council for the Disabled. The complexity of services now available suggests that the statutory services should undertake more advisory work of this kind, and should, where appropriate, assume the role of advocate on behalf of people who find it difficult to use services or to present their needs effectively. Many social workers now undertake advocacy work, but this is rarely seen as an integral aspect of their departmental duties.

The development of advocacy work requires more, however, than a knowledge of local resources. The service which offers advocacy may itself from time to time appropriately be the target of action. It is essential, therefore, that the staff should not only be fully aware of the powers and duties of their own service but should also achieve agreement among themselves about how these powers and duties should be interpreted and used. Furthermore, it needs to be remembered that the assumption by social workers of an advocacy role carries with it additional power in the lives of their clients; if clients are to make effective use of an advocate without suffering a loss of status, then they need to be more realistically informed than they frequently are at present about the provisions and duties of the service, the response expected of them, and the safeguards available to them. Without these attendant developments, advocacy can widen the distance between service and client rather than narrow it: the client may regard the social worker as atypical of the agency, ascribing all good outcomes to the personality of the worker and all disappointment or incomprehension to obstruction by more senior colleagues. Or the client may mistrust the benignity of the worker, and wonder how much iron is contained in the velvet glove; this can be a particularly intractable problem in 'detached' work, where the social worker's attempt to play down his differences from his client (in dress, speech, and way of life) may generate mistrust of his motives which becomes increasingly difficult to express; one can only wonder whether 'detached' social workers are as much loved by their clients as they sometimes believe. Or, again, the distance between worker and client may be increased by the worker's enthusiasm for his advocacy role; as one client said recently about her social worker's militancy, 'She's so busy fighting for my rights that she doesn't have time to listen to what I say'.

Secondly, social services could extend their activities to develop self-help and self-expression within local community groups, and to promote a sense of community participation in the formation of service policies. This again involves the dissemination of information about policies and alternative strategies. But in addition it offers a means whereby people may offer direct services to each other, may help to influence the development of services, and may bring about institutional changes. It implies, also, the responsibility for strategic co-ordination of a wide range of independent resources.

Thirdly, social services might seek to provide protection from the experience of social exclusion of various kinds such as unjust exclusion from benefits, social isolation within local communities or within Homes and hospitals.

Some of these functions require the development of skills other than those traditionally associated with social work; they present a challenge in the training of social service personnel as well as in the deployment of staff within agencies. At present, some of these responsibilities are being developed in some areas by the appointment of specially designated officers. They are community development workers, information officers, homes and hospital liaison officers, etc. An important task for the future is to integrate their work within the team structure of direct service, and to identify a common sense of purpose which unites their activities with those of the social workers. [See P. Baldock: *Community Work and Social Work* (last chapter), Routledge and Kegan Paul, 1974.]

Significantly, the discussion paper *Priorities in the Health and Personal Social Services* (HMSO 1976) suggests that, while it is necessary to increase the number of trained staff in the personal social services (in 1976, only 5100 of the 13,500 field social workers in employment are professionally qualified), the services should seek also to make greater use of ancillary and voluntary helpers, voluntary community organizations, and untrained support staff. 'Support for voluntary effort and the encouragement of self-help schemes may represent better value for money than directly provided service, and may also provide the means of continuing preventive work. By their diversity and the ingenuity they bring to the task, voluntary organizations can be an important adjunct to the authority's own direct services in getting help to people in need.' This is not simply a matter of economizing on expenditure; neither is it a denial of the importance of professionally qualified staff. It suggests, rather, that the continuing social relevance of permanent institutions such as the personal social services depends on the quality of their association with less formal patterns of help and of social obligation and responsibility.

3 The Size of Services and their Institutionalization

The growth of the personal social services, in terms both of real increases in their budgets and manpower and of their geographical organization [particularly following the Social Work (Scotland) Act, 1968 and the Local Authority Social Services Act, 1970, the reorganization of local government in 1974 and the combining of Probation and Aftercare Committee areas in 1974], has inevitably led to changes in their internal structures. Twenty years ago when services were small, staff sometimes worked in what were virtually non-hierarchical services: probation services, for example, were mostly two-tier organizations; the local authority services, although traditionally more hierarchical, were still sufficiently small to permit frequent and easy contact and a ready flow of information between managers and main-grade workers.

As we have seen, the growth of services has presented new challenges to management in terms of the deployment of staff and the planning of resources and services. An estimate made in 1971 of the manpower of services for the period 1970 to 1975 spoke of an annual growth rate of $3\frac{1}{2}$%, equivalent in real numbers to an overall increase of 300,000 (Rosenbaum 1971).

Growth of this kind introduces new organizational problems with which local services are at present grappling. First, as has been implied in a previous section, there may be a conflict between the need to manage the day-to-day routine work of main-grade workers and the need to plan ahead. In most services, this conflict is resolved by the separation of these functions: for example, in a social services department, one assistant director may be responsible for the general management of fieldwork and another for research and planning. While this is an administratively neat solution, it leads to a situation where the two functions can be viewed together only at directorate level; main-grade social workers may be unable to pass their knowledge, gained from practice, direct to the policy makers because of an administrative disjunction, and may feel entirely divorced from policy-making responsibilities.

135

Secondly, the growth of hierarchies, however essential administratively, tends to create the expectation that decisions are made only at the top, and that communication works only in a downward direction. Thus, professional knowledge and direct information about clients' needs, problems and attitudes may be unintentionally kept at the bottom of the pyramid of service and may remain unco-ordinated and unexpressed.

Thirdly, the career structure of services has necessitated that many highly qualified and experienced field practitioners should leave practice and become administrators, and this has led to a loss of expertise and lack of leadership at field level. Thus, although field workers may be supervised to assist their individual professional development, the development of a professional culture is left to external organizations (BASW, NAPO) rather than assisted within the employing body.

Fourthly, there may be an implicit conflict between the needs of the service structure and the needs of the individual professional worker. At a high level of generalization one will usually find compatibility of ideology and values between managers and field staff: both are concerned with the promotion of welfare and the meeting of needs. But there will almost certainly be differences in respect of the principles by which daily work is organized and assessed. Management must properly be concerned with the efficient use of the agency's resources, with the performance of the agency's duties conceived in precise and limited terms, and with the achievement of verifiable tasks. On the other hand, field workers tend to be more concerned with the use and development of relationship skills, to feel an unlimited commitment and responsibility towards some at least of their clients, and to be concerned to uphold professional values. In simple terms, the conflict may lie in the definition of successful work: success in management thinking is allied with the notion of efficiency; in professional thinking (especially when one considers clients who need considerable support to maintain their level of social functioning and who have little hope of improving their situations) success may often be assessed as the maintenance of a relationship and the achievement of small advances in self-sufficiency. This difference in perspective becomes apparent in defining the role of the supervisor responsible for the day-to-day work of the main-grade staff (i.e. the Senior Probation Officer in charge of a team, or the Principal Social Worker in charge of a small group of staff within a local authority area). There may be tension between his exercise of managerial authority (insisting, for example, that certain duties should be carried out in particular ways) and his use of supportive non-authoritarian techniques which recognize the professional autonomy of his colleagues and which are concerned with encouragement in 'unsuccessful' work situations. If supervisor and supervisee disagree about the professional handling of a case, should the supervisee be left to handle things his own way, or should be be instructed to change his approach? If he disagrees with the policy of his agency, is this disagreement acceptable as an aspect of his professional autonomy or is it interpreted as the disloyalty of an employee? If the supervisee feels acutely anxious or depressed about his work, can he be free to express these feelings in confidence (as to a professional colleague) or will he be concerned that any expression of negative feelings will block his promotion prospects? In short, it is difficult for a supervisor to ascertain how far he is a professional consultant and how far he is a manager; how far he should seek to maximize his personal contacts with junior colleagues or to remain sufficiently aloof to be able to exercise managerial power in situations where the agency's responsibilities are not being efficiently undertaken.

Issues of this kind raise further questions about the evaluation of field practice (by what criteria work is to be judged) and about the relationship between social service and social work. It can be argued on the one hand that the ideology of professional social work is wholly consistent with the ideology of the personal social services, that to be a social worker is to be a social service worker. Yet, as I have suggested earlier, it is possible to envisage a personal social service which does not contain professional social workers and whose values are incompatible with those of social work: the organization of Public Assistance in the 1930s would provide an example of this. Social work implies a constellation of values and skills which may be relevant and useful to the functioning of a personal social service but which are not wholly applicable to all the work of the service. If this view is accepted then it implies that the supervision of professional social workers needs to take two forms which, in the interests of clarity, might appropriately be separated in practice: on the one hand, there needs to be a managerial form of supervision to ensure that the statutory duties of the service are carried out efficiently; but in addition there is room for a more professionally-oriented supervision, concerned with the personal and professional development of the individual worker, with the extension of his knowledge and understanding of the needs and feelings of his clients, and with support in undertaking the tasks which are deemed appropriate to professional practice but which are not wholly contained (if at all) within the statutory duties. An examination of the work of any social service employee reveals a host of caring activities which are not essential to the performance of his official duties but which derive from his personally held values concerning obligations in social relationships. The institution of two supervisory systems would involve, however, a recasting of the hierarchies of organization which would run counter to the traditions of both local authority and probation services. (For alternative management structures see: Algie, 1970; Foren & Brown 1971; Kogan & Terry, 1969; Rowbottom et al., 1974.) It would necessitate also the recognition that the needs of the service and the needs of the professional are not always compatible and that some compromises are necessary. A simple example of this is the issue of specialization.

Before the Local Authority Social Services Act, social workers entered services specifically because of their interests in relatively narrow fields of human need, social problem or social work practice: child care, criminal behaviour, some form of handicap, etc. It was in the interests of the complexity of clients' needs, the growth of legislative responsibilities and the administrative neatness of services to abandon these forms of specialization. The word 'generic', which was originally used to describe the common training of caseworkers prior to their specialization in practice, was improperly transferred to describe their field work and became roughly equivalent to 'general'; that is to say, social workers were expected to work within an unlimited range of human needs and social problems, and to achieve professional competence in all aspects of their work. (It should be noted here that the Seebohm report, while advocating the appointment of general social workers, did not recommend the abandoning of specialization, though recognizing the inadequate ways in which specialization had hitherto been defined.) Many social workers, challenged to become jacks-of-all-trades, have been brought face-to-face with their lack of interest in, and personal unsuitability for, some areas of practice; some have resented their removal from the specialized practice in which they considered they had worked well. At a more fundamental level, the loss of opportunities for specialization have meant, for some social workers, the loss of the focus of interest which drew them into social work in the first place; significantly, one frequently finds when interviewing applicants for social work courses that their motivation derives from concern about a specific problem in social policy or about a certain kind of need. It has meant also the loss of the criteria whereby they were able to identify the development of their professional skills, and to evaluate the worth of their intervention.

Some social service and probation departments are now re-introducing opportunities for specialization which represent a compromise between managerial and professional needs; this has been most apparent in the appointment of community workers and in the permission given to medical and psychiatric social workers to remain based within their hospitals and clinics. It is likely that other forms of specialization will be introduced, possibly associated with the development of career opportunities for social workers who do not wish to transfer from field practice to administration when seeking promotion. But a case could also be made for permitting some specialization in the immediate post-training period in order to encourage the growth (and experience) of competence in a field of particular interest to the social worker before he is required to undertake more general responsibilities.

4 The Status of the Client

A further consideration in respect of the expansion and re-structuring of services is the status of the client, his involvement in the work of the agency, and his rights in respect of the agency's influence upon his life. One of the aims of re-organization was to simplify the processes of referral: the number of alternative sources of help was reduced and clients no longer needed to adapt the formulation of their needs to fit into a variety of administrative definitions of agency responsibility. These are important gains. On the other hand, clients can no longer 'shop around' if they are dissatisfied with the service they receive; they are confronted by monopolistic services of considerable complexity which must sometimes seem incomprehensible. If, as has been suggested, social workers feel increasingly remote from the policy-making of their departments, the distance of the client is more remote still. Rapid changes among field staff in the local authority services have affected the traditional continuity of help between social workers and their clients and have affected relationships between social workers, teachers, doctors and others working with the same family. Complaints about the inadequacy of social services are voiced by other professional workers who are no longer certain whom to telephone, and who regret the loss of long-standing colleagueship with former child care or mental welfare officers. Not surprisingly, therefore, the structural growth of services has been mirrored by the increasing organization of client-protection and reformist groups in which social workers play a somewhat ambiguous role (for example, Child Poverty Action Group, Claimants Unions, Voluntary Advice Centres). But efforts have also been made within the organization of services to offset the perceived disparity between large-scale bureaucratic structures and the needs, feelings and perceptions of the individual client and family: for example, the simplifying and co-ordination of information sheets and application forms in respect of various welfare facilities,* and the increasing use made of

* For an example of this development in Liverpool see *Community Care*, 17 September 1975, page 4.

advertisements for specific services. Perhaps the most important current development in many local authority departments is the decentralizing of services. The Seebohm Committee envisaged the establishment of area teams of about twelve social workers, based within communities of between 50,000 and 100,000 inhabitants. In some areas a further devolution has taken place towards a 'patch' system of working, by which social workers are within walking distance of their clients' homes and become personally well known within small neighbourhoods. The implications of this development are, first, the recognition that hierarchical structures are not ideally suited to all aspects of social service provision and should in part be replaced by the intimacy and delegated autonomy of small teams; and, second, that social workers by co-operation with local people should adapt the quality and scope of their services in response to area differences and personal aptitudes. One writer (Oakley 1975) has gone further still in suggesting that, having in mind the administrative difficulties of delegation and the limitations of autonomy within employer–employee relationships, social services might instead 'draw up a series of contracts for services to go out to tender' within small localities. By this means, local residents' groups, small co-operatives and communes, as well as the more established voluntary agencies, would contract to carry out part of the department's functions in return for grant-aid and would by this means offer potential clients alternative services within their own neighbourhoods. This suggestion would no doubt encounter many administrative and legal difficulties, but it offers an example of the radical thinking at present to be found among some social workers. While not compatible with traditional practice in local authorities, it echoes the concern of the Seebohm Committee to achieve a community base and community involvement in the policies and provisions of services; and it draws attention to a point made earlier that, particularly at times of economic stringency, it may be appropriate in respect of some needs to regard the services as a secondary rather than a primary resource.

At the present time, the decentralizing of services by the establishment of locally based area teams raises issues of accountability and ideology which are dealt with elsewhere in this book. What exactly is meant, in administrative terms, by an area team? And what should be the source of the rationale for its work? The alternatives are, first, to regard the locally based team as a 'caller station', implementing policies and maintaining patterns of service defined at headquarters; and, second, to regard the team as responsible for developing policies and services directly related to local institutions, resources and needs. Implicit in my earlier comments has been a preference for the second alternative. But this may well be an ideal to be approached rather than to be wholly achieved; for there are some important difficulties in it. First, although a local team may be best able to assess how local needs might be met, having regard to local traditions of voluntary action, no team can in isolation wholly grasp the wider influences of county or district politics, or can realistically comprehend the policies, resources and procedures of other services at work within, but not based in, the area. Secondly, the understanding of local needs may remain at a superficial level if local study is undertaken only by team members who are already hard-pressed by the volume of their day-to-day work. Most social workers would admit that their work is based more on the exercise of commonsense than on any systematic study of the social environment of their clients; there is no reason to suppose that more sophisticated insights would automatically derive from the delegation of greater responsibilities to local teams. Thirdly, there is the related problem of knowing how to define the needs which may be detected in a local neighbourhood in ways which prescribe appropriate action. Even in the unlikely event that local people agreed in principle on the priorities of needs or problems in a particular neighbourhood, the actions they prescribed to meet them might well have an incompatible variety based on a range of theories about the sources of stress or distress. For example, if the predominant problem were seen as violence or vandalism, intervention might be prescribed in respect of individual morality, family upbringing, the lack of adequate leisure opportunities, or the quality of the local schools. If a variety of modes of intervention were decided upon by the social work team, some would need wider support and resources than the local area could itself produce, and some might be seen by a substantial number of local peo ple as irrelevant or misguided. It is unlikely also that the team alone would feel confident that they had adequately defined either the needs or the solutions.

Locally-based area teams are, therefore, in an ambiguous position in defining and exercising their responsibilities. The simplest and neatest solution is to regard them as 'caller stations', but this undervalues their potential as monitors of local conditions and as sensitive instigators of local involvement in, and local responsibility for, the meeting of needs. The administrative challenge, therefore, is to find the right balance between centralized and delegated policy-making. No hard and fast rules can be formulated for how best to meet this challenge as much depends on the composition of the team and the needs and problems peculiar to the area. But certain minimal achievements by an area team are essential to realistic administrative decisions about delegation by headquarters staff: first, the team members need themselves to be clear in their opinions about local priorities, and be prepared to undertake enough study to substantiate their opinions; second, they need to clarify the particular skills of each team member, in relation to specific problems or particular styles of work, and be prepared to organize the team's work on this basis; third, they need to find ways of clarifying what goals are to be achieved, both generally in the neighbourhood and specifically in relation to known clients, so that firm criteria become established for continuing and withdrawing from cases, criteria based on the known competence of the staff and on the achievement of goals.

In considering the organization of social services we have seen that the making of social policy, whether at local or national level, does not culminate with an Act or White Paper. As Eyden (1969) has pointed out, the passing of an Act is the beginning rather than the end of debate about the logistics of service, the nature of co-operation between organizations, and the planning of future change. The debate starts with the purposes and objectives of specific services, but brings into focus wider issues: what means are most likely to achieve particular ends; what is the likely impact of service not only on the client but on local networks of social relationships; what is the source of moral (rather than legal) authority in providing a service? In the personal social services, the goals are often too vague to suggest precise actions; they are concerned with social justice, with welfare, with individual fulfilment. It is therefore only at the community level that one can begin to define which actions will have the desired effects. As the Seebohm Report suggests, the personal social services should be experiments; as such they need to combine the complexity of large-scale planning with ready responsiveness to social change, and to compatibility and incompatibility between individual and collective needs.

5 Personal Social Services and the General Public

One of the managerial dilemmas in all social services is that of finding an appropriate balance between mass provisions and discretionary responsiveness to individual and local needs. Social policy in respect of the personal social services has laid increasing emphasis on responsiveness to the needs of individuals and families and, more recently, of local communities. This emphasis may lead to organizational tension, however; attempts to achieve very localized responsiveness may seem at odds with the formulation of large-scale strategies of provision. The operational policies of a social services department may emerge as much from the accumulation of small tactical decisions taken at various levels in the organization in response to the presentation of need, as from the decisions made 'at the top' by the committee and directorate. The pursuit of local responsiveness as an ideal of service inevitably tends towards increasing the extent to which decisions are taken by main-grade workers with direct knowledge of local needs and attitudes and in personal contact with the general public. The delegation of decision-making has not been specifically formulated as a strategic policy for the personal social services, but it is an implicit by-product of the emphasis placed in recent years on three aspects of their functioning:

(1) preventive work,
(2) community care,
(3) and citizen participation in policy-making.

All three carry implications for the future of relationships between the services and the general public, and for the ways in which decisions are reached affecting the needs of local people.

PREVENTIVE WORK

From an administrative standpoint, the first dilemma is one of resources. Having in mind the high level of demand for immediate assistance to meet

143

urgent needs, it is difficult to determine how much effort and money should be devoted to activities where the effects, if any, will be long-term and often unpredictable. Secondly, it is necessary to differentiate the variety of processes contained within the concept of prevention and to relate these processes to the present functions of the social services.

Leonard (1971) has suggested that the concept can be usefully subdivided into primary, secondary and tertiary modes of intervention. Primary prevention is concerned with influencing the economic, social and political ideologies and structures in our social life which tend to increase the likelihood of poverty, distress and deprivation; such preventive work lies beyond the exclusive concern of the personal social services, though any service concerned with social justice cannot avoid some responsibilities in this area. Secondary prevention concerns more immediate 'at risk' situations, where as yet no damage has been done but where there is a combination of circumstances which, if not adjusted, will lead to the experience of need or suffering and the necessity of remedial services of some kind. Tertiary prevention is the prevention of a recurrence of need, suffering or socially unacceptable behaviour. The personal social services and social work have traditionally been concerned with tertiary prevention; clients have approached services, or have been referred to them, following some kind of social difficulty, and the service function has been to repair the situation and, where possible, to prevent its recurrence. Several recent developments in social service responsibilities have implied an extension of preventive work of this third kind. Resources under Section 1 of the Children and Young Persons Act 1963 to prevent the need for children to be taken into care, though formulated in terms of secondary prevention, are often used on behalf of families who are already receiving casework help and with whom it is hoped to prevent further distress or deterioration in family functioning. Community service orders (Criminal Justice Act 1974) and facilities for intermediate treatment (*Children in Trouble* 1968, Cmnd. 3601) are intended to help those who have already been in trouble to avoid further similar difficulties. Activities of this kind have two things in common: first, although they have the appearance of new and somewhat radical approaches, they represent an extension of the individualistic therapeutic model of social work help, by which social needs are dealt with in micro-environmental terms; but secondly they pre-suppose an acceptance by the public at large of the same value system as that of the personal social services, in particular the same approach to social justice. For example, a financial grant under the Children and Young Persons Act, 1963, may be made arbitrarily to a family whose financial resources are no different from those of their neighbours; it will be made therefore on the recognition of individual differences between people (in their abilities, for example, to cope with adverse situations) rather than on their similarities with their neighbours. When one interviews social service clients, one is frequently told of the injustice of the social services in giving more to a neighbour who has not deserved it. Similarly, community service orders and intermediate treatment offer interesting and often enjoyable experiences to those who, possibly in the eyes of their neighbours, should more properly be punished. A correspondent to the *Sunday Times*, 11 January 1976, said that one of the things she dreaded as an indignity of old age was having her garden cared for 'by young thugs on community service orders'. A further difficulty in developing preventive services, therefore, even at the tertiary level, lies not in their administrative and economic feasibility but in the possibility of discrepancy between the values of the service and those of the local community; effective preventive work depends in part on a shift in the services from preoccupation with the micro-environment of the individual client and his family to a concern for the value systems of the wider community environment and how to influence them. (A parallel situation has been found in the Government's sponsorship of job-creation for school leavers to prevent their immediate experience of un-employment; local authorities and voluntary social services have been sympathetic, but few jobs have been created in local industries.)

Moral dilemmas exist also in work concerned with secondary prevention. Such work implies the right of services to intervene *in advance of* the expression of the need for help. Furthermore, it raises problems of the confidentiality of information between, for example, a general practitioner who may foresee a growing marital conflict and a local probation officer. The problem is particularly acute in the detection of situations where children are at risk of neglect or injury from their parents. The NSPCC has achieved considerable success in its approach to these difficult situations; the general public accepts the society as a long-standing institution, well-intentioned and, though powerful in the courts, removed from direct association with central and local government. Similar preventive work through joint local government action has met with greater difficulties: the Co-ordinating Committees established in 1950 following the joint circular of the Home Office and Ministries of Health and Education became increasingly resented by social workers as places where confidential information was exchanged without control over its subsequent use. Families whose names appeared before the Committees risked both labelling as 'problem families' and also the experience of subtle changes in attitude towards them among those services represented on the Committees. Some social workers refused to attend meetings in protest against the labelling process at work within them. At the present time, the development and maintenance of registers of children who may be 'at risk' has encountered similar dilemmas and anxieties. This is another example of a situation where administrative efficiency may run counter to professional values, and where the values of both services and professionals may be at variance with those of the citizens they wish to serve.

Effective preventive work cannot therefore be regarded *simply* as an extension of the traditional concerns and policies of the personal social services. It owes its origins to the activities of caseworkers who have increasingly recognized the limited scope of their intervention. But it involves exploring the inter-relationships of a variety of value systems, and cannot be divorced from considerations of public participation in social policy. Preventive work cannot be effectively attempted merely as a management directive, for to some extent its authority can be derived only from the strength of horizontal relationships between social services, other agencies and professional groups, and the communities in which they work.

The complexity of preventive work is such, therefore, as to make its development a slow process, and thus to reduce the emphasis likely to be placed upon it by hard-pressed local authorities at a time of economic stringency. Yet the long-term economic consequences of any withdrawal from preventive work may well be considerable. Meacher (1976) has drawn attention to the dilemma of choice that exists between spending money now for which there is no immediate return, or saving money in the present and risking higher expenditure on remedial work in the future. For example, the National Children's Bureau study in 1972 indicated that 14% of 7-year-old children displayed symptoms of disturbance. It is at present often left to the voluntary sector to indicate the need for preventive work and to develop pilot schemes of intervention.

COMMUNITY CARE

This became an operational concept in the 1960s: it was initially associated with the policy intention (made possible by the growth of the local authority services and the availability of psychotropic drugs) to reduce the number of long-stay beds in psychiatric hospitals and to provide domiciliary services to enable patients to be cared for in their own homes or in small local hostels. A detailed account of this movement in psychiatric treatment may be found in the work of Kathleen Jones (1960) and, more recently, in a study by Bayley (1973) of the implications of 'community care' in situations of mental handicap. Initially the assumption was made that effective community care could be provided more cheaply than institutional care; this assumption is now questioned, particularly as the concept has been extended to cover alternatives to penal institutionalization and other forms of custodial care.

Effective community care rests on five factors:

(1) the willingness and ability of the family (where there is one) to shoulder a burden of care which may in some measure be disruptive of the needs of some members;

(2) the development by local authorities of alternatives to large residential institutions, for example, foster-care facilities and small-scale residential units;

(3) the acceptance by local people of the need for these facilities to be sited in close proximity to their own homes;

(4) the development of a wide range of domiciliary and related services

for those living alone or to support the care provided by families: in addition to social work support, home help, home-nursing, day care and recreational facilities, physical adaptations to accommodation, and readily available medical advice are all essential;

(5) the practical help and concern of neighbours: to help with shopping, to 'sit in' with the handicapped person, to offer friendship, excursions, relief to families in holiday periods, etc.

Clearly the capital and recurrent expenditure involved in this comprehensive view of community care is considerable. But in addition it requires careful negotiations and the development of patterns of co-operation at various levels: between the social services and voluntary agencies and groups in defining local needs and in planning the enlistment of 'good neighbourly' support; the development of a sense of partnership between teams of social workers, domiciliary workers and medical support services; defining the role and accountability of the local voluntary helper (whether he is to be regarded as an ancillary to the department or, as Bayley suggests, a central figure in the total process of care). This latter possibility has been given practical implementation in a volunteer scheme promoted by the Hillingdon Social Services Department. Here, since the passing of the Chronically Sick and Disabled Persons Act 1970, the authority has spent up to £30,000 a year on the installation of telephones in the homes of the housebound. In the installation, some voluntary help was offered by members of the Post Office Union. It was recognized, however, that telephones in themselves did not constitute an adequate provision; while it was useful for social workers and home helps to be able to telephone their clients, it was doubtful whether the telephones served much purpose in emergencies as, for example, following a fall. A volunteer scheme was initiated, therefore, with the limited objective of making brief but frequent calls to the housebound. It was found that short daily calls established genuine relationships between the housebound and the volunteers; more than 90% of clients and all the volunteers preferred a short daily call to a longer weekly one, and the satisfaction experienced by both is indicated by the continuing help of the volunteers over many months and the ease with which new volunteers are found to help man the scheme.

The department's conclusion from this scheme is that it is an effective method of safeguarding the security of clients; it is also considerably cheaper than the less frequent visits by social workers (it is estimated that the scheme costs 35p a day for each client as against £6 a visit by an assistant social worker). The scheme illustrates also three important aspects of the effective development of community care; the volunteer's contribution is seen as a central rather than a subsidiary function in the caring process; his task is clearly defined, so that he can commit himself to it without risk that it will become extended and too time-consuming; the usefulness of the task is self-evident, and the work is therefore satisfying.

The skills required to initiate a volunteer scheme within a community care programme are, however, considerable: they include the ability to call public meetings and enlist enthusiasm and support; to fit the volunteer to a definable task for which he is particularly suited; to help him to recognize the value of his contribution within the broader context of services; to offer immediate advice when he is confronted with an unexpected situation; to reconcile his motivation to help, and the form in which he is able to provide it, with the values and objectives of the department and of other contingent services.

This work is both skilful and time-consuming, and there is sense in delegating full-time responsibility for it to particular staff members; but the risk in doing so is that other staff members may then feel no direct concern for the work. An important difficulty in enlisting volunteer help for community care lies not in finding willing people but in the uncertainty of their subsequent relationships with the paid staff.

A further issue in the development of community care is to determine who the staff member or members should be. Should he be a qualified social worker? In the probation service, staffed entirely by social workers, this is not in doubt. But within a local authority department it may be argued that a trained community development worker is, on the face of it, more likely to possess the initially essential skills in public relations and in enlisting public enthusiasm, although he is not directly in touch with the individual clients and families with whom the volunteers may subsequently work. The development of an effective community care programme may therefore require some consideration of the relationship of community workers to social work teams, and more fundamentally of the relationship between community work and social work. There has been a tendency hitherto to assume that these are separate and even alternative modes of work. It is certainly doubtful whether anyone can effectively master the skills of both methods of intervention, but the maintenance of their professional and ideological separation serves purposes other than community welfare. It is doubtful whether anyone in need of help recognizes which kind of intervention he requires in methodological terms; similarly it is unlikely that an effective promotion of community care can be achieved if the enlistment of volunteer help is linked exclusively to one particular kind of practitioner.

It might be argued therefore that the promotion of volunteer help should be the responsibility of several people in the organization according to the nature of the care required and offered. For example, social workers might enlist volunteers whose interests lie in problems of family relationships and in the need for professional services; community workers might look for those concerned with community action programmes, play groups and recreational facilities, or participation in local planning; and home help organizers might enlist the help of those who wish to offer neighbourly service of a practical nature, for example, such as shopping, sitting-in services, friendly visiting. The case for regarding the home help organizer as a key figure in community care provisions and in the enlistment of voluntary help has been stated by the Volunteer Centre following the publication of a consultative paper by the Central Council for Education and Training in Social Work and the Local Government Training Board on the training of home help organizers. The Centre has argued (*Social Worker* 1975) that, since the transfer of the Home Help Service to the Social Services Department in 1970, the service has increasingly developed community or neighbourhood-based schemes of help. In Sheffield, for example, the home help service employs 120 salaried street wardens to provide direct services to the elderly and housebound and to mobilize community resources. It may be, as the Centre suggests, that the home help service is at a cross-roads in its development: at worst it may become an encapsulated administrative unit, divorced from the assessment of needs and from community life, or at best a focal point for the development of local caring services, based on the values of local people and fostering a sense of mutual responsibility within neighbourhoods.

So far attention has been given to the importance of voluntary and informal help in the development of community care, and to some of the issues which the enlistment of this kind of help may raise in professional and organizational terms. Community care may be promoted also by established voluntary agencies and groups, through Church organizations, Councils of Voluntary Service, local old people's welfare committees, for example. Such action may lack the degree of central co-ordination that it is possible to achieve in schemes organized by the statutory services, but they have the compensatory advantage of permitting the emergence of a variety of neighbourhood patterns of service devised by people with intimate neighbourhood knowledge. Local groups may be able to enlist the help of those who would not think of volunteering at the Town Hall. For examples of community care schemes of this kind see Cheeseman *et al.*, 1972; Ferguson & McGone, 1974; NCSS, 1972.) Other forms of community care may be provided by informal services which work on the basis of communes. The work of the Simon Community and the Cyrenians with vagrants and alcoholics has shown that, with appropriate group support, considerably demanding work can be undertaken by untrained volunteers. Women's Aid Centres offer an example of the important level of community care which can be provided by those who themselves have needed help.

In view of the variety of auspices and patterns of community care, it is not easy for the statutory services to find ways of relating their own provisions to neighbourhood and community schemes. Some local authorities provide support by small payments to known voluntary helpers (see Age Concern 1974); others have recognized that to make maximum use of informal community caring may involve a restructuring of services, both geographically and, in a sense, culturally. Some statutory advice services are now located in local shops and public houses in order to meet 'good neighbours' in their own local setting. (See Darvill 1975.)

Two general points arise from this brief consideration of community care. First, the traditional mode of work of the personal social services, based on exclusive relationships between individual social workers and families is now being extended, as service workers recognize the availability and complexity of local resources, towards the development of community teams, made up of people with different but complementary interests and skills. Secondly, and arising from this, a new balance needs to be found between the centralized functions of statutory departments (setting standards, allocating resources and achieving concerted action) and the autonomy of local teams in responding to the needs and resources of the neighbourhoods within which they work.

CITIZEN PARTICIPATION

The preceding section has been concerned with citizen participation in the provision of service. An ideal expressed by the Seebohm and Skeffington (1969) Reports was that citizens should participate also in the formation of service policies; the Seebohm Report, for example, spoke of the involvement of clients in the work of old people's welfare committees. To what extent is public participation in policy making possible? At present there is a growing body of experience in mobilizing public opinion and action in respect of town planning programmes and the redevelopment of neighbourhoods. Community workers employed by voluntary agencies (Councils of Voluntary Service or churches, for example) or by social services departments have for some years been active in encouraging local people to make representation when a slum clearance programme or a road development was inimical to the life of their community. Similarly, it is now commonplace for local people to be helped to develop their own recreational facilities, community newspapers and neighbourhood services on a voluntary basis.

To what extent can these processes be applied to the development of policies in administratively complex social services departments, or in probation and after-care where policies and functions are defined in law? The role of the community worker (especially in a statutory service) is ambiguous in this respect. He may find it easier to mobilize community opinion and action in respect of the work of another department than of his own employing authority. This is not simply a matter of his self-preservation; it is related more particularly to his awareness of the complexity of responsibilities of his department, the relative shortage of resources to meet them, and the essentially competitive situation when new developments are considered. He has a choice of roles, therefore, when complaints are voiced about an inadequacy within his own service: either to be a mediator identifying with and explaining the policies of the department in the context of its wide responsibilities, or to enable the case to be put as strongly and effectively as possible, dissociated from agency policy, but to leave the final decision where it rests at present, in the power of the Committee and managers of his agency. This second alternative, i.e. the formation of a pressure group, is by no means an ineffectual activity. Pressure groups, both nationally and locally, are ways of enhancing the relatively small political power of individual complainants; they may make new and relevant information available which has not hitherto been considered; they may be persuasive in arguments; they may influence the voting behaviour of their members in the next local or national election; and they may have access to the mass media.

The accountability of a service cannot, however, be related simply to its responsiveness to local pressure groups. The function of a pressure group is to compete single-mindedly for resources, and thus it may tend to increase inequalities of provision, to the detriment particularly of those who are unable to represent their needs as effectively or to exercise power and persuasion. The responsibility of a statutory service, on the other hand, especially one committed to the general promotion of welfare, is to achieve an equitable distribution of resources based rather on the seriousness of a problem or need than on the power of complainants. A pressure group may seek to promote change through a conflict of interests, whereas a service usually seeks to effect social change through co-operation between competing interests.

The pursuit of co-operation draws attention, however, to the ambiguous role of the expert (whether he is a manager, researcher or social worker). Although the expert sees more of the total pattern of resources and needs, and has more knowledge of 'how things work', is his decision necessarily the right one particularly in respect of the experience of need? It is necessary here to distinguish between accountability to the users of services and accountability to the general public. Experts may know more than consumers do about resources and processes, but cannot be expert in how a service *ought* to be used by the individual consumer or how the consumer ought to feel about his situation. Only the consumer knows what the service means to him and how he has experienced it; he has therefore a contribution to make to the processes which exist, at least in part, to further his well-being, and a right to have his criticisms considered. This is a different matter from trying to achieve general public participation in debate about priorities in the overall use of resources.

At the same time, it has been suggested, in considering the promotion of community care, that some measure of responsibility for the form services take should be delegated to the local area team in association with local residents. One might envisage a situation, therefore, where the use of some resources (those associated with a particular neighbourhood) might be planned in co-operation between staff and local pressure groups, or groups of actual or potential users of services. By this means, services would derive part of their authority from the communities they serve; they would be based on a kind of consumer syndicalism. Similar processes are already being tried in some residential establishments, in the work of day training centres, and in some local offices where facilities are made available to local people irrespective of their formal designation as clients.

The issue of public participation is related, therefore, to the problems of sharing power and to defining the source of authority within services. The impression is sometimes given (in respect, for example, of frauds among claimants of supplementary benefit) that the public needs to be protected against the tyranny of social service consumers. Consumers and potential consumers of services may in turn equally need protection from the beneficent rule of centrally-based experts on social needs and provisions and from the elusive but considerable power of individual public employees. The elected representative offers some protection, but his protection is usually based on the isolating of the individual applicant as a special case. An additional need is therefore for group consumer representation and consultation, related to the activities of services in local neighbourhoods. How this can best be promoted is still a matter for experiment and research.

It has been suggested above that the role of the community worker, especially one employed by a statutory service, is ambiguous and complex when he seeks to involve local residents in issues of service-policy rather than simply in the development of local service-provisions. All community work is based on the assumption that participation is good, in that it represents more effective democracy, precipitates social change, and ensures that the management of resources is related to the experience of need. These principles are somewhat easier to comprehend when they are left at a high level of generalization and abstraction than when they are pinned down to specific situations. Rodgers and Stevenson (1974) have suggested that social workers (they include community workers in this title) are appointed to offer direct and definable services to people and to preserve *individual* rights. Since concern for the promotion of local democracy and social change may all too readily lead to coercion by the community worker or by majorities within particular localities, and to the danger that the values and needs of certain minority groups will be ignored, they are led to the view that a distinction must be drawn between social work and political activities and processes. On the other hand, some writers would define all social work as political (for examples see R. Bailey (ed.): *Radical Social Work*, Arnold 1976), and it has been suggested earlier in this book that one cannot separate the policies, functions and activities of the social services from wider social and political considerations. Among community workers, the current debate, therefore, is whether or not the social changes they seek to achieve should be based on gradual reform or on more dramatic and 'radical' processes; any social change has, in some sense, political implications.

The central issue in defining the role of the community worker is whether he should regard himself as a political leader, rather than whether he should regard himself as 'involved in politics'. Community workers usually become engaged in local situations because they are appointed by an organization. Their appointment is based on the assumption that they possess certain kinds of knowledge and skills relevant to the social needs of a particular community, not on their personally held political ideology. Inevitably, their involvement leads to a measure of identification with the interests of those they serve; role ambiguity may therefore arise in a wish to serve the community *either* on its own terms *or* in the ways defined or expected by the employing agency. (This ambiguity is present in all social work, though usually in a less dramatic form.) Yet this ambiguity is a necessary outcome of work, and much of the supposed value of community work would be lost if the ambiguity were denied or resolved by a simplistic loyalty to one side or the other. The community worker is the channel by which certain resources are made available to local people. But by his intervention, local people may become more than just the recipients of the agency's service; they may in addition become a social resource available to promote the welfare of others. (See Seebohm Report, para. 2.) What may have started as the means of accomplishing a defined task may have spin-off effects which were not contained in the original definition of the work to be done; if these effects are related to the meeting of needs, then they should not ideally be divorced from the social responsibilities of the employing service. Where prolonged conflict arises between the community worker and the employing agency, this is likely to be related to one or more of the following possibilities: that the community worker's activities are not related to felt needs, or that there is a discrepancy between the agency's operations and its expressed intentions, or that there is a lack of resources, or disagreement about their allocation, or that there are inter-agency tensions which need to be resolved at committee level by the elected representatives.

Community work has achieved importance in recent years, first as a way of developing local voluntary resources and latterly as a means of securing the involvement of local people in the policies and decisions of local services. Community workers have appropriately drawn attention to the political implications of their work and to the occasional relevance of conflict-strategies. What needs to be clarified in the future, however, is the relationship between these strategies and the legitimate welfare concerns of the employing agencies; why conflict arises or becomes necessary, and the extent to which community workers usurp the functions of elected representatives. On this last matter, I have implied that the functions of the community worker and elected representative are complementary rather than overlapping, though both profess to speak on behalf of their local communities. But there are many divergent views on this issue which have yet to be adequately recorded and evaluated.

THE MEETING OF CLIENTS' NEEDS

At an earlier point it was suggested that the problems with which the personal social services deal have both individual and social characteristics: they are experienced in different personal ways by individuals but are perceived by society as a whole as intolerable, in terms either of the degree of suffering they cause or of the threat they pose to community well-being. In the preceding sections we have seen similarly how the meeting of needs is concerned with, and has practical implications for, both the individual citizen and the local community in which he lives: the functioning of the personal social services may often appear to be individualistic (concerned with the protection and care of individuals), but yet effective care can be achieved only if attention is paid to the relationship of the individual and of the services themselves to local community relationships and values. At times the needs and values of individuals and those of local communities will be opposed; at other times they will be similar. In the former instance, the services have a choice, either to share in the social isolation of their clients (that is to say, to continue on an individual basis without regard to local criticisms) or to devote time to public relations in the hope of generating greater acceptance of the 'deviant' individual.

At the same time, services derive all their authority and resources from the communities in which they work, and social workers frequently experience tension between their concern to help the 'deviant' individual and to emphasize his rights to service, irrespective of whether he is perceived by his neighbours as deserving of help, and their desire to subscribe to and identify with the generality of values about social obligation and duties. Social work is rooted historically in moralistic judgments about the deserving and undeserving poor, and although the development of psychological and sociological insights has made these notions unacceptable in theory they may still exercise some influence (however unwitting) in day-to-day practice: for example in the extent to which one may exercise moral pressure to change behaviour (whether or not one understands its causes) which is generally regarded as unacceptable.

The role of central government in influencing the policies of the personal social services has therefore been important, not only in the promotion of standards of provision but in helping local services and their staffs to maintain a sense of purpose and direction in situations where individual needs and community values conflict. Since 1950, Government has increased the sophistication of its information services (note, for example, the publication of *Social Trends*), has developed processes of consultation with local authorities, and has appointed professionally qualified staff to advise and inspect the operation of services (as in the Probation Inspectorate of the Home Office and the Local Authority Social Work Services division of the DHSS). Through White Papers (for example, *Children in Trouble*, *Better Services for the Mentally Ill*) and the establishment of committees (for example, Seebohm) central government departments have become centres for the formulation of expert and professional policies.

In spite of support of this kind, however, there are (perhaps inevitably) disjunctions between agreed purpose and daily practice. To begin with, local performance in the personal social services will be affected by the policies **and resources** of contingent services: as has been noted earlier, for example, many thousands of children are in local authority care because of homelessness or bad home conditions; in March 1974, 1151 London families were in bed-and-breakfast accommodation at a weekly cost of between £30 and £40 per family. Secondly, the skills and knowledge of local staff may be inadequate to achieve agreed purposes: a paper on Legal Studies in Social Work Education (CCETSW Paper No. 4, 1974) has estimated that in respect of social work duties alone there are now 55 Acts of Parliament or statutory instruments that need to be considered. The British Association of Social Workers has commented that "Too much may now be demanded of social workers in terms of skill and knowledge in the light of the unending and fragmented demands placed upon them." (BASW evidence to the Butterworth enquiry on work and pay of probation officers and social workers 1972, Cmnd. 5076). It is sometimes argued that only by a return to some specialization of task can an appropriate level of knowledge and skills be acquired and maintained; but on the other hand, it is difficult to promote specialization without creating artificial boundaries of task which distort the needs of some clients. As Kogan (1969) has written, the personal social services are living "in bracing times, and those who get through will be able to say, with the survivors of Agincourt, 'I was there'."

Because of the gap between agreed policy and actual practice, it is often easier to define the purposes of local services by reference to White Papers and legislation, or to theories and assumptions drawn from psychology, sociology or politics, than from a study of their day-to-day practices. But this again leads to a regrettable position where purpose and policy seem divorced, in theory as well as in planning, from the concerns of the field workers and their clients. If one's nose is always kept to the grindstone one has little time to think about the total purpose of one's work; fieldwork practice is often experienced by practitioners as merely the accumulation of small disjointed achievements with isolated individuals or groups, rather than as the practical demonstration of social purpose and social policy.

There are, it seems to me, three ways in which at the field work level of operation one might begin to define a sense of purpose which would infuse the work situation rather than seem remote from it. The first is to clarify who the beneficiaries of service are; this matter has been considered earlier but requires further exploration. The second is to encourage research into the outcome of intervention of different kinds. And the third is to clarify the role of the client, his right to service and the rights of the authority to intervene in his life. Little progress has so far been made in any of these, and the following notes are intended as statements of the present uncertainties rather than offering firm guidelines.

Who are the beneficiaries?

In an ideal work situation the beneficiaries would be both the designated client (whose rights are upheld and who is assisted towards a constructive experience of social relationships) and the community (whose values are endorsed, and which feels protected from disruptive behaviour). This situation may apply, for example, when work leads to the willing reconciliation of a married couple, to the relief of the social isolation of an elderly person, to the successful fostering of an ill-treated child. In some cases, however, as we have already seen there is uncertainty about the beneficiary: some probationers, for example, accept the terms of a probation order only because its alternative is worse, while others accept the Order as a positive contribution to their own well-being. A child whose behaviour is disruptive of family or school life may be taken into care; though designated as a client he may not see himself as the primary beneficiary of the intervention, though he may well be regarded as such. To designate the client as the primary beneficiary in *all* social work is, therefore, to overlook the qualitative range of attitudes and needs to be found among clients and the different kinds of 'entitlement' to service which are applied in different situations. Even when an entitlement of service is clear-cut (no client would be turned away from a social services department who sought help in some aspect of the care of his children) the kinds of help received may vary considerably in the extent to which they are perceived by the client as relevant to his needs and in the extent to which the client regards himself as a beneficiary.

In defining the purpose of service, therefore, a fundamental concern for field workers is to clarify the general dilemma of allegiance. When the scope of work and service offered by agencies was limited, narrowly defined and readily comprehensible, agency policy and function provided the resolution to ethical dilemmas of allegiance and the question of whose interests should be the primary concern of the worker. With expansion in the scope of work and in the variety of modes of intervention, 'agency function' has ceased in many areas of social work practice to be a useful guide: one would be hard put to it to define the 'agency function' of a social services department except in very broad generalizations, yet it is through the agency that the social worker must remain accountable to the tax payers who pay his salary. The responsibility now rests therefore with the workers themselves to come to grips with the question of primary allegiance. As far as those designated as clients are concerned, it is well recognized that to be a beneficiary has meant to make oneself available to be changed in some way. As Pinker (1971) has said, 'clients are those citizens who receive what the social services call help and who live with the consequences of that help.' If, as is suggested, beneficiaries may be people other than those formally designated as clients, it may be argued that they too should be engaged in processes of change. In short, it may not be the function of the field worker merely to adjust the behaviour of client-groups in the interests of other groups or institutions but to promote beneficial changes in social attitudes and relationships based on an awareness of the relative gains of the various beneficiaries. This suggests an unexplored middle ground between two opposed factions among social workers: those whose practice represents an unquestioning advocacy of the client's rights to help within what is perceived as a corrupt 'system' and those who act as if 'the system' is broadly satisfactory and clients need help with adjusting to it.

Anxiety is sometimes expressed about the abuse of social services and the abuse of the good will and trust of field workers: some deny that abuse exists or is relevant; others look for more rigorous safeguards against it. How far should social workers be trusting or suspicious? Nobody knows the answer to this dilemma; nor shall we know until more work is done on the impact of social work practice on the various beneficiaries associated with each case.

The outcome of intervention

There are two main areas of study concerning the outcome of intervention: the first which judges its effectiveness on the basis of the clients' subsequent behaviour measured against external criteria, and the second which monitors clients' reactions to intervention and their own evaluation of it. In neither area has much progress so far been made, and thus we have available no clear guidelines on certain issues fundamental to the effective delivery of services and to the development of good social work practice: for example, little is known of the relationship between particular styles of intervention and the achievement of specific outcomes; nor has a satisfactory arrangement yet been found by which the evaluation of intervention can be built into the day-to-day work of agencies; where research workers have been appointed, their relationship with service practitioners is unclear, and often clouded by misunderstanding.

There are three general problems in promoting research into the delivery of services. First, there is uncertainty about what constitutes success or failure in the outcome of work. Plowman (1969) has suggested that these concepts of success and failure need to be broken down into three measurable criteria: the achievement of a pre-determined social adjustment (for example, not committing further offences over an agreed period of years), the relief of symptoms of distress, and the achievement by the service user of increased insight. Similarly, Goldberg (1970) has proposed four component activities in the assessment of success/failure: measuring the client's behaviour on certain dimensions, measurements of change in personality, socio-metric tests, and the monitoring through questionnaires of the client's satisfaction with services.

But in both these proposals there are certain difficulties when one applies them to the whole range of services now available. First they relate essentially to a casework orientation of practice; that is to say, effectiveness is measured primarily by reference to change in the client, and some practitioners (notably community workers) would deny that changes of this kind are always a desirable outcome of intervention. Furthermore, evaluation of services needs also to take into account the attitudes and perceptions of the practitioners, concerning how their activities relate to the problems and needs which *they* perceive, which outcomes are primarily desired, whom they define as beneficiaries, to whom they feel primary allegiance, and the extent to which their practice is assisted or impeded by resources and factors which lie outside their relationships with their clients. Evaluation of the outcome of service is inevitably linked to social values about what constitutes appropriate behaviour and about how people ought to function in particular situations, and these values may well be differently defined by different practitioners within an organization. The social services are concerned with some sort of betterment, but betterment is not easily defined or assessed. Gottschalk & Auerbach (1966) have suggested that no ultimate success criteria have yet been identified in psychotherapy, and the same comment is no doubt true of the provisions of social services.

A further problem affecting the promotion of research into the effectiveness of the personal social services concerns the validity of retrospective evidence. Short of conducting controlled experiments which would affect the whole social functioning of people, our main sources of information about the effectiveness of services and about people's attitudes towards them are retrospective—we try to judge the effectiveness of activities after they have taken place. There is some evidence, however, that in evaluating social work practice both clients and workers tend to over-estimate the changes that have taken place (Meyer, 1965). One study concludes 'we found no correspondence between measured outcome and the positive evaluation of the programme made by the boys and the counsellors' (Powers & Witmer 1951). Conclusions of this kind are usually interpreted simply as indicating both the low utility of the social worker's practice and also his over-estimation of the value of his work. But life is more complicated than that. Many probation officers, for example, record cases as failures in their statistical returns (if a probationer re-offends, or an ex-prisoner is recalled to prison, or if marriage partners separate) while maintaining with confidence that in emotional terms and in terms of the attitudes of clients their work has not been wholly unsuccessful. Here again, therefore, one encounters dilemmas of value and purpose; few if any probation officers choose their careers because of their concern to combat the crime-rates, though this has been the major criterion used hitherto in evaluating their work.

It is reasonable to suggest, therefore, that the evaluation of social service intervention is made well nigh impossible by the problems of measuring *at one time* all the factors which should be included as relevant. Evaluation ideally needs to consider 'on what basis and to what end will who do what to whom, for how long, with what effects, at what costs and with what benefits' (Mullen, Dumpson *et al.*, 1972). Because of this complexity of variables, research has hitherto been concentrated on the arbitrary combination of certain factors to the exclusion of others. In general, the extent to which a wide range of factors has been included depends on the clarity with which a particular service can be defined and on the relative simplicity of the value-complex associated with the needs of the client-group. The provision of services to old people, for example, is more readily separated from the broad complexity of provisions and values than services to assist delinquents or multi-problem families. Examples of service-evaluation hitherto have fallen, as noted earlier, into two main areas, studies of outcome and studies of process, and these will now be briefly considered.

The studies of outcome

The outcome of intervention has been assessed first in relation to objectively perceived changes in the clients' later social behaviour. Examples of this are the work of H. Meyer (1965), G. E. Brown (1968), the Cambridge–Somerville Youth Study (Powers & Witmer, 1951), and the experiments conducted by the Home Office in matching client's personal characteristics with the characteristic modes of intervention by the social workers (the MESPA experiments). In all these studies, outcome has suggested only minimal work effectiveness, but the three American studies show weaknesses in their approaches to evaluation: they discount the validity of clients' feelings; they assume that good social work practice is simply intensive casework; they ignore the context in which casework is undertaken; and they lump together both clients and workers as if they formed homogeneous groups (the first group all needing the same kinds of help, and the second all working in the same ways) with the result that variations in practice and outcome are statistically flattened. As has been shown in the studies of Reid & Shyne (1969) and Mayer & Timms (1970), the same methods of work will in some situations do good and in others do harm. These outcome studies offer no guidance in this dilemma.

A second group of studies has assessed outcome in relation both to objectively perceived changes in behaviour, to clients' feelings about the outcome, and to the presence of emotional and physical changes. The work of Goldberg (1970) should particularly be studied in this respect, not only for its intrinsic methodological merit but as representing a successful attempt to unite the separate areas of evaluation. Butrym's study, *Medical Social Work in Action* (1967) relates the retrospective impressions of clients to the initial expectations of referral agents. Though objectively defined changes may seem small in these studies, both indicate that, as a result of skilled intervention, clients' morale was heightened and their experience of need reduced.

Studies of client's feelings related to the processes of intervention rather than its outcome

Reference should be made to the work of Hewett (1970), Mayer & Timms (1970), McKay *et al.* (1973), and Sainsbury (1975) where particular attention is paid to the impressions and feelings of clients, and to the work of

Rogers (1965) and Truax & Carkhuff (1967) whose emphasis is on the qualities of workers' relationships which promote changes in clients' feelings about their situation. Hewett showed the emotional importance to the client of combining practical advice with sensitivity and caring; Mayer & Timms and Sainsbury particularly draw attention to the importance for the client of compatibility between the way he presents his needs and the worker's mode of approach to the case. Both have regard especially to the complexity of feelings experienced by clients at the time of their referral to services. The work of Rogers and his colleagues has suggested that the attitudes of social workers which most affect the feelings experienced by their clients are warm acceptance of the client (leading to openness and spontaneity in the expression of feelings by both sides), accurate empathy (generating in the client the feeling of being wholly and intimately understood), and congruence between the worker's *expression* of concern and commitment to his client and the client's actual *experience* of this concern.

Most of these studies have been undertaken with relatively small groups of clients or with clients who overtly share certain characteristics. More ambitious work in this field, which attempts to study the experiences of a random group of clients, has been started with the Hampshire Social Services Department at Southampton. The first report (McKay *et al.*, 1973) which studied 305 clients, demonstrated the inadequacy of clients' knowledge of services when they approached the Department for assistance, the complexity of uncertainty and anxiety which accompanied their referral, and the significance which they attached to the personality characteristics of the workers they met. The frequency of contact between client and worker was found to be important in building a relationship of trust, and in overcoming the initial barriers created by differences of perception and expectation.

In evaluating services, therefore, research appears to demonstrate that social workers may play a significant and helpful role in the lives of their clients, but that this helpfulness is more evident in the area of feelings (in helping to allay anxiety, in encouraging self-esteem, and in promoting the value of the individual) than in achieving objectively validated changes in social behaviour. If one regards the primary function of the social services as the solution of social problems, objectively and administratively defined, then the role of the social worker within the service is uncertain. If, however, services are seen as more concerned with the promotion of satisfying social relationships between people, then the role of the social worker becomes more central to organizational purpose.

If a balance is to be achieved between these two viewpoints, future research will need to concentrate first on the use of samples of clients to provide research and control groups; the ethical problems of offering service to one group and withholding it from another are considerable, but an alternative way forward is suggested by Goldberg's work, *Helping the Aged*, where research and control groups were both offered service but of definably different kinds. Related to this, we need to identify the exact content of the services offered, so that evaluation can be made of the different components of a service. Thirdly, we need to be more explicit about the nature of success; this requires a comparison of the values held by organizations, individual workers, professional groups, clients and others in the community. And finally, we need to consider the relationship between the activities of researchers and the work of practitioners within the services. Statistical analysis of caseloads and of measurements of behavioural change may not relate to the values which practitioners exemplify and uphold in their work;* from the standpoint of the social worker concerned with the needs and feelings of an individual client, effectiveness may not always be measurable by statistical criteria. Moreover, statistical information about the 'disposal' of clients and the costs involved in the disposal, while providing clues to aspects of service which merit further study, may not provide indicators of the success of a service in achieving its global purposes. For example, the number of children taken into care may reflect the special social conditions of a geographical area rather than the quality of service provided within the area; or it may tell us how effective the social workers are in detecting children's needs; or how ineffective they have been in preventing the break-up of families.

The promotion of research within the social services might at this stage best be regarded as a means of defining which areas of policy and practice merit intensive future study rather than as the means of evaluating what is being done. This is particularly true of studies concerned with clients' reactions to services; the value of these studies is generally agreed, but more as an article of faith than because they are regarded as having direct relevance to the policy of services. The uncertainty which at present surrounds the relevance of clients' evaluations of services is, perhaps, a further indication of the uncertainty of their status as beneficiaries of services.

THE ROLE OF THE USER OF SERVICES

The user of the social services may be known by several different titles: applicant, patient, consumer, person in care, probationer, client. Except possibly for the last, these descriptions all imply that in some sense he is having something provided for him or done to him. It is rare for him to be regarded as a participant in services. Certainly he is a recipient of service as he is at the receiving end of provisions, but he has three other roles: as a definer of his own needs, as a fellow citizen and as a potential provider of service to others. The extent to which, and the manner in which, these various roles are combined rests on certain issues. First, the more services are regarded as concerned with the isolated needs of a minority of inadequate people, the more likely that the recipient role will over-ride and

---

* See, for example, the evidence of the Home Office to the Royal Commission on Local Government 1967: 'There is no statistical criterion of effectiveness . . .'.

possibly exclude the other roles. If, on the other hand, services are regarded in the terms of the Seebohm Report as an experiment involving a wide complexity of social relationships within community living, the more likely it becomes that the client's other roles will be recognized. The development of community service orders within the probation service is an example of this, in that they combine the traditional purposes of probation—to modify the attitudes and social behaviour of clients—with the involvement of the client as a provider of service and as a citizen contributing to the welfare of others. The care of mentally disordered people in small residential units, particularly in flatlets where they are encouraged as far as possible to look after themselves, represents a shift in the client's role from that of patient to that of citizen. A study recently undertaken of the families known to a Family Service Unit illustrated how effectively, through group meetings, clients were able to help each other in ways equivalent in outcome, though not in methods, to the intervention of a social worker; it showed also the eagerness with which some clients wished to contribute to the service they were receiving (Sainsbury, 1975).

Secondly, the combining of roles within the status of client depends on the extent to which he is regarded as inadequate not only to meet his own needs but also to define them. The definition of an illness is essentially an expert function; the patient of a doctor will sometimes (not always) know that he is ill, but will not be expected to be able to define his illness nor to account for its development. Similarly, the more the assessment of need made by the social services focusses on the deviance or abnormality of the client's behaviour and on subtle definitions of the aetiology of this behaviour, the less contribution is expected from the client in terms of self-help and self-assessment. The work of Mayer & Timms (1970) has shown how some clients may receive 'help' based on a system of assessment which is neither disclosed nor understood.

Thirdly, the status and role allotted to the client will depend on the extent to which his behaviour is seen as a threat to the good order of society, or as bizarre in some way. An important function of pressure groups on behalf of minorities is to emphasize the normality of those they represent and their equality as citizens. A similar process is at present at work, under the influence of government policy, in the treatment of juvenile offenders.

Social services are the products of their age and are responsive to changes in public opinion; thus at different times and in different agencies the 'client' role may be differently formulated. At present, if one is the client of several services, one is likely to be treated in a variety of ways according to the prevailing definition of the client-role and the emphasis given to particular components within this role; one may be treated as equal or dependent, as the victim of pressures or as the exploiter of service, as the patient in need of treatment or as a person capable of self-help. These uncertainties in the client-role have led to considerable debate among social workers, between those who wish to abandon the word 'client' as stigmatizing and those who wish to transform it so that clients become real clients—that is to say, they enter into a contract with the service, based on a clear understanding on both sides about the length, focus and goals of contact. In practice this means that, at the time of referral, the client is encouraged to formulate not only his needs or problems but also the tasks necessary to overcome them. These are *his* tasks, to which the helper contributes by joint agreement. Time-limits of work are established at the outset. If on moral or agency-related grounds the worker is unable to agree to help in the defined tasks, then this is stated unequivocally and new tasks jointly established or the contact ended. It is evident that in this system of working the emphasis is removed from the aetiology of behaviour and from the expert definition of need in favour of joint planning for future action. The worker moves from the role of primary provider of service to that of the client's assistant. The extent to which this approach is successful or unsuccessful with particular client groups has been monitored in recent research in the United States (Reid & Epstein, 1972; Fahs Beck & Jones, 1973). No similar research has yet been undertaken in this country, though some social workers on an individual basis or in intake terms are beginning to work in this way.

It is doubtful whether this approach is universally applicable: not all clients may be able to define tasks; some may suggest tasks which the worker can foresee would be destructive in some way. There are problems not only in respect of the care of the very young children and the severely disordered, but in cases where, for example, an aggrieved wife is unable to define her needs beyond the wish to see her husband punished or morally condemned. Nevertheless this general model serves a useful purpose by suggesting that some social service can be time-limited (an important factor in a period of rapidly increasing work loads) and in reminding us that clients can make positive contributions to the defining and provision of services. The emphasis moves in this model from the client's perceived inadequacies to his areas of social competence and self-help.

The model serves to question also the authority by which services are provided. It is not in dispute that, by legislation and statutory instruments, services have authority to intervene to prevent or allay suffering. But emphasis on the client's contribution reminds us that the client also may properly exercise authority over the extent of intervention and the precise form the intervention takes. It enables the worker to steer a balance in practice between two opposed images of man; one which would see him in mechanistic terms (in which free-will and choice are illusory concepts) and the other which would tend to stress his free-will and to lose sight of deterministic elements in behaviour-formation. Furthermore, at a time when statutory services have become monopolistic, vast and largely incomprehensible to the general public, an emphasis on the client's definition of the tasks to be undertaken opens up some freedom of choice between alternative strategies of help; it increases the possibilities of participation and personal **auto**nomy, and it promotes the recognition that the services' responsibilities to bring about change are not limited merely to altering the individual lives of their clients.

Conclusion

This section has raised a host of problems, and has indicated briefly the range of complexities which confront policy makers and social service workers at the present time. Starting from an apparently simple statement of purpose, that is to ensure minimum standards of living and to promote certain life opportunities, it has become apparent that the implementation of this purpose raises issues of planning, organizational structure, relationships and responsibilities between workers, their clients and the general public, the evaluation of effectiveness and the role and status of the service-user. The key problems, which all these issues exemplify in different ways, are concerned with the location of decision-making and the sources of authority and power: to what extent decisions should be taken centrally, delegated to local teams, or locally shared between team members and the local communities in which they work; to what extent the authority of a service derives both from its statutory foundations and also from the people who use it. A study of the work of social services departments, undertaken by the Social Work Service of the DHSS (1975), has shown how different local authorities are dealing with these problems. In some authorities, local area teams have been given considerable autonomy, to the extent that the structure of service has become federal rather than hierarchical. But change of this kind introduces new challenges, of how to maintain equal standards of provision in different areas, how to prevent flexibility leading to organizational fragmentation. The greater the local autonomy within a service, the more difficult it becomes to find equitable ways of allocating resources such as residential places and money, which are not exclusively related to particular geographical areas. Effective channels of communication are necessary not only within the organization but with other services, other professions, and local neighbourhood groups: lateral communications of these kinds may need to take place at various levels in the organization, and shifts in the delegation of authority will affect decisions about who communicates with whom. To what extent, for example, should residential and day care workers be directly linked to particular local teams (although the services they offer may be available to several teams) or linked to each other through the headquarters of the service? Which specializations should be team-based and which based centrally? As specializations develop, should they relate to particular client-groups (the handicapped, the elderly, the delinquent teenagers) or to the promotion of specific skills (in organizing groups, in short-term crisis work)? Assuming that there is need for both kinds of development, how should such specialists be linked with the general work of local teams, and with the work of other professional groups?

Issues of these kinds cannot be resolved in advance of the formation of services. They arise as a result of the work done. Each question formulates the issues in a new way and requires a new working equilibrium. But there are no final answers.

PART IV

Social Workers and Social Work

1 Introduction

Frequently throughout this book it has been necessary to talk about what social workers do. But we have not yet considered what social work is, the values held by social workers and how social work practice fits into the work and purposes of the personal social services. There is considerable doubt at the present time about all these issues, and it is fashionable to speak of the 'crisis in social work'. The purpose of this section is to present the main elements of debate.

It is important at the outset to recall that social work originated in the work of voluntary societies and did not become a major element in the work of the local authority services until after the Second World War, notably with the establishment of Children's Departments in 1948 when the concern, characteristic of social work, with individual needs and differences in need was introduced into the policy and legislation governing the care of deprived children. Until that time, local authority services had dealt with *categories* of people assumed to share particular characteristics; the focus of their work had been on the control of social problems, and homeless children, for example, had been regarded more in terms of the problem they presented than in terms of their individual suffering and needs. Social work by contrast has always been related to the meeting of individual needs and to the recognition of individual differences in need. The Charity Organization Society in 1926 for example provided a client with the instruments necessary to earn his living by playing in a jazz band; no such individualistic provision would have been envisaged through the statutory services. Before the Second World War, social work's only major links with public welfare provisions had been as a secondary service to the work of other professions: for example, probation casework as a development within the law, medical and psychiatric social work as developments within medicine. Similarly, moral welfare casework was a service within the Church.

The emphasis on an individualistic approach to need, perhaps inevitably, drew the attention of social workers away from involvement in the criticism of those larger social institutions and social attitudes which gave rise to the needs with which they were concerned. Their numbers were small and their power to influence economic and political thought and action was limited, even when as individuals they recognized the extent of social injustices and the relatively small contribution to social change that could be made on a basis of individual casework. In general, their work was concerned with the moral regeneration of individuals and families rather than with wider forms of social change. Thus, social work came to be seen by its critics more as a social sedative than as a dynamic means of righting injustice. There were of course exceptions to this: the settlement movement within social work represented concern with the relationship between social classes; leading nineteenth-century social workers, such as Edward Denison and Canon Barnett as members of the Charity Organization Society, recognized that the needs of individual applicants for help were frequently symptomatic of the 'economic derangement' of society and of the social victimization of the poor. But individual social work (casework) was the major method of intervention, and this primacy was re-inforced before and after the First World War, first by the attitude of social workers who sought to preserve voluntary charity as a major means of poverty relief, and second by what has been described as the psychiatric deluge in social work in the 1920s and 30s. This was when workers, impressed by the need for psychotherapeutic forms of help and influenced by the recent translations of the work of Freud, moved their attention from moral regeneration to techniques of emotional therapy and adjustment. Their work thus became, if anything, more intensely individualistic (see Woodroofe, 1962). Their allegiance to psychiatry, both for theory and for technique, promoted a model of professionalization based on diagnosis and treatment rather than on social reform.

There have been several consequences of this theoretical stance, some good and some professionally and socially limiting. On the positive side, social workers have developed skills in forming caring relationships which many of their clients have found supportive; for some, the relationship with the social worker comes nearer to consistent and reliable friendship than any other relationship in their experience (see Sainsbury, 1975). The social worker's emphasis on relationships has provided clients with some guarantee of individual concern within the mass provisions of urban society (see Meyer, 1970). But on the other hand, the assumption of a medical model in social work practice has led to a tendency to define some general social problems inappropriately in terms of the deviance or inadequacy of the individual client, and to assume a social consensus as to what constitutes appropriate and normal social behaviour. For many years, for example, the sources of all forms of juvenile delinquency were sought in terms of mental ill-health; while this may be an appropriate approach in respect of some delinquent acts, there are others where it may equally be argued that delinquency is explicable (if not inevitable) as a social response to environmental conditions which in various ways are destructive of the development of the individual. Furthermore, professionalism is a process in which problems become defined partly in terms of the professional skills available to deal with them; thus, a profession linked closely to a psychiatric model of intervention will tend to use psychiatric techniques irrespective of the extent of their relevance in specific situations. The more the skills are developed, the more they will be applied, and in the process of application the less comprehensible they may become to the clients and to the general public. Expertise and mystique often, unfortunately, go together.

Thus, although the practice of social work is partly concerned with the creation of social relationships as a means of meeting human needs, much of the history of social work practice has seen the limitation of this function to the creation of individual relationships set in isolation from wider networks of social interaction and from broader issues of need and injustice.

Several observers and critics of social work practice at the present time would suggest that social work has not changed: that social workers still remain professionally aloof from public opinion, from an awareness of social injustice and from the need to promote social change. For example, Robinson (1975) talks of 'the failure by social workers to come clean about what they are trying to do'. The editor of the *Sunday Mirror* has spoken of the need for greater communication between social workers and the popular press as essential to better public relations. A study by Glastonbury in 1969 has shown that, of 385 families interviewed, only 45% knew what a social worker did (Glastonbury *et al.*, 1972).

Although criticisms are variously expressed, they can be traced fundamentally to one major problem in social work theory and practice: that, in spite of the post-war growth within statutory services concerned very largely with the setting of behavioural standards and the control of social problems, social work has failed 'to incorporate a political dimension ... it is in danger of being unaware of the influence which political situations inevitably exert upon it ... It may find itself in the position of forwarding alien political objectives under the impression that these are congruent with the needs of clients and the values of the profession' (Warham, 1973). Social workers find themselves attacked for their promotion of norms of behaviour which may rob their clients of self-determination and choice, for their apparent unwillingness to devote their energies to changing social institutions, and for their use of therapeutic relationships as disguised forms of power. They are accused of collusion with power groups in denying their clients certain liberties: it is sometimes said, for example, that there are few opportunities for clients to participate fully in the decisions made about them, few sources of reliable information about their entitlements, and few opportunities for redress against the individual social worker's inappropriate use of discretion. It is perhaps indicative of the seriousness of these attacks that community workers have been at pains to establish an identity outside the label 'social worker' and outside the British Association of Social Workers; they are at present debating whether their training courses should lie outside the recognition of the CCETSW, and should offer awards other than the Certificate of Qualification in Social Work.

It may be that this loss of confidence in social work cannot be healed. Some authors have forecast the death of the profession (see Kahn, 1974). But more optimistically one can see signs of change in the attitudes and values of social workers which go some way towards meeting these criticisms.

2 Changes in Theoretical Emphases

In professional training courses at present, and in the quality of articles in the social work journals, there has been a move away from an exclusive interest in the skills and techniques of interviewing (in the processes of individual change) towards a consideration of the social and political objectives of intervention and towards a social rather than a psychological definition of the work done. Social workers increasingly provide their clients with information about the services available, offer advocacy services on behalf of their clients either directly (as when representing a client at a tribunal) or indirectly (as when a probation officer's report to the court includes a recommendation about the disposal of a case), and encourage self-help activities in local groups. The development of work with groups of clients has helped not only to relieve the isolation of the individual client in his experience of need, but also it goes some way towards overcoming the relative isolation and asymmetry of power of the caseworker–client relationship by linking that relationship to the wider life experiences of the client.

Secondly, there is greater recognition than in the past that the form taken by services and the solutions they offer are determined less by the client's actual need or suffering than by the kinds of help that happen to be available. It has been suggested by Romanyshyn (1971), for example, that services may be organized to deal with the symptoms rather than the underlying causes of social problems. From this standpoint, many social workers would now argue that social work is not an effective way of dealing with all the social problems and needs within the remit of the personal social services; that it is necessary for social workers to define the areas of need in which social work is appropriate and those other areas where it represents merely a social palliative, or where it may tend to consolidate a career of deviant behaviour or client-dependency—for example, by isolating a pattern of behaviour for specific treatment and divorcing it from the values and behavioural norms of the client's social environment. A client who graduates from supervision order to a closed community home, to Borstal, to prison, and to the after-care service will find it hard, with the best will in the world, to re-establish himself in community life and to have his needs considered afresh and comprehensively when he approaches a social agency. The environment of a residential Home or the regular supportive visits of a social worker may in one sense promote a client's freedom from anxiety about certain aspects of his life; but at the same time it may limit other freedoms, may encourage dependency and sometimes prevent active self-help. All social workers have met the situation where a close relationship with a client is accompanied by the perpetuation rather than the alleviation of his difficulties. In common with many other social relationships, social work may promote the self-esteem of individuals while at the same time inhibiting self-realization. It may turn people into cases (see Scheff, 1966; Balint, 1957).

It is not my intention to endorse a common and fashionable standpoint which argues that social work practice concentrates on personal need when it ought to concentrate on political and social processes. This finds its extreme expression in the claim that casework with individuals and families is apolitical and conservative while community work is political and radical. But rather I would argue with Pearson that "Social work operates at the intersection of what is 'personal' and what is 'political' " (Pearson, 1975); that the private troubles of individual clients have full meaning for the social worker only if they are understood in the context of more general public issues, and vice versa (see Wright Mills, 1947).

In practical terms, social workers are concerned with people's social competence: social competence is enhanced when a systematic effort is made to develop inner resources and capacities, to promote a positive sense of the self, to enable the full use of a wide range of social resources, and to facilitate flexibility in social relationships and in the performance of a variety of social roles. In the course of his work, the social worker may be required by some of his clients to accept a high level of temporary emotional dependency. Considerable skill is necessary for the social worker to determine how far dependency should be accepted, to manage his own feelings in attempting to help people in considerable emotional distress, and to regulate appropriately the use of his own personality and powers. The social worker's task is to help convert people's passive reactions to the stresses of their environment into creative response and personal initiative. The reference to task-oriented social work practice in the previous chapter is an example of this kind of movement.

THE CHANGING VALUES OF SOCIAL WORK

Social work had its origins in Charity. Its institutionalization within the statutory services, the increased numbers of social workers and their higher status have all offered a challenge to re-think the values of charity and to enlarge the value—basis of practice. The first concern of the social worker must still be with the relief and prevention of material and emotional poverty among his clients; but added to this there should be a concern to help enhance the life—chances of the client and the value he ascribes to his own life. This has been apparent in changes in the way social policy has been formulated since the last war. The Children Act 1948 was concerned with the well being of all children seen as individuals; the Seebohm Report offered an approach to family welfare so comprehensive as to include everybody. The concern of social policy has moved during this century from the disposal of social problems by repression, through an emphasis on individual therapy and rehabilitation, to the wider advocacy of community planning for the development of social relationships and obligations. *Social Work and the Community* and the Seebohm Report were concerned not merely with the comprehensive meeting of needs but with patterns of living in local communities.

There are three problems for social workers in playing their part in this shift of concern. The first lies in their constant absorption in the alleviation of urgent small-scale needs; it is difficult to maintain equal concern both for immediate specific needs and for general social purposes.

Secondly, there is a problem of relating together, in practical terms, theories and values which are all useful in some situations but which, taken together, are divergent and discrepant. For example, some clients need emotional or behavioural help for which psychodynamic or behaviourist theories are relevant; this help may achieve changes in a client's situation by means of a temporary period of emotional dependence on the social worker. Other clients present situations which can best be helped by environmental changes or self-help actions by the client in which emotional dependence would be wholly inappropriate. Expressed in terms of values, social workers in different situations may be concerned with the promotion of their clients' freedom and rights, *or* with the acceptance of emotional or social powerlessness and dependence, *or* with the imposition of behavioural controls. Similarly, the social worker's mandate may be in different cases derived from his agency or his client; either way, his duty will be as much to react to the situation he finds as to initiate changes in the way it is perceived and defined.

The third problem lies in the public expectation that social work is concerned with the achievement and maintenance of a kind of consensus. Social work in a marital dispute, for example, will often be evaluated on the basis of whether reconciliation is achieved between the spouses; work on behalf of deprived children is judged to be most successful if it leads to the re-uniting of a family; social workers are expected to work not only in co-operation but also in increasing good will with other professions and bodies whose values may be at variance with their own. I am not suggesting that their work situation should be different from this, but only that the constant pursuit of consensus may lead social workers to wonder what their own values really are, particularly when the support of an institution (marriage, the family, the local school, the Government's policy on employment) may appear to run counter to the needs of their clients.

It is now increasingly realized that social development to alleviate suffering and injustice requires a re-thinking of the role of the social worker as an agent of consensus. Social work is not possible without the promotion of agreement about some superordinate values that link people together in mutual responsibility; but neither is it possible if it denies the expression of conflict as sometimes an essential step in moving people, institutions and organizations towards more creative adaptations to each other's needs and purposes. A wholly consensus view of welfare may mean the promotion of an artificial harmonization which ignores legitimate differences of need and purpose, whether between individuals, groups or power structures.

It might therefore be argued that the importance that social workers have traditionally attached to individual needs and to the promotion of satisfying relationships should sometimes appropriately be subversive of norms, values and policies where these are concerned with the maintenance of institutions rather than with the promotion of individual human values. Pinker has associated the ethos of social work with the view that 'the real test of a civilised society is the degree of decency with which it treats its minorities, irrespective of their lack of effective political power' (Pinker, 1971). He sees the persistence of injustice as most likely to arise from the indifference of the relatively prosperous majority towards the needs of a minority of poor people. If this is so, then the values of the social worker may well be subversive of those of the majority of citizens. Whether subversion necessarily means open conflict is another matter. Subversion may be orderly or it may be destructive. But the values of the social worker, particularly his concern with individualized justice, lead him to become both a buffer between opposed sets of values in the individual case situation and also an agent of social change in his wider professional orientation. Inevitably there will be times when his mediation between opposed values draws attention to dehumanizing practices within the social services themselves. While appointed to regulate the use of his agency's resources he may also inevitably become his agency's most severe critic.

It would be unrealistic, however, to expect that the values of the profession of social work should not be tempered by the values of employing organizations, with their rules, their legally defined mandate for the provision of services, their formalities and hierarchies. It is probably not accidental that individual casework has progressed in status more than other forms of social work, for it more readily adapts than, say, community work to the structures and traditions of pre-existing institutions such as hospitals, the courts or the local authority services. Nevertheless, however mildly a social worker may in practice interpret his mediating role, and however much he may seek to avoid conflict, he represents values which challenge any glib assumptions about the justice of existing institutions: for he stands for—or should stand for—a holistic conception of man, for the satisfaction of physical, emotional, cultural, economic and aesthetic needs, for the rights of the least powerful, and for the interdependence of the individual and the community.

3 The Accountability of the Social Worker

This is a difficult issue. It draws attention to a fundamental and inevitable weakness in all formulations of social work theory—inevitable in that there is no comprehensive social science model for understanding the individual person in his whole life situation. Social workers are concerned both with the inner dynamics of people and with their social functioning; they draw upon a range of social sciences which offer theoretical choices rather than the integration of understanding. The dichotomy that has grown up between work with individuals and families (casework) and community work illustrates the lack of theories to enable us intellectually to link together the individual and the society in which he lives. It is difficult to resolve the issue of accountability in the absence of an intellectual integration at the level of theory or at the level of purpose.

On the face of it there are four choices: accountability to the employer; accountability to the profession; accountability to clients; or a mixture of these. The first of these carries with it a limitation in the extent to which the social worker can question and act against his agency's ways of working, or can challenge the social values which legitimize both the agency's standing and his own appointment. On the other hand, if one accepts that one of the functions of social workers is to exercise control in certain situations (for example, when a child suffers ill treatment or a man is terrorizing his neighbours) then employee status defines the duties, supports the worker in carrying them out, and invests him with the authority to act. Accountability to an employer means that the scope and aims of social work tend to change over time in response to shifts in legislation and in public opinion; this does not necessarily imply that practice is codified to the point where no professional discretion is possible, but it limits the extent to which one can properly speak of professionalism, in that no ultimate statement of professional purpose in social work could be formulated which was not subject to externally determined changes. A similar problem arises in the evaluation of social work practice, in that what might be desirable practice from a management viewpoint may not accord with the worker's personal view. For example, a social worker may be required to help a family to function adequately in the face of seriously adverse material and social conditions; it may appear to him that the situation requires radical appraisal and action beyond the willingness of his agency to consider. Any complaint he might make about the agency's policy, or his refusal to contain and 'talk out' the complaints of his clients, might be interpreted as a problem in his acceptance of the agency's authority. While one would not wish to dispute, therefore, that the social worker is accountable to the agency that employs him, one could argue that exclusive accountability of this kind may lead to conflicts at the very centre of the social worker's structure of values.

The issue whether social workers should be accountable primarily to their employers is sometimes debated in terms of the extent to which they should be agents of social control. 'Control' and 'advocacy' are sometimes used as if they were antonyms, the former wholly bad and the latter wholly good, and the assumption made that accountability to the employer implies the exercise of authority and power which limits the rights of the client and effectively controls his behaviour in the interests of existing power structures. This polarization is a naive one if we consider the actual effectiveness of social workers as agents of social control; there are no indications that the social problems with which social workers are concerned have been reduced in size by their intervention, or that their activities have promoted greater behavioural compliance. Furthermore, all close relationships contain controlling aspects; this is true of marital and family relationships and peer group relationships as well as of the more formal relationships of doctor and patient, teacher and pupil, social worker and client. The extent to which relationships imply control does not depend *simply* on whether they are statutorily based or backed by the authority of an employer; it depends also on the extent to which one person identifies with, and internalizes, the authority of the other. From this point of view, a social worker in a voluntary agency or a community worker who sees himself wholly accountable to his client-group may exercise controls and authority which are quite as influential as those of a statutory social worker. Accountability to an employer may carry with it the exercise of statutory power, but this *of itself* does not indicate the amount of control that the social worker effectively exercises. The point at issue, therefore, needs to be seen not simply in terms of the exercise of control but in terms rather of the impact of employee status on the implementation of certain values and the denial of others. The effect of being accountable to an employer may well be to limit the activities of the individual social worker; he may become 'caught up in the system' and unwittingly set aside certain values which as a free-lance social worker he might wish to uphold. But if social workers act collectively, and collectively define the values which are important to them, they may succeed in achieving general changes in the way social services are organized and delivered, more effectively than would be possible if their accountability to the employer were wholly denied (Leonard, 1976).

Accountability to a profession offers an external reference point in dilemmas of value, of appropriate action and of inappropriate demands from inside or outside the employing body. For example, BASW has published a code of ethics and a code which attempts to relate social work practice to social protest and action. A professional group may co-ordinate the experiences of practice within different employing situations, and thus draw public attention to inappropriate pressures on employees: a letter from the General Secretary of BASW to *The Times*, 12 January 1976, set out the range of social work responsibilities in the local authorities, commented on the present and future rate of increase in work loads, and stated categorically (which perhaps few employers or social workers would be ready to state individually) that 'no authority is able to meet its minimal statutory obligations at the present time'.

On the other hand, by its nature, a central professional association can deal only with generalities rather than with local variations of need and practice. Social work must be related to and responsive to very localized situations at the level of the family and neighbourhood, and neither codes of practice nor the formulation of techniques and skills in general terms can satisfy the necessity for local variations. One problem of professional accountability, therefore, is its seeming irrelevance at field level at times of local crisis in work-load management and practice.

This last point suggests the main attraction of the view that social workers should be accountable to their clients. This permits unlimited possibilities of local variation in techniques of work. It recognizes that clients' understanding of services and the ways in which they formulate their needs are of primary importance in the practice of social work, and are rooted in local experience and local networks of relationships. (By and large, people learn more about services from their neighbours and relations than from publicity.) It serves also to help reduce the stigma which clients experience when they approach social services: as Pinker (1971) has pointed out, the degree of stigmatization varies inversely with the degree to which people feel near to the norms of society; if, therefore, the social worker (as, in a sense, the representative of the wider society) presents himself as primarily accountable to the client, the stigmatizing process is reduced and the client's self-esteem safeguarded.

Accountability to the client implies also that the worker will seek a more open and equal relationship with those he serves than is perhaps possible if he invests himself with the status of a local government officer or a professional. He is more likely to feel able to accept and confess his inability to deal with all the needs presented to him and to admit his need for co-operation with unofficial and non-professional resources. Accountability to the client implies advocacy of the client's needs and rights on his own terms, and recognition of the complex and sometimes painful emotional processes involved in seeking help from a service.

The dilemma of this position, however, lies in its fragmentation of values and help. Particularly at a time when resources are short, and when, in effect, clients are in competition with each other, the social worker offers no mediation between competing needs; the help offered to a particular client will tend to rest on the skilful advocacy of his particular social worker rather than on the worker's judgment of priorities of need between different clients. In short, there is a fundamental conflict between client-centred and service-centred approaches to practice in the definition of priorities and in the use made of scarce resources. This process of fragmentation may be in part off-set if social workers define their accountability to groups of clients rather than to individuals (see Jordan, 1973), or seek to make their primary relationship with a particular neighbourhood or small community. But the problem remains that some major resources need to be allocated with reference to a wider geographical area and a wider range of needs than any local combination of social workers can wholly comprehend.

In considering these three forms of accountability, therefore, we find internal as well as mutual conflicts: conflicts associated with the values basic to social work practice; conflict between the wish to serve and to represent particular clients and the importance of maintaining a broad view of social needs, social problems and the allocation of resources; conflict concerning the appropriate auspices for defining 'the good of the individual', and the relationship between 'individual good' and 'common good'. At present the accountability of the social worker is an uneasy blend of responsibilities to his service, his professional colleagues and his clients. Social workers tend to feel uncertain about the goals and values of their intervention, their right to intervene and the criteria by which the effectiveness of their work should be judged. The task of management to harmonize the work of agencies in order to achieve agreed goals is made all the harder by these kinds of uncertainties about the accountability of one section of their employees. The Seebohm philosophy embodied 'a wide conception of service, directed to the well-being of the whole of the community and not only to social casualties, and seeing the community it serves as the basis of its authority, resources and effectiveness.' The dilemma facing the relationship between employing bodies and social workers is what is meant by accountability to the 'community' in this context: the larger the sphere of one's operations the larger the 'community' to which one tends to refer. Thus, for management, the concept is of a different order from that of the social worker, preoccupied by the needs of individual families and with the networks of relationships within neighbourhoods.

It is therefore not profitable to think in terms of a simple, single line of accountability for social work. Neither, similarly, can one define unitary objectives, strategies and techniques: the social worker's practice represents a mixture of direct individual help, improving the quality of social life, and ameliorating adverse personal and social conditions. The social worker will at various times—even within the handling of a single case— be concerned with situations of emergency, of prevention and of social development, and with the attempt to mediate between a variety of value systems. In so far as he stresses one value above others, this will be concerned with the client's standing within the network of services: to advocate for the client a role in which he is not simply the object of intervention, but rather a social resource who, in personal interaction with the social worker, contributes to his own good, to the good of others, and to the achievement of certain social objectives implicit or explicit in legislation and statements of policy.

The last point raises a further question, however: namely, the extent to which and the manner in which the social worker is accountable to the state as a whole. It has been implicit in what has been written above that conflicts may occur between the three kinds of accountability; as employee, as professional and as helper. Thus, for example, a group of social workers may reach the view that the Social Services Committee and Directorate have inappropriately defined priorities of expenditure. But in what sense is the word 'inappropriately' used in this case? At the present time, this is usually answered by reference to professional values, or to *ad hoc* evaluations of pressing unmet needs among the service's clientele, or to certain political ideologies. There may, however, be occasions when such a point might be made by reference to divergences between local and national policies, and to the social worker's accountability to central government's definitions of social policy. From this point of view, the social worker's involvement in an organization such as NALGO is of importance, in that it provides him with an additional basis for the evaluation of his work and the work of his service, and with a platform for the discussion of policies at the level of central government and the local authority associations.

4 The Content of Social Work

The activities of social workers may be described under four headings: first, to assess needs by discussion with the client, and to support and assist the client to remove obstacles (whether in feelings or attitudes) which impede his use of services and the achievement of his potential for a satisfying life; secondly, to mobilize resources within the individual, the family and the community in order to maximize the client's participation in community life; thirdly, to influence the ways in which services are co-ordinated, so that they give freedom to the natural processes of self-help and self-realization; and fourthly, to offer technical and professional advice.

All four activities represent a complexity of involvement in the lives of others and the recognition of multiple causation of need. In social work practice there are no single and discrete causes of distress. To take a simple example, a marriage does not run into difficulties *simply* because a husband beats his wife, or becomes a drunkard, or simply because the couple have stopped loving each other. All human behaviour is 'over-determined', in the sense that one can find multiple causations in any act of behaviour, as the different social sciences amply demonstrate. At the same time, this complexity of interlinking causation is one source of success in social work practice in that a single action may have multiple effects; some effects may be positive and some negative, and the single most important professional skill of the social worker is to direct his efforts in ways that produce multiple positive effects.

The complexity of social work practice (in the mode and direction of intervention, and in the accountability of the worker) has increased significantly in recent years, particularly in the local authority services. Paradoxically, the Seebohm Committee's recommendation of a 'more unified provision of personal social services' has made more complex the definition of the task of the individual social worker (in both field services and residential care), because of the merging of hitherto distinctly administered client-groups. To a lesser extent, the same tendency may be found in the work of the probation service, which is now responsible for probation, prison welfare and after-care, parole and suspended sentence supervision, welfare work associated with marriage breakdown, community service orders, day training and hostels. As recently as ten years ago, the source of professional identity for social workers lay in the clarity of agency function in respect of a single well-defined client group; social workers defined themselves in terms of their agency's duties (Child Care Officer, Mental Welfare Officer) rather than as a more-or-less united professional group. Articles in the professional journals reflected this—authors wrote about their performance of specific duties more frequently than about common and divergent practice-issues in work with a wide range of client-groups.

Partly in the interests of professional unity, and partly as the result of the search for a common basis of practice at a time when 'agency function' has expanded to a virtually indefinable complexity, recent social work theory has moved towards the definition of a unitary model of practice, capable of embracing all modes of intervention irrespective of agency setting. (See Pincus & Minahan, 1973; Goldstein, 1973.)

SOCIAL WORKERS AND MANAGERS

The development of a unitary profession may in one way indicate a movement parallel and complementary to the unification of service provisions; but it carries with it the possibility of increased tension between a strong profession and a strong employer, particularly as the development of service has led to more complex managerial structures. A recent article in *Social Work Today*, for example, describes social workers as 'cannon fodder in the age of administration' (Glastonbury, 1975), and examines critically the relationship between main-grade professional practice and hierarchical structures. The author argues that senior staff tend to define tasks administratively rather than professionally, are out of touch with direct experience of social work practice, and endorse conditions of work which may be contrary to the personal needs of professional staff. It is not suggested that problems in relationships between professionals and administrators are the result of insensitivity or ill will, but rather than they are an unavoidable by-product of bureaucratization, and the author questions whether large-scale organizations are appropriate for the delivery of professional services.

Yet, as we have seen, the efficient use of scarce resources seems inevitably to imply a need for planning over large geographical areas. There seem to be two ways of meeting this dilemma, both of which have been mentioned elsewhere in this book. First, by considering the extent to which managerial decisions can be delegated to field level; and, second, by building into the organization a double system of supervision, one essentially managerial and concerned to ensure that the agency's statutory duties are undertaken, the other essentially professional—divorced from managerial issues and concerned with the professional definition of tasks (which may extend beyond the performance of a statutory duty) and with the professional development of the individual worker. An issue which would need to be resolved in both networks of supervision is that of specialization. It is not suggested that all social workers should be specialists, but it needs to be recognized that limiting the responsibility of a social worker may in some situations help him to develop that 'distinctive competence' which is the hallmark of the specialist. It may help him to develop his own professional satisfaction and ensure a higher standard of performance in his statutory duties. It may promote the ability among more social workers to look objectively and in detail at the impact of the work of the organization on the lives of particular client-groups. Specialization by the definition of tasks may be appropriate among both skilled and unskilled workers. Helen Bosanquet once commented that there are two kinds of specialists: those who can do only one thing, and those who can do one thing better than others. Recognition of both kinds of specialization may offer a way of linking managerial and professional interests and accountability.

Specialization cannot, however, be considered without regard for the way in which a social service links with other services. Should the specialist worker be based within the structure of his own service, or should he by virtue of his specialization operate from within the structure of another service—as medical social workers are based in hospitals, for example, and some probation officers are based in the prisons. The advantage of this kind of attachment are that the worker can more easily develop his understanding of the host organization and is more readily available for the support of clients particularly at times of crisis; he may also become more acceptable, where this is necessary, as an agent for policy changes within the host organization. There is some uncertainty about this last point, however: attachment to another organization inevitably weakens the support that a social worker would normally expect to receive from his colleagues; the social worker may feel isolated, and his role may be strongly influenced by the host organization. The development of specialization by means of 'attachments' is therefore an area of considerable disagreement from both management and professional viewpoints.

Greater progress has been made in the promotion of specialization within the structure of organizations; this is often of an informal kind, for example, at team meetings where new work is allocated there is often a tendency for particular kinds of problems to be given to certain workers. Thus, one may envisage a time when, by informal processes, a team contains several specialists. Specialization may be of two kinds within professional practice: it may be based upon the form of presentation of a problem, or upon the need for a particular kind of interventive skill. Social workers may become accepted therefore as specialists in work with a defined client-group (for example, the mentally ill) or in such skills as the development of group-work, the understanding of welfare benefits, the problems involved in marital breakdown. The development of managerial skills may be considered in this context. These too need to be learned and one may envisage this learning as a gradual process of specialization. How far management is a specialization *within* professional social work is far from certain, however; at the present time, becoming a manager is most frequently seen as a change of status rather than a professional role-specialization and the hierarchical structure of agencies tends to re-inforce this view.

In the 'pre-Seebohm' period, when professional interest and agency function were inextricably linked (when for example, a person sought professional recognition precisely in order to become a child care officer), it followed automatically that managerial status implied a more advanced *professional* status. Perhaps a time has been reached in the development of services when this equation needs re-examining: managerial responsibility may not represent the most appropriate career development of the skilled professional; and professional skills in social work are certainly not all that is required for effective management.

PROFESSIONALISM

It will have become evident that, in considering the relationship between social work and service organizations, the problems are both technical and ideological. Ideological problems lie at the heart of the process of professionalization in social work, and many social workers feel uneasy about being known as professionals—for obvious reasons: professionalization is frequently associated with the endorsement of an asymmetrical power structure between professional and client; the professional may become encapsulated in theories and definitions which diverge from the 'common sense' of his client;* his interest may become focussed on the skills of the job rather than its purpose ('the operation was successful but the patient died'). Professionalism is frequently associated with the pursuit of status by the process of mystification. By the employment of professional social workers within public service agencies, there is at least no risk that they will become wholly divorced from social and political accountability; but this allegiance in itself may increase the relative powerlessness of the client and the relative authority of the social worker.

There is certainly a dilemma for the professional standing of social work if that professionalism becomes *wholly* identified with planned statutory provision and with the preservation of dominant social values. Critics of professionalization have drawn attention to the possible results of such an

* R. M. Titmuss (*Essays on the Welfare State*, pp. 23–4) commented on the tendency of the professional to 'create' the need for his help. A related tendency to define need in terms of the skills available to meet it is demonstrated by H. Meyer: *Girls at Vocational High*.

identification—for example, the loss of spontaneity in relationships, the concentration on adjustment rather than advocacy, an avoidance of controversy about broader issues of policy and planning.

Those who defend professionalization, on the other hand, do so on the basis that it provides the only realistic alternative to bureaucratic absorption: it provides a standpoint outside the employing agency from which to judge competence, to criticize decisions and to uphold the rights of clients and potential clients.

Professional associations of social workers originated in the 1930s with the Institute of Almoners (later the Institute of Medical Social Workers), the National Association of Probation Officers, and the Association of Moral Welfare Workers. At that stage professional associations were linked with the organizational setting and focus of practice; although in 1936 a British Federation of Social Workers was founded to provide a forum for the discussion of common interests, membership of the Federation was available only through membership of the affiliated organizations. Uncertainty about the boundaries of social work was evident in the affiliation of the Health Visitors Association and the Association of Housing Managers. In 1951, interest in the possible development of generic training for caseworkers (cf. Younghusband, 1947, 1951) and the emergence of two new professional associations (the Associations of Children's Officers and Child Care Officers) led to the formation of the Association of Social Workers which, unlike the earlier Federation, invited direct individual membership. The Association produced a series of booklets which drew attention away from the different settings of casework practice in favour of the discussion of general issues directly related to the nature of a developing and independent profession: for example, on the education of social workers, on ethical and moral dilemmas, on the need for a register of qualified practitioners. It was largely through the inspiration of ASW that regular meetings were held between representatives of the various professional organizations from 1959. These culminated in 1963 with the formation of a Standing Conference of Organizations of Social Workers to which were affiliated ACCO, APSW, IMSW, NAPO, the Associations of Moral Welfare Workers and Family Caseworkers and the Society of Mental Welfare Officers. The formation of the British Association of Social Workers in 1968 (contemporaneously with the publication of the Seebohm Report) was based on the work of the Standing Conference, particularly the Conference's second discussion paper which examined alternative models for the formation of a unified profession; all the earlier organizations except NAPO wound up their affairs at that time in favour of the new Association.

BASW employs a full-time secretariat and publishes three journals, the *British Journal of Social Work, Social Work Today* and *Parliament and Social Work.* (These represent the merger of three earlier journals: *Case Conference, Medical Social Work* and *Mental Welfare.*) Members meet in sixty-eight local branches, and specialist interests are catered for by the work of four sections concerned with General Health, Mental Health, Child and Family Care and the Treatment of Offenders. In addition, there are central committees concerned with parliamentary and political issues, salaries and conditions of service, membership, professional development, international relations, education and training, and publications. As one might expect of a new and more-or-less united profession, major attention has been given to the formulation of codes of ethics and practice for social workers, the definition of the social work task and the role of the social worker, particularly in respect of social and political action.

The risks attaching to the process of professionalization have been mentioned, and some social workers are dissatisfied with the direction taken by BASW, particularly in regard to the restriction of full membership to those holding professional qualifications. *Community Care* magazine in August 1975 reported that a group of social workers in Devon were considering establishing a new organization; and an implacable opponent of BASW has been the marxist organization and journal Case Con. Whether it is appropriate for social workers to follow the traditional pattern of professional growth is a matter for continuing debate. It has been suggested, notably by Etzioni (1969) and Toren (1972) that social work cannot achieve full professional status because of the short length of training required of social workers, the limitations placed on their use of discretion by employing bodies, and the relatively low status within service organizations of the front-line workers. Social Work is therefore commonly defined as a semiprofession.

The professional ambitions of social workers need to be seen also in relation to the relatively large proportion of unqualified staff who hold social work posts, particularly in the local authority services. Proportions of qualified field work staff in 1975 varied between 78.36% and 1.8% in the local authorities, and in regional terms the variation lay between 46% in the southwest and 25% in the north of England.

Qualification is, of course, no guarantee of competence; but it remains one of the essential bases of professionalism and of the respect offered to a profession when it speaks critically about social injustices and about the structures and institutions which contribute to injustice. The next chapter will be concerned with the education and training of social workers; but it is appropriate to note in the present context that, as training courses increasingly introduce the study of sociological and political issues in social service provision, so we may expect to find an increasing professional commitment to the study and alleviation of social injustice. Pearson (1973) has found in a recent study that 25% of a group of social work students had been motivated to enter social work by a strong sense of social injustice. The long-standing separation between professional social work and social reform may now be at an end.

5 The Present State and Future of Social Work

Reference was made at the start of this chapter to the present crisis in social work, and comments have been made about certain areas of conflict and change: in theories, values and accountability; and in the growth of professionalism. Social work at the present time is the cross-roads for a range of social service developments, and for various expressions of concern about the social implications of theories drawn from the social sciences. For many years, the basis of knowledge and practice for social work was made up of the legislation and structure of the social services and the psychodynamic study of human behaviour; other studies such as philosophy, sociology and economics, were regarded as contributory rather than central to understanding and performance. Since the mid-1960s, the study of social service administration has been amplified to include a greater concern with social policy and the politics of welfare; new sociological perspectives have challenged the primacy given to psychodynamic insights; and within the study of psychology social workers have recognized the relevance of, for example, learning theory and transactional analysis. The secure professional model offered by psychiatry, upon which so much social work theory and practice have been based, has itself been challenged by anti-psychiatric movements, particularly associated with the work of Ronald Laing (1967; 1960; Laing & Esterson, 1964) and David Cooper (1967), and by new insights into the role of the family in the genesis of psychiatric disorder. Thus, the security of the knowledge-base for social work practice has been undermined. This has happened during a period when, in administrative terms, the organization of social services has changed rapidly and has produced its own uncertainties, aspirations and dissatisfactions, particularly in respect of the specific/generic issue and the development of hierarchical structures (see Jones, 1975). The British Association of Social Workers itself represents a dramatic change from single-function to multi-purpose professional allegiance.

During this same period there has been a development in the political activities and militancy of pressure groups (for example, Child Poverty Action Group, Disablement Income Group, Age Concern) and of client groups (for example, Claimants Union, the Preservation of the Rights of Prisoners). The response of social workers to this activism has been mixed, and the profession stands divided on the comparative relevance of consensus and conflict strategies in various work situations. Community work, until recently seen as a method of intervention within social work, and one which might have built a bridge between traditional forms of practice and the new political and sociological perspectives, has been concerned to establish a separate identity. However, it is itself divided between movements which, broadly speaking, support the work of the social services (for example, by the development of neighbourhood help and the promotion of self-help through community associations and informal groups), and those which seek to promote radical change in socio-political structures, and to train local people in activism and in the complexities of political power (see Baldock, 1974).

The future of social work depends on the ability of the profession to achieve a broad unity of support among social workers allied to a wide range of theoretical and political views. Secondly, and related to this, it depends on the profession's ability to establish an identity which is not seen simply as an extension of the aims and requirements of local authority services as the major employers. Thirdly, it depends on recognition of the interrelatedness of various kinds of intervention, irrespective of superficial divisions of technique and method, of formal and informal auspices. Social work may become an integrating power in the pursuit of social justice and social change. It could, equally likely, become merely a way of describing the benevolent activities of a minority group of social service employees.

Social work as a profession is concerned to encourage the availability, relevance and use of formal and informal social resources, to co-ordinate resources, and to respond sensitively to people's needs and obligations. The practice of social work offers one possible bridge between resources and consumers, and one means whereby information can flow between those who need help and those who have services to offer. If social work is at present under attack for its failure in any of these tasks, these attacks need to be seen in the context of growing caseloads, uncertainties in social policy, bureaucratic muddles, a rapid expansion of staffs (a problem of quantity versus quality), and traditions of organization and practice which have given insufficient weight to the right of consumers to be heard when the services they receive are experienced as inadequate.

Furthermore, the failures of social work are symptomatic of wider failures to revise service ideologies and practices concerning the promotion of welfare. Welfare can no longer be equated simply with the specific provisions of specific agencies with limited and clearly defined structures; yet the work procedures so far devised since 1970 represent a modification of earlier practices rather than a radical review of purpose and of the most appropriate means of promoting welfare in the community at large.

6 The Education and Training of Social Workers

The status of a profession is associated with the quality of training received by its members. Social work education has had a complex history in Britain: until the mid-1950s all professional training and practice was closely linked to the needs and functions of specific kinds of agency practice (probation, child care, medical and psychiatric social work) rather than the development of a united profession. The extent to which training was available (both inside and outside the universities) depended entirely on the amount of money or other resources made available for it by central agencies, notably the Home Office, the Ministry of Health, the Institute of Medical Social Workers and the Association of Psychiatric Social Workers. For some forms of social work practice (for example, education welfare, work with the handicapped) very few training opportunities existed. A further difficulty was the indecision of the universities about the academic standing of this kind of vocational teaching. This indecision was the result of two major dilemmas: first, the uncertain relationship between theory and practice; there was—and is—no systematic body of theory which illuminates all aspects of the practice of social work and which relates exclusively to social work; second, the uncertain relationship between academic studies and field training; students spent a considerable part of their time in social agency practice over which the universities neither had nor sought any educational control. In the first half of this century, many universities developed courses offering a basic education in social studies with a more-or-less specific concern for the pre-training needs of social workers; these were principally at non-graduate or post-graduate levels. But as late as 1959, of the twenty-four universities which offered this kind of basic education, only six offered also some form of professional training, and only three of these were concerned with generic social work education.

Thus, until within the last twenty years, social work lacked the academic leadership of the universities, both in the development of research into processes and practice and in the formulation of methods of social intervention which would transcend the specialization of interests required by the agencies. Training was limited to work with individuals and families, reflecting the modes of intervention demanded by the services; even today, training opportunities for residential work, group work and community work are seriously underdeveloped.

Eileen Younghusband (1951), concluded that, in social work training, 'academic freedom coupled with the rich luxuriance of professional training bodies has led to something approaching chaos'. At that time, no courses offered generic training, and the specialization of professional training was increasingly at variance with the general education in social studies offered to students at the pre-professional stage of their education. For lack of a comprehensive understanding of social needs, qualified social workers were able to make little contribution to discussions of new policies and social legislation in the post-war period. The first Chair of Social Administration was established in 1948 and the second in 1951; development of undergraduate studies in this field was not directly linked with the interests and needs of professional education and practice; and it is difficult to see how it could be, given the breadth of studies in the one and the narrow specialization of the other. Although many graduates in social administration sought training as social workers, there were few attempts made to develop a coherent pattern of continuing education.

A pioneer generic course of training for caseworkers was started at LSE in 1954 which provided a model upon which professional education (Applied Social Studies) in other universities has been based. But the links between these courses and undergraduate teaching in the social sciences remained uncertain and often tenuous. The rapid development of social work courses in the universities during the 1960s reflected, as before, the willingness of Government to make special funds available rather than an academic commitment to the development of a new profession. Nevertheless, the effect of the establishment of generic courses in the universities has been to shift the focus of training from the acquisition of specific technical skills related to the needs of particular client-groups to the development of professional education linked to a systematic study of the social sciences. Significantly, a continuing anxiety among university teachers has been the extent to which the purpose of students' field work practice should be to illuminate and make practical use of *academic* studies, and how far the evaluation of a student's performance in a course should be based upon his ability to fit comfortably *as a colleague* within the particular agencies where he undertakes his practice.

The development of social work education in colleges of further education and polytechnics followed the report in 1959 of a working party, set up by the Ministry of Health (HMSO, 1959) under the chairmanship of Eileen Younghusband, to investigate the manpower and training needs of local authority services for the physically handicapped, the mentally disordered, the aged and the homeless. Social workers in public health and welfare departments had not hitherto been offered the range and scope of training courses equivalent to those available to probation and child care officers (sponsored by the Home Office) or to medical and psychiatric social workers. Local authority health and welfare services had hitherto relied to a large extent on the administrative skills of former relieving officers, on the piecemeal availability of emergency training schemes for work with clients suffering from specific handicaps, and on the recruitment of untrained staff from university courses in social studies and the social sciences. For this group of workers, the only systematic and comprehensive studies were those offered by NALGO and by courses leading to the award of the Diploma in Municipal Administration.

The scope of the report was wide: in addition to surveying for the first time a complex network of services, the report defined the purposes and methods of social work; the professional functions of social workers were identified in relation to the intensity of the needs of different clients and the complexity of skills required to meet those needs. It was estimated that an annual recruitment of 500 trained social workers for ten years would be necessary to meet the requirements of the services in respect of the broad middle-range of clients' needs. Courses were therefore developed, initially called Younghusband courses, in colleges of further education under the auspices and guidance of the Council for Training in Social Work, established in 1962 by the Health Visiting and Social Work (Training) Act as an independent publicly-financed body. The Council was charged with responsibility for promoting and 'recognizing' courses, for setting standards and for awarding a national Certificate of Social Work.

In addition, in 1961, the National Institute for Social Work Training (now the NISW) was jointly established, in accordance with the recommendations of the Report, by the Nuffield Foundation and the Joseph Rowntree Memorial Trust. This was to act as a national staff college for social work training, with a governing body representing the professional social work organizations, the universities and central and local government bodies, and incorporating individual members with special knowledge of social work education. In addition to its programme of courses for administrators, managers and supervisors in the social services, the Institute has undertaken the sponsorship of research and publications on social work and social policy, and has filled the need for co-ordinated study of social policy and social work which the universities had failed to meet for many years.

At the time of the publication of the Seebohm Report, therefore, there were three national councils responsible to Ministers for different specializations within social work training: the Central Training Council for Child Care, the Advisory Council for Probation and After-care, and the Council for Training in Social Work. Courses existed also under the auspices of the Institute of Medical Social Workers and the Association of Psychiatric Social Workers. Graduate courses in the universities which were generic in emphasis therefore needed to seek 'recognition' by more than one of these bodies; the non-graduate courses in colleges of further education and the polytechnics were more specialized; those offered externally by the Home Office and other bodies were wholly specialized. The Seebohm Committee recommended the integration of responsibilities for training, and by an amendment to the Health Visiting and Social Work (Training) Act of 1962, the Central Council for Education and Training in Social Work was established in 1971 as an independent publicly-financed Council with direct access to the Minister for the Social Services. The Chairman of the Council is appointed by the Privy Council, and membership includes representatives of the employers of social workers, of educational institutions and social work teachers, and of professional associations; eleven members are appointed by Ministers. The Council has now assumed responsibility for the training of social workers employed in health and education services, probation and aftercare, voluntary organizations and in the whole range of daycare, domiciliary services, field work and residential services of the local authority social services and social work departments. In addition to the promotion of training facilities and the recognition of courses, the Council awards the Certificate of Qualification in Social Work, exercises a developmental function in respect of social work education, and publishes information on careers in the social services. Following the merging of the Social Work Advisory Service (an independent charity) with the CCETSW in 1975, the Council now offers also a clearing house for applications to social work courses of all kinds. The Council establishes working parties from time to time to consider various aspects of syllabus-content in social work education and to publish discussion papers on new training needs in the field of social service.

The Council inherited responsibility for a wide range of courses at various lengths, various degrees of specialization, and a range of academic standards and auspices. It inherited also various forms of partnership between the earlier Councils and professional associations and the educational institutions within which courses were based. These partnerships have certainly been profitable, in that they have led to higher and more consistent standards of education and to a large increase in the number of course-places. They have also survived a complexity of compromises between the educational autonomy of universities, the needs of employers to recruit staff trained in particular skills, and the promotion of particular welfare policies by central government. Within the university sector an important adaptation in the last decade has been the merging within postgraduate education of the earlier separate courses in social studies and applied social studies: although this is not a universal development, it is now possible for many postgraduate students to receive their general and professional education in single integrated courses, and this has helped to promote greater similarity in the provisions of universities and polytechnics. Similarly, in both sectors of education, there are now some integrated four-year courses for undergraduate students which unite studies in the social sciences with professional education and training. In all these developments, success has depended on co-operation between the central government agencies and the courses. Two important focal points for co-operation and discussion between the CCETSW and social work teachers are provided by the Association of Teachers in Social Work Education, which offers individual membership to academic and field-teachers of social work students and provides a forum for debate about educational practices; and by the Social Work Education Committee of the Joint University Council for Social and Public Administration, which is made up of representatives of social work courses in the universities and polytechnics affiliated to the Council, and is concerned with all matters relating to the organization and future development of social work education.

The main preoccupations in social work education since 1971 have been to increase both the number and size of courses and to achieve a greater coherence in training patterns in the length of courses, their content and their general relevance to the needs of all services, than existed before 1971. The usual length of the total training period for social work is now two years, and the qualification on completion of all full professional courses is the Certificate of Qualification in Social Work. Particular attention has been given through working parties and sponsored research to the teaching of law, the value-basis of social work, the relationship between social work and community work from an educational standpoint, the relationship between generic and specialist components in basic training, and the organization and standards of field work within courses.

But in addition to the achievement of coherence in patterns of education, attention has been given to specific practice needs, particularly in the local authority services. It was recognized at an early stage that only about 4% of the 65,000 staff caring for the 395,000 people in residential establishments had received any training (CCETSW Report No. 1, 1973), and, following the publication of a report on the need to develop residential work training, special facilities have been introduced into several CQSW courses. In addition, a new pattern of training, based on a combination of academic and in-service study and leading to a Certificate in Social Service, is now being promoted which will cater particularly for residential and day-care staff, and for those who wish to develop skills in one or two aspects only of social work practice, for example, in work with the handicapped or the elderly. In addition to this form of specialized study at the level of basic training, plans are in hand also for the promotion of postqualifying studies for practitioners who have been in post for two or more years, to assist the development of specialized knowledge and skills at a higher level of professional competence.

Detailed information about developments in social work education may be obtained by reference to the Reports, Leaflets and Bulletins published by the CCETSW; but it is appropriate here to outline some of the current issues debated by social work teachers.

First, the acceptance by universities and polytechnics of responsibility for vocational education for social work has been accompanied by the transfer of financial responsibility from special earmarked funds to general funds within the educational institutions. This has already taken place in polytechnics and colleges of further education and will be completed in the universities in 1977. Social work education, which has hitherto been financially protected, will therefore need to compete with other educational provisions. In this competition, social work courses are at some disadvantage: the organization of students' field practice is an expensive (and, for the universities, unconventional) activity; similarly, staff–student ratios need to be such as to permit the maintenance of intensive tutorial and field work support. Within the universities, it is possible that these special needs will militate against the acceptance of further development in the size and educational scope of courses. Within the polytechnics, there are difficulties of a different kind: since the report of the Houghton Committee on the salaries of teachers (1974), it is now more rewarding financially to teach on courses leading to degrees and to Diplomas in Higher Education than on the two-year non-graduate social work courses; the difficulty of obtaining adequate academic staff for social work education is therefore likely to increase. Furthermore, the award of maintenance grants to non-graduate students lies wholly within the discretion of their local authorities; in the present economic climate, fewer students may be given the means to train as social workers.

Second, the expansion of courses has taken place at the same time as a rapid growth in the scope of work of the social services—notably through the implementation of the Children and Young Persons Act 1969, the Criminal Justice Act 1972 and the Chronically Sick and Disabled Persons Act 1970. Thus, while coping with larger numbers of students, social work teachers have found it necessary to expand the content of training within the time-limitations of their courses. The tension between quantity and quality in relation both to size and to content of courses has therefore been considerable. Many teachers express the anxiety that their students are no longer sufficiently prepared for the complexity of tasks that await them on qualification. An essential development for the future, therefore, is to devise some way of continuing the training of newly qualified staff during the early years of their appointment as social workers.

Third, concern for the development of community resources, combined with a greater sociological and political emphasis in social work training, has led to a relative reduction in teaching based on a treatment model of practice, in favour of studies devoted to social policy and to community development. The focus of generic education has moved from an exclusive preoccupation with casework towards the formulation of 'generic social work', of which casework forms only one part of a complex pattern of intervention. While this may be a sound development in theoretical terms, it is—one hopes only temporarily—out of line with the ways in which social workers are used by their employing agencies. The link between training and practice is more tenuous than it was when training was directly related to the function of specific agencies. Furthermore, students sometimes find themselves ill-equipped to cope with situations in which pathological behaviour is a central factor. (See for example the report on the Meurs case, reported in *The Times*, 16 January 1976.)

Related to this, a matter of current concern in social work education is how to bring together the increasing variety of theories and insights now available within the social sciences, and to employ them systematically as a basis for assessing and meeting human needs. There is a fundamental educational issue involved in this: one may expose students to a variety of ideas in the hope that each student will be able to develop from them a personally useful synthesis; but is a two-year training programme long enough for this? Or one may pre-select material and process it in such a way that students have a clear conception of the relevance of what they are being taught; but does this not then do violence to the academic integrity of the subjects?

Fifth, there is the problem of field supervision. The rapid movement of well-qualified practitioners into managerial posts has meant that social work students are now frequently supervised by relatively inexperienced and recently qualified staff. The development of a 'career grade' for practising social workers will in time overcome this difficulty; but at present, generations of practitioners are being trained whose training-supervision has been inadequate and who will themselves within two years become field teachers. Courses are no longer able to rely on a stable group of field work teachers; each generation of students is accompanied by a new generation of inexperienced supervisors.

The answer to some of these dilemmas might be *either* to lengthen the courses offering basic training *or* to develop opportunities for further and advanced study after initial qualification. Both are difficult to achieve at a time when the demand for training is unabated (it is not unusual for courses to have a 7:1 ratio of applicants to places) and the resources available cannot be much expanded. In the summer of 1975, vacancies for social workers in local authority departments numbered 15,000. During the preceding three years, 7325 students qualified as social workers. The target of the CCETSW for student places on all courses in 1976–7 is 4000. The shortage of qualified social workers will therefore remain an issue for some time, and may preclude any extension in the length of training.

The education and training of social workers cannot be separated from wider considerations of the organization and functions of the personal social services. The report of the Seebohm Committee recommended that an advisory council should be established which would be concerned both with the policy of the services and with training, in much the same way as were the earlier Advisory Councils on Child Care and Probation and **After-care** at the Home Office. The training function was, as we have seen, made a separate concern by the establishment of the CCETSW in 1971, while what the Report had envisaged as the parent body was set up in 1973 as the Personal Social Services Council. This Council's task is to advise Ministers on policy issues over the whole range of personal services, both statutory and voluntary, and, like the CCETSW, it is an independent body. It provides a service only for England and Wales, but works in co-operation with the Scottish Advisory Council on Social Work and with the advisory committee of the Department of Health and Social Services in Northern Ireland: its geographical scope is more limited than that of the CCETSW which covers the whole United Kingdom.

The Personal Social Services Council's main tasks are to promote research and debate which will assist the formulation of priorities of intervention and the development and management of community resources of all kinds. The Council is concerned also to promote relationships between the personal social services and other services and professional groups. The staff of the Council and the money available to it are small, and thus it is likely to be essentially an enabling rather than executive body, concerned to co-ordinate and publicize information and ideas from a variety of sources, and to present what its first Report describes as 'a broad synoptic view' of services. Its independent status will enable it to promote a critical analysis of service-provision and to draw attention to the interdependence of services without association with any established interests. It is hoped that the Council, more than any other existing body, will be able to represent the needs and opinions of those who use the services. The development of education and training in social work, and the pursuit of relevance in training both to the needs of consumers and to the interests of employing bodies, will depend very considerably on the links and information-sharing between the two Councils and on the quality of their future relationships with both the educational and service institutions.

PART V

Current Work and Future Trends

'By 1973 the personal social services accounted for approximately 1.6% of all public expenditure and 0.8% of the Gross National Product' (Cmnd 5879). This represented a doubling of their share of national resources during the preceding five years. In terms of all local government expenditure the level of resources available to the personal social services in 1973 was 5.6%. The Government's review of *Public Expenditure to 1978–79* (Cmnd 5879) indicated, however, that current expenditure will be levelled off and that there will be a fall in capital expenditure.* Thus, the economic climate of the personal social services has worsened. This was particularly felt in the year 1975–76, and although the rate support grant for 1976–77 permits an increase in expenditure of £30 million (an increase in real terms of 3.9% over the actual expenditure of the previous year) the next few years will be lean ones and will present a challenge to local committees and managers in determining precise allocations. We need, therefore, to think of the present and future work of the personal social services in this context, to consider ways of dealing with a situation of economic stringency, and to review some of the assumptions and principles of current practice which may need to be re-thought.

* Report of the Personal Social Services Council, 1975. See also *Priorities for Health and Personal Social Services*, HMSO 1976, which indicates that the overall growth rate, 1977–80, will be 2% p.a., and that capital expenditure will be cut by 50% (from £100 m in 1974/5 to £44 m in 1979/80). The paper proposes that annual spending should be increased by 2% for field work (with special emphasis on the needs of the mentally disordered), 2.6% for residential care, and 5% for day care.

1 Towards a Consolidation of Service

This is more easily said than done. A central difficulty for the personal social services is that there is no single principle or purpose upon which all their work can be based; there is not the same conceptual unity which one might hope to find in education or medicine. During the period of economic growth, services developed in direct response to the local expression of needs or to legislation. Legislation was not accompanied by guidance from Central Government about the relative importance to be attached to specific needs or problems, though, as we shall see, there have been recent signs of change in this respect, and the concept of need was generally used to provide a focus and a mandate for activity. The close association between welfare policies (nationally and locally) and the values and conceptual framework of professional social work has created a situation where agencies and staff respond to any expression of need with a sense of responsibility.

There have been two flaws in this development: first, the presence of a need has been assumed to carry the implication that it ought morally to be met by the statutory services; and, second, that the best way of meeting the expression of need is by some form of social work intervention. The more effective the detection of needs, the greater has been the demand for qualified social workers.

But 'need' is a difficult concept to use; its definition has no clear boundaries, and individual experiences of need are virtually incapable of comparison with each other. Not surprisingly, social workers, whatever their level of appointment within the services, find it difficult to compare people's needs and to rank them in order of priority. As we have seen, when they attempt to do so, they achieve answers which do not always accord with their personal interests as social workers or with the exercise of the professional skills in which they have been trained. On the whole, it has been easier to go on working harder than to ask questions about the purpose, relevance and appropriateness of this or that particular kind of professional intervention.

It may well be impossible to find a single unifying principle around which to define and consolidate the activities of the personal social services (see Roberts, 1975), but some movement towards consolidation could perhaps be achieved by reference to the cost-effectiveness of particular provisions, and by the wider recognition that the existence of a need may not always be a justification for statutory intervention nor for the use of social workers.

COST-EFFECTIVENESS

If we assume that statutory intervention is justified in a specific situation, then there are choices to be made concerning the form of that intervention. The policy has been established in all social service legislation since 1948 that, on both humanitarian and economic grounds, it is preferable to offer help to those in need within their local communities rather than in large-scale residential institutions, by domiciliary support and day services. While it is appropriate to uphold this general policy on humanitarian and ideological grounds, further research is necessary to establish that 'community care' really does meet needs and resolve problems in specific situations. Certainly, community care is an economical alternative, but part of its cheapness may be related to its inadequacy; and in some forms of implementation it may perpetuate rather than resolve difficulties. Hawkes (1975), writing about the care of the mentally ill, has suggested that the *therapeutic* value of community care remains an unproven assumption, and that without more research it is inappropriate to assume that by increasing the number of social workers one will create more effective community-based therapy. Bayley's work with the mentally handicapped (1973) has voiced a similar doubt. This is an area of development both in policy and practice, therefore, where consumer research is necessary to discover what relationship exists between the actual experience of need and the structure and costs of effective provision. Furthermore, community care by the provision of domiciliary and day care services may take many forms: the involvement of a social worker, social work auxiliary or voluntary helper; the services of home helps, home nurses, home wardens; the work of doctors and medical auxiliaries; clubs, day centres, day-patient facilities and Meals-on-Wheels. Very little is known about the differential use of these various kinds of manpower and about the most effective ways of co-ordinating their work. To what extent are the different interventions perceived by consumers as useful and relevant? To what extent can one form of service substitute for another? To take a simple example, could the person delivering a meal, given more time or more preparation, offer a service broadly equivalent to that of the social worker, or act as an assessor of the need for other forms of intervention? Different activities and interventions, even when offered by the same department, are frequently regarded as separate and functionally unrelated. This separation is even more apparent when several agencies and auspices are involved. To establish the cost-effectiveness of the 'help' given and received requires that the various inputs of service should be regarded as the united work of a team rather than as the activities of separate individuals and agencies. From time to time, the social services come under critical public scrutiny because of the death of a child or old person; it is not unusual to find that several public servants and professionals have been involved, some of whom are unaware of the activities of others. The problem here is not simply a failure in the effective co-ordination of information, though this is important; a more fundamental difficulty lies in the failure to recognize that a group of services and workers has the potential to function as a team, in that their activities (like the needs experienced by their clients) are inter-related, and in that different workers are able in part to substitute for each other. Reference was made in an earlier chapter to the recent advocacy by the DHSS of more effective co-operation between health, education and the statutory and voluntary social services; an aspect of this co-operation and of the cost-effectiveness of provisions is the definition of those aspects of help in which substitution is possible.

The public provisions of local authorities are now subject to processes of inter-departmental corporate planning. This increases the possibility that community welfare provisions of all kinds may be made more effective by the establishment of agreed objectives and priorities of service. Whether corporate planning will develop in this way is yet to be seen. As the Chairman of BASW has suggested, this constructive use of corporate planning provisions may be submerged beneath a more limited interest in exercising budgetary controls over the work of individual departments (BASW Conference 1975.)

Further research is necessary, also, to define the skills specific to particular kinds of worker within the personal social services, and how these skills may be most efficiently and economically used. This is not a plea for the functional separation of workers: the emphasis should be on team work and on the extent to which jobs can be linked together. But the definition of skills would help to determine whether the worker assigned to a specific situation actually has the ability to do effective work within it. Research on work with the elderly or handicapped, for example, may indicate a need in particular situations for more or fewer social workers, more or fewer home helps. Are the skills in which a social worker has been trained properly and necessarily used in alleviating the loneliness of these particular clients? Jordan (1975) has recently suggested that social workers should be called upon to help only in those situations where their skills are actually known to be helpful. He doubts, for example, whether most social workers have the skills required for some forms of community care in which they become involved, and condemns the tendency among social workers to take on all work irrespective of whether they can effectively do it.

A competent social worker will have a variety of skills and methods of intervention available to him. Cost-effectiveness lies also, therefore, in the choice he makes of these available skills, and in his recognition that a choice of skills actually exists.

This is a difficult matter, and one which lies at the heart of effective professional supervision within the services; for each social worker, and this is no doubt true of other forms of service, develops his own characteristic ways of working. However intensively he may have been trained to use a variety of modes of intervention, he will tend to use only a small selection of those modes, irrespective of their effectiveness in meeting the difficulties and needs of his clients (see Mayer & Timms, 1970). The most common mode of intervention at present is that of 'continuous service': that is to say, contact is made between social worker and client which continues until such time as all the client's needs are ostensibly met, or until the worker is satisfied that it is safe to end the association. On this basis, social workers find it considerably easier to open cases than to close them; the relationship between worker and client may become a source of pleasure for them both, so that neither wishes to end it; long-term goals of work may be overlooked in a seemingly never-ending series of small tasks (see Sainsbury 1975); the client may continue to present needs and feelings in which the worker feels it appropriate to be interested. Yet it may sometimes be the case that long-term associations of this kind are counter-productive. There is evidence to suggest—though further research is essential in these matters—that continuing contact with the social worker may increase rather than reduce dependency, dissatisfaction and depression (Reid & Shyne, 1969), that male clients particularly are often resistant to long-term intervention, that the sex of the worker in relation to the sex of the client may influence the speed with which a productive partnership is achieved, that the increments of change in the client's whole situation may cease to be significant after a relatively small number of interviews (Fahs Beck & Jones, 1973), and that the co-operation of the client with the intention of the worker may be particularly influenced in the immediate post-referral situation (Sainsbury, 1975). If these and similar findings are substantiated by further research, then the process of assessment and the differential use of skills are important contributions to the promotion of efficient and economic work.

The effectiveness of intervention relative to its costs may also require a change in the perceived status of the client. It has been found in residential care that groups of clients can be effectively used as a resource for identifying and meeting needs through the development of a sense of colleagueship with staff (see Editorial 1976). Both in residential and field services, the more the clients are assumed to be dependent, the greater the dependency they tend to express. Holman (1975) has argued that clients who are treated as inadequate and incapable will respond in these ways; that, in practice, their capacities for self-help and collective action are frequently underestimated; and that stereotypes are sometimes created in the minds of social workers not by the proven incapacity of clients but by the ways in which they express their needs—ways at variance with the thought-process of the social worker but not necessarily inappropriate or inaccurate. Similarly, Jordan (1975) has advocated that honest and frank discussions between social worker and client, involving the open recognition of what the social worker and his agency can and cannot offer in terms of effective service, tend to reduce the stigmatizing of clients and at the same time to enhance the self-help capacities of the client and the professional integrity of the worker. Thus, cost-effectiveness may be increased by reducing areas of inappropriate or inefficient intervention and by increasing the self-reliance of the client.

Arguments of this kind are closely associated with debate concerning the justification for statutory intervention. Statutory personal social services exist partly to meet needs and to deal with problems which cannot be met or resolved by the less formal processes of self-help, family help and neighbourhood help. They exist also within a broader framework of social provision to help right social injustices and to promote more equitable life-opportunities through the redistribution of resources. These are not incompatible ideas. To regard the client (defined as individual, family, group or community) as a resource rather than as a passive recipient of services is to enhance the likelihood of strengthening those social movements concerned to promote equity and redistribution. This is amply demonstrated in the practice of group work and in the establishing of groups which, in the pursuit of additional neighbourhood resources, develop skills in negotiation, in exercising pressure on central and local authorities, and in establishing their own services.

Community workers in various settings find that the principal challenge of their work lies not in enlisting neighbourhood help and concern, but in assisting people to define their goals. Similarly, in work with individuals and families, the major difficulty is to define the tasks on which co-operation between client and social worker may be based; it is comparatively rare to encounter in a client a total lack of concern about the need or problem presented to the agency or a total inability to do something about it. Thus, in many aspects of the work of the personal social services, there is no lack of human resources, inside or outside the context of 'the case'; the problem is one of harnessing and focussing resources to the definition of tasks. This process, however, takes time. It is often quicker and easier to reach a decision and to undertake all the work oneself than to share the making of a decision and to encourage other people in the realization that they have the potential to undertake the necessary tasks. The situation is, however, complicated in all forms of social service by a prevailing uncertainty about the legitimacy of the clients' definitions of their needs and, in the matter of enlisting local voluntary help, by issues of confidentiality.

It is possible, therefore that the practical justification for some of the activity of paid staff in the statutory services rests paradoxically on a desire to save time in handling situations, on uncertainty how far the defining of social needs should be regarded as an expert task, and on moral dilemmas in the sharing of information. Certainly, if client and community are to be regarded as resources, then the initial phase of work will be longer and more intensive than in those forms of practice in which the social worker assumes responsibility for defining needs and meeting them. But there is some evidence to suggest that, in casework at least, the speed of later change is significantly increased by taking the time at the outset to involve clients in defining the tasks to be undertaken (Reid & Epstein, 1972). The same may apply, *mutatis mutandis*, in other forms of intervention.

It has been suggested in this chapter that, in consolidating and finding a focus for the work of the statutory social services, one of the areas of debate is the justification for statutory intervention, particularly prolonged intervention, by paid staff in situations of need. Two points have been made: that the skills of social service workers can and should be deployed in ways which tend to shorten the time in which they need to be directly involved; and that services and individual workers need to consider how far the essential tasks can be made the responsibility of the clients themselves, or can be appropriately delegated to volunteer helpers. The eleventh report of the Expenditure Committee of the House of Commons (Cmnd 5879, 1975) has suggested that 'it is possible that social workers are . . . carrying out functions which do not need social work skills and which other people could do just as well if not better'.

But a third issue is implicit in what has been said so far: namely, the appropriate nature and extent of 'democratization' in devising and providing services. 'The vitality of progress depends upon imaginative intervention, and, to ensure this, the right to innovate is diffused throughout society (Marris & Rein, 1974). The consolidation of provisions in the personal social services depends on the willingness of a very wide range of other services and community groups to find ways of uniting and using the abilities and insights of all kinds of people: administrators, professionals, formal and informal networks of helpers, planners, researchers and other employees. Part of the difficulty experienced by the personal social services in defining the boundaries of their own work lies in the uncertainty of response from other agencies and groups. The Chairman of BASW (1975) has commented that, within local authorities, the failure of contingent services to define agreed policy objectives, together with the recent expansion of social services departments, may have led to the withdrawal of housing and education departments from some of their legitimate welfare concerns and to an increasing number of referrals to social workers. Similarly, the responses of voluntary agencies and groups to developments in the local authority services are frequently unknown and not seen in reciprocal terms. Decisions within the National Health Service are sometimes made without adequate external discussion, irrespective of their effects on public welfare and on the work of the local authorities. Yet, in any geographical area, the ability of a personal social service to define the scope of its own work must depend on agreements with other services and groups on their overall objectives. The case for the appointment of community development workers and liaison staff is frequently based on this need.

But is it also possible, as is often argued, to extend democratization in policy-making to local neighbourhood groups by the appointment of community workers and by the local community involvement of area teams? It was noted in an earlier chapter that some movement of this kind has already been achieved in many areas; but the difficulties of combining inter-service liaison with local democratization are more considerable than is sometimes recognized. To begin with, where an individual or group stands personally in relation to a social need and to the formal processes of planning will inevitably affect his or their perception of how resources ought to be provided, harnessed and used. Community work and community action often depend on the use of conflict strategies, and it is difficult to combine these strategies with an argument in favour of open planning and administration between services. Conflict tends to make administrators close their ranks, not to open them. Furthermore, there is little evidence to suggest that local community interest in planning can be maintained in general terms rather than in terms simply of *ad hoc* complaints; yet the formulation of policy objectives suffers already from too much specificity and too much restriction, in Titmuss's words 'to the immediate, the intimate, the precise and the manageable.' (1968.)

There are, in short, fundamental difficulties in relating together democratic forms of planning with professional forms of planning, particularly when the scope of a service extends well beyond the local interests of a specific community group. It is hard to see, for example, how one could effectively democratize the work of Regional Planning Committees for Intermediate Treatment, or how one might deal democratically with newly emerging problems and needs towards which there is no guarantee of local public sympathy, or where there is a high risk of the stigmatization of future clients: for example, in respect of the growing dependency on alcohol,* or of increasing acts of vandalism. Voluntary organizations often provide an essential link between the formal planning of services at professional and administrative levels and the involvement of the general public in understanding and contributing to the work of the services. But it remains difficult, as was noted earlier, for statutory services to negotiate with all the voluntary agencies active in their areas, each with its own traditions of service and frequently lacking a federal structure to promote the kind of debate about policies and objectives which would serve as a frame of reference for defining the scope of the statutory services and the reciprocal involvement of local people.

---

* Helping Hand Organization: *Female Alcoholism*, 1976: there are now 150,000 female alcoholics, and this number is growing rapidly.

2 Relationships between Central and Local Government

So far we have considered some of the issues involved in identifying and consolidating the functions of local statutory services and in deciding where to focus resources in order to achieve greater efficiency in their use. The role of central government has until recently been ambiguous both in co-ordinating the various policies underlying separate welfare provisions and in giving guidance on their unified implementation. In some aspects of personal social service there is considerable government intervention—for example, in the inspection of the work of probation departments, in the appointment of directors of social service, in the endorsement of proposals to institute new capital expenditure programmes. But little help has until recently been available to determine priorities of service or to shape a unified policy for local authority intervention. Griffith (1966) commented that 'the refusal or failure or reluctance of government departments to make policy explicit is the most complicating factor in relationships between government departments and local authorities'. It was noted earlier that the Health and Welfare White Papers requiring local authorities to devise ten-year plans for the development of services, 1963–73 (Cmnd 1973) and 1966–76 (Cmnd 3022), offered few guidelines and made no reference to the likely availability of resources. During the present decade, more direct guidance has been available on the shape of services for 1973–83 (Circulars 1976). More specific statements of policy have been made, for example, concerning the treatment of mental disorder and physical handicap; greater attention has been given to the problems of inter-departmental planning, both centrally and locally, in the recognition that comprehensive provisions to meet problems and needs extend beyond the scope of the personal social services. The Cabinet Paper, '*A joint approach to social policy*' 1975, defined social policy in terms of the promotion of realistic public expectations, the achievement of economies, and the promotion of efficiency rather than expansion: attention was particularly drawn to the need for more effective implementation of policies concerned with the care of children and of young people before and after they leave school. As noted earlier, recent Government statements have quantified minimum standards to be achieved, based on the greater availability of information concerning variations in services in the country as a whole. (See Davies 1968; Harris, 1971.)

There remains, however, the need at central government level, particularly in the formulation of long-term plans, to co-ordinate the separate intentions of all related services—welfare, education, health, housing, employment, income maintenance—and to agree priorities and objectives for local guidance. Ambiguities of responsibility continue to exist. This becomes apparent at local level when, for example, Section 1 payments under the Children and Young Persons Act 1963 are used to pay rents to housing departments and to supplement Supplementary Benefits; when education authorities make independent appointments of social workers to work in schools and in the youth services; when hospitals discharge long-stay patients for whom alternative accommodation is not available. The DHSS working party on Social Work Support for the Health Service provided one example of a welcome trend towards more unified policies in the initiation of services (see Birch, 1975). In the light of this situation Roberts & Smith (1976) have recently suggested the need for a Central Government social welfare service to unite all these concerns. This may sound an attractive suggestion from some points of view, but there would be difficulties in implementing it, even if it were acceptable to the local authority associations: the boundaries of such a service would in the end still need to be arbitrarily drawn, and its size would probably lead to a functional separation of its various parts. The problem about the promotion of welfare is that, essentially, it is everybody's business, and no merger of existing structures could wholly contain this kind of comprehensiveness. Nevertheless, there is certainly a need for greater co-ordination of policies, not least in regulating the flow of legislation so that it does not, as at present, exceed both the resources and the skills available to implement it. There is need also, nationally and locally, for a more imaginative use of the resources we have, so that solutions are not sought in compartmentalized terms. Whatever else we need, we do not need *simply* more of the same.

Central government guidelines on social policy, however, cannot of themselves provide a guarantee of local implementation. When, in January 1976, government advised a 3.9% growth rate in local authority social services for the year 1976–77, authorities responded by proposals above and below this figure. An assistant secretary of BASW commented: 'We would like to see central government monitoring local authority programmes as they do capital programmes requiring loan sanction'. (*Community Care*, 4 February 1976.) In the light of this situation Judge (1976) has recently advocated more extensive central government intervention, particularly to promote equitable standards of service between different areas, by the replacement of undifferentiated rate support grants by earmarked grants to individual local authorities for the development of specific provisions. This would constitute greater control by central government over the affairs of local authorities than has hitherto been regarded as acceptable. There would also be practical difficulties in determining the relative size of these specific grants for individual local authorities: presumably such a scheme would mean that, in the interest of achieving national minimum standards, local authorities who had already achieved good standards of provision would be economically at a disadvantage in the promotion of new work. Judge suggests also that, as an aspect of national policy, further consideration should be given to the charges levied by local authorities on the users of particular services, and to variations between authorities in the extent of their use of charges—for example, for home helps and for meals. This suggestion is, however, full of complexities, even though one would wish to see greater equality in the provision of local services: it raises issues about the appropriate level of central government control; it would exacerbate the vexed ideological and practical problems of means-tested services by not acknowledging variations in local political viewpoints. Judge's proposals imply also the re-iteration of another fundamental ideological issue: how far services should be responsive to local variations in the expression of need, or, alternatively, how far their levels of provision should be related exclusively to economic considerations determined centrally.

In the relationship between central and local government, in the transmission of guidance, and in the formulation of a unified policy for the personal social services, the Social Work Service of the DHSS plays an important role which might usefully be strengthened.

The Social Work Service was formed in 1970 from the professional staff of the Children's Inspectorate of the Home Office and the Social Work Division of the DHSS as an allied development to changes in the organization of the local authority social services. The Service has a central staff of about forty and a larger regional staff based on the seven regional planning areas for children's services established by the Children and Young Persons Act 1969. The Service provides for the dissemination of ideas between authorities and between services on the use of provisions; it incorporates an inspectorial responsibility in respect of the performance of statutory duties; and it advises on the implications of central government statements of policy for the planning of services in local areas.

Hitherto the work of the service has been characterized by its informality of approach. The role of the individual officer has not been clearly advertised, and the advisory function of the service is more apparent than the functions of inspection and regulation. Here again, the delicacy of relationships between central and local government is an important issue. It is relatively uncontroversial to relay information about how services may be developed, about their use and structure in different areas, and about local and national policies; but it may be argued that, in the economic uncertainties of the next few years, greater weight should be placed on the monitoring and regulation of standards of service. Without this, the *ad hoc* expansions of the past may be succeeded by a variety of *ad hoc* reductions in the future. Guidance will be necessary, for example, in achieving equitable adjustments in the number of different kinds of staff if the maintenance of one kind of service is not to be achieved inappropriately at the expense of another.

In addition, as has been suggested, the form taken by local services has frequently reflected the methods of intervention available rather than a direct acknowledgement of the experience and gravity of social need or a broad appraisal of the nature of social problems and their sources. This has been particularly apparent in work associated with delinquent behaviour; only recently have attempts been made to relate the form of services to the whole life experience of clients, and even in these attempts the concept of 'treatment' appears sometimes to have been misapplied. There are now new challenges to be faced by the personal social services: the community care of the chronically sick and disabled; possible increases in the problems of violence and vandalism; new philosophies of citizen participation in planning and delivering services; the increasing recognition of the immediate needs of certain client-groups (for example, the homeless, the young unemployed, the alcoholic, the single parent); the new emphasis on welfare rights and entitlements; day care, day-patient treatment and various forms of group work. Guidance is necessary, therefore, on the development of new skills and techniques of intervention, on the deployment of existing staff within changing patterns of work, and on the promotion of new kinds of service-relationships. The activities of the Social Work Service could with advantage be strengthened to offer guidance to administrators and field staff and to those responsible for training and re-training programmes.

3 The Nature of Social Work

Finally, it is necessary to consider the future of social work as a profession. What is its present and future nature and purpose? For much of its history, it has been associated, on two dimensions, with the administrative identification of specific client-groups, and with the development of artificially separated 'methods of intervention' (casework, groupwork and community work) and the clarification of techniques and skills within each method. One reason for the relatively low status of residential work hitherto has been the difficulty of defining its scope by reference to an established social work 'method'. Fortunately the separation of 'methods' is now being critically re-examined, at least in theoretical terms, in the development of unitary models of practice based on the general applicability of specific skills.

Secondly, social work is concerned with social stability and social change, and a central issue for the future is the appropriate balance of these two functions. What is the professional commitment of social work? Should social work be concerned with experiment in intervention and with extending the scope of its involvement in social affairs; or should it concentrate on the refinement of proven skills, and limit its involvement to those aspects of work in which it is demonstrably effective? Should its scope extend beyond, or be contained within, the duties of employing services?

One of the folk myths of social work answers these questions by relating them back to the 'methods': community workers are said to be innovatory, caseworkers are thought to be concerned with the conservation of their skills. On the other hand, it may well be the case that the attitudes of social workers vary more according to their ages than to their methods-orientation. This has implications for employers, in that the scope of social work practice in their organizations may have less to do with how they define jobs (community worker, caseworker) and more with the particular combination of ages within the work-team. For example, the growing enthusiasm among social workers for their advocacy role is particularly associated with the younger age-group for whom advocacy has become a

professional value which infuses all their work rather than an optional practical extension of their main function. Significantly, all the principal papers
of the BASW Conference in 1975 were concerned in various ways with advocacy as a central professional responsibility, and this may well indicate
the future scope and orientation of the profession. If so, this will inevitably
have an impact on the relationship of social workers to their employers. The
more they identify with the clients or the local communities whose needs
they are advocating, the greater the possibility of conflict in respect of
decisions or procedures which appear to deny those needs, and the more
difficult it may become to perpetuate departmental loyalties of a traditional
kind. As Coates and Silburn commented following the publication of the
Seebohm Report, 'Social work is about to embark upon a series of changes
which could substantially remodel its contribution to society. Social workers
are, however, situated within the political fabric of the community, and their
professional freedom of action is liable to be substantially curtailed to suit
the convenience of their political and administrative chiefs. . . . Alone, the
social worker can do little, but in alliance with real forces in the community,
a great deal can be achieved.' (Coates & Silburn, 1970.)

A related aspect of the future of professional social work is its growing in-
tellectualism. The educational basis of social work training is now broader
and deeper than in the past. Social work students are encouraged, for a
short time, at least, to get to grips with a broad range of the human sciences;
they have the capacity to form an intellectual elite. How will this elitism be
used? The indications are that it will be used not to increase professional distance and mystique, but to speak with increasing authority on the form of
services necessary to meet needs and how they should be provided. This
may, as Coates and Silburn have suggested, lead to conflict with political
and administrative chiefs: but it may alternatively lead to a new kind of
relationship between elected members of committees and their professional
employees. Some BASW branches have recently negotiated informal
meetings between social services committee members and professional
social workers, outside the management structure of the services, to consider matters of local social service policy and practice. If such meetings
become commonplace, they will represent a new form of social action,
capable both of promoting social reform and of drawing attention to the unmet needs of certain consumer-groups; they may serve also as a means of
uniting intra-professional concerns with the development of advocacy and
with political intervention. As Rein has suggested, the future of social work,
depending on the use made of its professional structure and the academic
quality of its members, may lie in becoming 'a unique research–action activity, assessing and analysing the directions of change in social life and its
impact on individuals. The job is that of social criticism: the merger of
scholarship, social justice and passion' (Rein, 1970).

There are, however, many complexities and issues to be resolved before
the profession of social work can develop effectively in the way envisaged by

Rein. 'Social work is distinguished, firstly by the disparity of norms in a profession which is not yet fully fledged . . . and secondly by the stress and uncertainty of the job.' (Rodgers & Stevenson, 1973.) Disparity of norms is apparent not only in the variety of values and techniques which social workers use. It exists also in the range of public expectations of the functions of social workers: for example, in the extent to which they are expected to exercise power in different situations; in the extent to which they are expected to be able to solve social problems and to meet needs, irrespective of the complexities of their causation. A great deal remains to be done to promote public awareness that social problems cannot be solved simply by training and employing more social workers, and that some (perhaps many) of the situations in which they are involved are created by social forces and structures beyond the scope of the personal social services, however well coordinated and expertly staffed they may be. Similarly, the stress and uncertainty of social work are related not only to the intensity of suffering which social workers frequently encounter, but also to the gulf that exists between understanding and action. Social workers may indeed form an intellectual elite within the personal social services; but their elitism is based on their direct knowledge and understanding of the nature of problems and needs, rather than on the development of skills which are demonstrably effective in all the areas of intervention with which they are now concerned. I do not wish to imply that social workers do not offer a helpful service; they frequently do. But not all their intervention is effective in the way that the general public expects it to be; nor is it all effective on the criteria which social workers would define for themselves. The knowledge-base of social work has certainly enlarged considerably in the last twenty years; but the defining of skills, and of the criteria for using and evaluating these skills, has not kept pace.

The reasons for this disparity are themselves complex. One cannot readily separate the practice and evaluation of social work from the practices of the employing services. As we have seen, there has been a growing association of the two since the last war; services are now judged by the public in terms of the quality of the social worker's practice, and social work is judged by its relevance to service requirements. This association will, I believe, steadily increase; few training courses now accept social work students who have not had experience of working in a social service; these students, for economic reasons, frequently elect to be trained as seconded employees and some, regrettably, see their training as nothing more than a chore to be accomplished to satisfy the requirements of employment and to guarantee their standing on their return to their authorities. While it is true that the CCETSW and many employers perceive training as an opportunity to strengthen professional wisdom and skills, the self-interest of employers who are disbursing large sums for the training of seconded staff naturally requires 'value for money'. Primarily they want their staff to be able to cope personally with the stresses of the job and to possess the skills and know-how necessary to undertake the duties that are defined for them; they do not want their staff to be primarily identified as agents of general social reforms which might call into question some of the functions and duties of the services themselves.

A further difficulty in the development of the profession lies in the relationship between problem and need, to which reference was made earlier. Social work is concerned with meeting individual and local needs. Sometimes this process helps to solve wider social problems; and similarly, solving problems sometimes helps to meet individual needs. For example, if poverty or the inaccessibility of resources are regarded as social problems, then meeting the needs of an individual client offers a small contribution to solving the social problem; social action to increase the entitlements of poor people in general will at the same time meet their individual needs. But this relationship between need and problem is considerably less certain when one considers the social problem of delinquency and the therapeutic and rehabilitative measures at present established to deal with it. No doubt some people commit crimes because of personal unhappiness or emotional disturbance; meeting their therapeutic needs is thus a valid contribution to dealing with crime. But not all criminal behaviour can be defined in these terms, and while the social worker may help to meet personal needs brought to his attention because a crime has been committed, there is no direct link between this activity and the general social problem of criminal behaviour. We cannot assume that all offenders are unhappy, deprived or disturbed people, even though they may be a considerable social nuisance. Thus, for example, Intermediate Treatment may be effectively therapeutic in combating the delinquent behaviour of one child, while for another it may be merely an intrinsically interesting experience (in that it may offer new activities and new associations) unrelated to his delinquent behaviour.

One of the tasks of social work, therefore, is to achieve greater certainty about its purpose and to define the situations where meeting individual needs is directly related to the resolution of social problems. When there is greater clarity about the validity or invalidity of therapeutic and rehabilitative models of practice in different situations, the profession will be more able than at present to define its effective scope and to decide whether and in what ways to extend that scope.

Finally, there is a good deal of work yet to be done to define the profession in terms of its component skills and, therefore, of its membership. As we have seen, this has changed over the years: residential work is now regarded as social work, while health visitors, who were eligible for membership of the British Federation of Social Workers in the 1930s are not eligible for full membership of BASW. The greatest uncertainty at present in this respect concerns the membership of community workers and the nature of community work—whether it is a form of social work, and, if not, how it relates to social work. It is ironic that, at a time when social workers **of all kinds** receive generic training, promoted by a single Central Council, and have achieved a measure of professional unity in BASW, community workers are working towards a wholly separate identity, both through the Association of Community Workers and by the Association's current (1976) proposals for a separate training Council. With hindsight, one wonders whether the structure of BASW, particularly of its sectional specializations, might have been ordered differently to give a more specific right to membership among community workers. As the matter stands now, however, it is likely that theoretical attempts to achieve a unified basis for all forms of social intervention in personal social service work will be offset by renewed emphasis on a kind of methodological separation which bears no relation either to the experience of need or to the promotion of social reform. Training courses for social workers may in future find that, if they wish to train community workers and social workers within a single framework, they will need to seek the recognition of two central councils rather than one; while courses in which the training of social workers and community workers is wholly separated will risk the perpetuation or renewal of mutual ignorance about purposes, values and techniques.

The future of social work is, therefore, uncertain, both within the profession itself and in its relationship with employers and the general public. It may in time, as Rein suggests, constitute a source of social criticism and social action which effectively unites pressure for social reform with the provision of individual care. Or it may become simply a way of describing the techniques used by some employees in the personal social services.

4 The Promotion of Welfare

This brief study of practices and policies in the personal social services and social work has shown that, in recent years, there has been a movement in the direction of understanding and meeting the needs and difficulties of individuals and families in a broad social context. While the deprivations suffered by individuals and the problems which individual behaviour presents to social order are still frequently (and sometimes appropriately) dealt with by means of an *individual* service provided by *one* member of one social agency, the 'case' is increasingly seen to represent fundamental problems in social organization and processes. That is to say in the way we, as a society, define and allocate social roles and responsibilities, in the economic, political and professional climate of the times, and in social attitudes. The circumstances and needs of those who use the personal social services have, therefore, to be seen on two dimensions: they are particular and special to individuals in certain respects; but they are also in part symptomatic of what life in our society, at this point in time, does to people.

The implications of locating individual need and problems in this broader social context may be studied on several dimensions in the current organization and delivery of social services. Although it remains convenient, administratively and professionally, to maintain a range of different services to meet specific needs, their relevance to the promotion of individual and social welfare depends to a large extent on two matters: first, on their agreement on matters of policy, objectives and priorities of work; and second, on their recognition that they are at best contributors to welfare rather than its exclusive providers.

On the first matter, there are encouraging signs of shared policies and planning within the social services. The Government's recent policy statement (*Priorities for Health and Personal Services in England*, HMSO 1976) proposes, for example, that the health authorities should give financial support to the local authority social services (£15 m a year) in respect of community care provisions for patients; there are regional joint planning committees for the care of children in which a range of statutory and voluntary services are represented; in the country as a whole one can find many examples of shared planning between authorities, departments and organizations concerned with the welfare (and not merely the defined needs) of particular groups of people. In short, it is recognized that individual needs cannot be dealt with in isolation from each other, and that social service makes better sense if it responds to the whole life style and situation of the users. On the second matter, however, there is still much thinking to be done. *Priorities for Health and Personal Social Services, 1976* recognizes that the presence of a need may not be sufficient justification in itself for statutory intervention (particularly in view of the present economic stringency), and draws attention to the present limitations of the statutory services in meeting needs. In particular, the report emphasizes that increases in current expenditure to provide more community care and preventive services (increases of 3.2% p.a. for the elderly, 2.2% for children and families, 2.8% for the mentally handicapped and 1.8% for the mentally ill) can be achieved only by cutting capital expenditure (on, for example, buildings). Standards of need are redefined in terms of what the country can afford. 'Authorities and their staffs will continue to have hard judgments to make between needs which it is essential for the services to meet and those which individuals and families must themselves be left to cope with. The development of a manageable order of priorities also requires recognition on the part of the community generally that there are limits to what the social services can do to alleviate social need.' There is a note of regret in these sentences which is in part appropriate but not wholly so. One can accept that it is a misfortune if services to meet need have to be restricted or curtailed in any way; but the opportunity has yet to be seized to define alternative and effective models of provision which would place the contribution of the social services in a wider context of debate about the nature of welfare and its promotion. Significantly, statutory services are said to 'meet' and to 'alleviate' need; individuals and families only 'cope' with it. If we accept that the social services have something to do with the promotion of welfare (in Scotland this is made explicit in legislation), then it is necessary to think more clearly than hitherto about the relationship between this promotion and the meeting of needs. There can be no dispute that by meeting needs some contribution is made to the promotion of welfare; there can be no welfare if basic human needs are not met. But the cumulative process of defining and meeting more and more needs is not itself the same as promoting welfare. A parallel may be drawn at the personal level in respect of leading a good life: one would not say that one was enjoying a good life simply because one is fulfilling all one's social roles and other people are fulfilling all theirs in respect of one's defined needs. Welfare and the good life imply creativity; meeting needs and fulfilling roles *may* be creative activities, but creativity is not an essential component in them. The present economic difficulties affecting the social services may regrettably be used only to excuse the inadequacies of statutory provision to meet needs, whereas they could be more constructively used to review the whole basis of welfare promotion and to clarify the role of the services as contributors to, but not providers of, welfare.

The report goes some way towards this creativity of thinking in its references to voluntary action: 'Support for voluntary effort and encouragement of self-help schemes may represent better value for money than directly provided services, and may also provide the means of continuing preventive work. By their diversity and the ingenuity they bring to the task, voluntary organizations can be an important adjunct to the authority's own direct services in getting help to people in need.' But it is a matter for debate whether this creativity of thinking goes far enough.

The location of individual needs in a broader social context of thinking about welfare has, as I have suggested earlier, several political implications. One may regard individual needs and difficulties as symptomatic of social processes about which political action as well as individual service is necessary. One may set services to individuals in the framework of a broader recognition of the life-style, social and political aspirations and creative contributions both of the clients themselves and of their local communities. But service developments of this kind at present merely represent additional socio political dimensions in the work of professionals, volunteer helpers and voluntary groups; they do not sufficiently call into question the attitudes and responsibilities of the politicians themselves—those who sit on social service committees and who frame social policies for national or local implementation. The promotion of social welfare (rather than simply the cumulative definition and meeting of needs) is frequently ill-matched with the present entrenched attitudes of the political parties: the left have sought increasing resources for the statutory services, but often to the extent of regarding voluntary action in respect of welfare as residual, or irrelevant, or tolerable only as supplementation of statutory effort; the right has emphasized the importance of voluntary services (in non-political terms), at the expense of resources in the statutory sector. Neither stance is relevant to the view that the promotion of welfare requires creative, egalitarian partnerships which can tolerate ideological divergence as well as agreement. Neither does the solution seem to lie in the present performance of politically extremist radical pressure groups, which in varying degrees play love–hate games both with the statutory social services and with the welfare of individual citizens in need of help—for example, by advocating the democratization of services while rejecting the acceptability of ideological disagreement, by demanding greater resources to services while rejecting the power which those additional resources will inevitably confer, by riding into political battle on the shoulders of the socially deprived whose current needs are met only by promises of post-revolutionary millenarianism.

The promotion of welfare is an ideal which challenges also the role and functions of professional employees, particularly during this period of economic constraint. For social workers working with individuals and families the principal questions for the future must be concerned with how they use their time. For example, how far do their different activities actually contribute to the welfare of those they serve? There is some evidence to suggest that their skills are sometimes misused on tasks which could be done as effectively or more cheaply or more appropriately by other people (Younghusband, 1951). A surprisingly small proportion of their time seems actually to be spent on their main function of face-to-face help (see Burns & Sinclair, 1963). Furthermore, there is reason to believe that the potential effectiveness of much of the work done is offset by a lack of skill in influencing the environmental factors which contribute to the stresses experienced by their clients (Davies, HMSO 1974). In short, casework services need to be both broader in conception and approach, and more precisely related to studies of effectiveness in respect of the special needs of individual clients; there is a need to combine generic principles of intervention with the enhancement of special and proven skills. (See Younghusband, 1973; Triseliotis, 1973; Vickery, 1973.)

The community worker faces different problems. Economic constraints will make it irrelevant to promote local action groups whose sole purpose is to demand more resources for a particular neighbourhood unless at the same time he or his groups are prepared to form a view about which other needs should be neglected and about how resources should be re-deployed. An important platform for community workers has been their emphasis on the decentralizing of social service and probation departments, the importance of locating sub-offices near to the focal points of local community life (e.g. clinics, playgrounds, schools, shops) and the importance of the physical accessibility of social work teams. However much one may applaud this view—and few would wish to oppose it or to praise the impersonal architectural monoliths in which some services are housed—it is unlikely that reduced capital expenditure will permit the building of specially planned neighbourhood offices in the foreseeable future. Social workers may have to choose between the principle of community involvement, irrespective of the accommodation and facilities available to implement it, and the achievement of physically better working conditions.

Finally, the promotion of welfare requires a reappraisal of the relationships and respective roles of service staffs at all levels and their clients; and of the extent to which it is possible and desirable to redefine the distinction between roles, in recognition that the promotion of welfare is not an exclusive responsibility of the professional, and (though it may require the contribution of certain expert skills) it is not in itself an expert function. Mrs Barbara Castle, speaking of pre-school playgroups in 1976, described them as 'universalizing the parent–child relationships of the more fortunate'. It is possible to make a generalization from this comment. She was not implying that good parenthood is an expert function which confers status and power, but that competence in bringing up one's own children can be extended to serve the welfare of other children and other parents on equal terms. Similarly, the personal social services contain a fund of skills and resources which can be shared; but these skills and resources need not, in all situations, carry with them special power or status. A social services department can offer resources to a self-help group without actually having to possess, control or manage the group. The Manpower Services Commission provides the funds necessary to pay the living expenses of Community Service Volunteers, but it does not manage the volunteers or control their employment. The promotion of individual and social welfare is concerned with the sharing of resources and responsibilities between people, between groups, between organizations and those who use them. An important issue for the personal social services and for their employees at the present time is the extent to which, and the circumstances in which, this sharing of resources and responsibilities can be conceived in terms of the delegation of tasks and duties, and how far delegation can and should be accompanied by the willingness to concede power and control.

References

Adamson, G. (1972). *The Care Takers*, Bookstall Services Publications

Advisory Council on the Penal System. (1974). *Young Adult Offenders*, HMSO.

Age Concern. (1974). Good Neighbours.

Algie, J. (1970). Management and organization in the social services, *British Hospital Journal* LXXX, p. 1245

Aves Report. (1969). *The Voluntary Worker in the Social Services*, NCSS.

Baldock, P. (1974). *Community Work and Social Work*, Routledge & Kegan Paul.

Balint, M. (1957). *The Doctor, His Patient and His Illness*, Pitman.

Barr, H. (1971). *Volunteers in Prison Aftercare*, Allen & Unwin.

Baugh, W. E. (1973, 1975). *Introduction to the Social Services*, Macmillan.

BASW (1973). *Intermediate Treatment*.

Bayley, M. J. *Mental Handicap and Community Care*, Routledge & Kegan Paul.

Bell, K. (1973). *Disequilibrium in Welfare*, University of Newcastle-upon-Tyne.

Birch, R. A. (1975). Social work support for the Health Service, *Health Trends* 7(1).

Borland, J. (1974). In *Management in the Social Services*, edited by Olsen, R., University College of North Wales, Bangor.

Broady, M. (1968). *Planning for People*, Bedford Square Press.

Brockington, F. & Lempert, S. M. (1966). *Social Needs of the Over-Eighties*, Manchester University Press.

Brown, G. E. (1968). *The Multi-Problem Dilemma*, Scarecrow Press.

Brown, R. G. S. (1975). *The Management of Welfare*, Fontana.

Bruce, M. (1961). *The Coming of the Welfare State*, Batsford.

Burns, T. & Sinclair, S. (1963). *The Child Care Service at Work*, The Scottish Education Department.

Butrym, Z. (1967). *Social Work in Medical Care*, Routledge & Kegan Paul.

Caplan, G. (1969). *An Approach to Community Mental Health*, Tavistock.

Carrier, J. & Kendall, I. (1973). Social policy and social change, *Journal of Social Policy*, 2, 3.

CCETSW (1975). *Day Services*, CCETSW, Paper 12.

Chairman (1975). BASW Conference, *Social Work Today*, 6, 15.

Cheeseman, D. *et al.* (1972). *Neighbourhood Care and Old People*, Bedford Square Press.

Circulars (1976). 35/72, DHSS. 197/72, Welsh Office. See also *Priorities for Health and Personal Social Services*, HMSO.

Cmnd 6922 (1946). *The Care of Children*, HMSO.

Collins, J. (1965). *Social Work in General Medical Practice,* Pitman.

Cooper, D. (1967). *Psychiatry and Anti-Psychiatry*, Tavistock.

Council for Children's Welfare (1975). *No Childhood.*

Davies, B. (1968; 1971). *Social Needs and Resources in Local Services*, Michael Joseph; *Variations in Services for the Aged & Children's Services*, Bell.

Davies, M. (1971). *Volunteers in Prison Aftercare*, Allen & Unwin.

Davies, M. (1974). *Social Work in the Environment* (Home Office Research Unit), HMSO.

Davies, M. (1975). A Different form of Probation, *Community Care*, 29 October.

Davis, L. F. (1976). Education welfare—the patchwork service, *Community Care*, 18 February.

Darvill, G. (1975). *Bargain or Barricade?* The Volunteer Centre.

Department of the Environment (1976). *Local Government Financial Statistics*, HMSO.

DHSS (1975). *Study of Play for Children in Hospital.*

Donnison, D. V. *et al.* (1975). *Social Policy and Administration Revisited*, Allen & Unwin.

Editorial (1976). *Social Work Today*, 6, 20.

Etzioni, A. (1969). *The Semi-Professions and their Organisation*, Free Press.

Eyden, J. L. M. (1969). *Social Policy in Action*, Routledge & Kegan Paul.

Fahs Beck, D. & Jones, M. A. (1973). *Progress on Family Problems*, FSAA (US). See also Schuerman, J. (1973). Do family services help? *Social Service Review*, Chicago.

Ferguson, I. & McGone, P. (1974). *Towards Voluntary Action.* Manchester Council for Voluntary Action.

Finer Committee (1974). *One-Parent Families*, HMSO.

Forder, A. (1975). In Mays, J. *et al., Penelope Hall's Social Services of England and Wales*, Routledge & Kegan Paul.

Foren, R. & Brown, M. (1971). *Planning for Service*, Charles Knight.

Freeman, M. D. A. (1976). *The Children Act 1975*, Sweet & Maxwell.

George, V. (1970). *Foster Care*, Routledge & Kegan Paul.

Glastonbury, B. *et al.* (1972). *Policy and Politics* No. 3.

Glastonbury, B. (1975). *Social Work Today* 6 (10).

Goldberg, E. M. (1968). *Helping the Aged*, Allen & Unwin.

Goldberg, E. M. (1970). *Research and Social Work*, BASW Monograph No. 4.

Goldstein, H. (1973). *Social Work Practice*, University of South Carolina.

Gostin, L. O. (1976). *A Human Condition*, MIND.

Gottschalk, L. A. & Auerbach, A. H. (1966). *Research in Psychotherapy*, Appleton–Century–Croft.

Griffiths, J. A. G. (1966). *Central Departments and Local Authorities*, Allen & Unwin.

Hagenbuch, W. (1958). *Social Economics*, Nisbet.

Hall, A. S. (1975). *The Point of Entry*, Allen & Unwin.

Handler, G. (1968). The Co-ercive Children's Officer, *New Society*, 3 October.

Hargreaves, D. (1967). *Social Relations in Secondary School*, Routledge & Kegan Paul.

Harris, A. I. (1971). *Handicapped and Impaired in Great Britain*, Office of Populations Censuses and Survey, HMSO.

Hawkes, D. (1975). Community care, *British Journal of Psychiatry*, September.

Hersov, L. A. (1960). Refusal to go to school, *Journal of Child Psychology and Psychiatry* 12.

Hersov, L. A. (1972). School refusal, *British Medical Journal*, Vol. 3, 8 July.

Hewett, S. *et al.* (1970). *The Family and the Handicapped Child*, Allen & Unwin.

Heywood, J. & Allen, B. (1971). *Financial Help in Social Work*, University of Stirling.

Holman, R. (1973) *Trading in Children*, Routledge & Kegan Paul.

Holman, R. (1975). Personal View, *Community Care*, 3 December.

Home Office (1975). *Probation Statistics 1973*, HMSO.

Hutton, D., Imber, V. & Mitchell, H. D. (1974). *Journal of the Royal Statistical Society*, 137 (4).

Ingleby Committee (1960). *Children and Young Persons*, Cmnd 1191, HMSO.

Jackson, M. P. (1974). *Financial Aid through Social Work*, University of Stirling.

Jenkins, R. (1972). *What Matters Now*, Fontana 1972.

Jones, H. (1975). ed. *Towards New Social Work*, Routledge & Kegan Paul.

Jones, K. (1960). *Mental Health and Social Policy*, Routledge & Kegan Paul.

Jones, K. (1972). *History of the Mental Health Services*, Routledge & Kegan Paul.

Jones, K. (1973). *Health and Social Service Merry-Go-Round*, MIND occasional paper number 1.

Jordan, W. (1973). *Paupers,* Routledge & Kegan Paul.

Jordan, W. (1975). Is the client a fellow citizen? *Social Work Today* 6, 15.

Judge, K. (1976). How to cope with zero growth, *Community Care*, 14 January.

Kahn, A. (1974). *Shaping the New Social Work*, Columbia University Press.

Kilbrandon Committee (1964). *Children and Young Persons* (Scotland), Cmnd 2306, HMSO.

Klein, R. *et al.* (1974). *Social Policy and Public Expenditure*, Centre for Studies in Social Policy.

Kogan, M. (1969). *The Government of the Social Services*, Charles Russel Memorial Trust.

Kogan, M. & Terry, J. (1969). *Organisation of a Social Services Department*, Bookstall Publications.

Laing, R. D. (1960). *The Divided Self*, Tavistock.

Laing, R. D. & Esterson, A. (1964). *Sanity, Madness and the Family*, Tavistock.

Laing, R. D. (1967). *The Politics of Experience*, Penguin.

Leonard, P. (1971). The challenge of primary prevention, *Social Work Today*, 2 (5).

Leonard, P. (1976). *Poverty, Consciousness and Action* (Sheila Kay Memorial Lecture), BASW.

Lubove, E. (1965). *The Professional Altruist*, Chicago.

Morris, P. & Rein, R. (1974). *Dilemmas of Social Reform*, Penguin.

Marshall, T. H. (1965). *Social Policy*, Hutchinson.

Marshall, T. H. (1969). The Role of the Social Services, *Political Quarterly*, 40. 1.

Martin, F. M. (1976). Children's Hearings, *New Society*, 12 February.

Mayer, J. & Timms, N. (1970). *The Client Speaks*, Routledge & Kegan Paul.
See also Maas, H. S. (1971). *Research in the Social Services*, National Association of Social Workers (USA).

Maynard & Tingle (1975). *Journal of Social Policy*, IV2.

McKay, E. M. *et al.* (1973). Consumers and a Social Services Department, *Social Work Today*, 4. 6.

Meacher, M. (1976). Before the crunch comes, *Social Work Today* 6, 20 January.

Meyer, C. (1970). *Social Work Practice—A Response to the Urban Crisis*, Free Press, New York.

Meyer, H. (1965). *Girls at Vocational High*, Russell Sage Foundation.

Ministry of Health (1967). *Centres for the Physically Handicapped.*

Ministry of Health (1968). *A Model of Good Practice.*

Morison Report (1962). *Departmental Committee on the Probation Service*, Cmnd 1650, HMSO.

Morris, P. (1975). *Community Care,* 22 August, 1976.

Mullen, E. J. *et al.* (1972). *The Evaluation of Social Intervention,* Jossey–Bass.

NCSS (1967). *Caring for People,* Allen & Unwin.

NCSS (1972). *Time to Care,* Bedford Square Press.

Newton, G. (1975). We must make an awful choice, *Community Care,* 29 January.

Oakley, P. (1975). Should we de-nationalize the Social Services? *Social Worker,* 30 October.

Packman, J. (1968). *Child Care—Needs and Numbers,* Allen & Unwin.

Parker, R. (1969). *Political Quarterly,* 40(1).

Parker, R. A. (1967). Social administration and scarcity, *Social Work,* April.

Parker, R. *et al.* (1975). *Changes, Choice & Conflict in Social Policy,* Heinemann.

Pearson, G. (1973). Social Work as the privatized solution to public ills, *British Journal of Social Work,* 3(2).

Pearson, G. (1975). *The Deviant Imagination,* Macmillan.

Personal Social Services Council. (1975). *Living and Working in Residential Homes.*

Pinker, R. (1971). *Social Theory and Social Policy,* Heinemann (1971).

Pinker, R. (1974). Social policy and social justice, *Journal of Social Policy,* 3(1) January.

Plowman, G. (1969). *Social Work,* 26 January.

Powers, E. & Witmer, H. L. (1951). *Experiment in the Prevention of Delinquency—The Cambridge Somerville Youth Study,* Columbia University Press.

Pratt, M. (1975). Stress and opportunity in the role of the prison welfare officer, BJSW, 5, 4, Winter.

Ralphs Report (1973). Committee on *The Role and Training of Education Welfare Officers,* HMSO.

Reid, W. J. & Epstein, L. (1972). *Task-Centred Casework,* Columbia University Press, 1972.

Reid, W. J. & Shyne, W. (1969). *Brief and Extended Casework,* Columbia University Press.

Rein, M. (1970). *Social Policy,* Random House, New York.

Rein, M. (1970). The Crossroads for Social Work, *Social Work,* 24 (4).

Report of the Work of the Prison Department (1973). Cmnd 5814, HMSO.

Roberts, A. (1975). *Long-Term Planning in the Personal Social Services* in *Management in the Social Services,* edited by Olsen, R., University College, Bangor.

Roberts, T. & Smith, J. (1976). A National Social Welfare Service, *Social Work Today,* 6 (20).

Robinson, T. J. (1975). The tarnished image of social work, *Community Care,* 8 January.

Rodgers, B. N. & Stevenson, J. (1974). *A New Portrait of Social Work,*

Heinemann.

See also Spencer, C. (1970). Seebohm Problems and Policies, *Social and Economic Administration*, 4 (3).

Rogers, C. (1975). *Client-Centred Therapy,* Houghton–Mifflin, Boston.

Romanyshyn, J. (1971). *Social Welfare*, Random House, New York.

Rosenbaum, S. (1971). Social services manpower, *Social Trends*, 2.

Rowbottom, R. (1973). Organising Social Services, *Public Administration*, 51.

Rowbottom, R. *et al.* (1974). *Social Services Departments*, Heinemann.

Runciman, W. G. (1966; 1972). *Relative Deprivation and Social Justice*, Routledge & Kegan Paul; Penguin Books.

Sainsbury, E. (1975). *Social Work with Families*, Routledge & Kegan Paul.

Scheff, T. J. (1966). *On Being Mentally Ill*, Weidenfeld & Nicolson.

Seed, P. (1973). *Expansion of Social Work in Britain*, Routledge & Kegan Paul.

Social Worker (1975). page 3, 30 October.

Social Work Service, DHSS (1975). Social Services Departments, June.

Social Work Services Group, Scotland (1970). *Children's Hearings*, HMSO.

Speed, M. (1972). Year Book of Social Policy in Britain 1971, edited by Jones, K., Routledge & Kegan Paul.

Thorpe, D. (1976). A half-hearted act of treatment, *Community Care*.

Titmuss, E. (1975). *Provision for the Disabled*, Blackwell.

Titmuss, R. M. (1950). *Problems of Social Policy*, HMSO and Longmans.

Titmuss, R. M. (1958). *Essays on the Welfare State*, chapter 2, Allen & Unwin.

Titmuss, R. M. (1968). *Commitment to Welfare*, p. 133, Allen & Unwin.

Titmuss, R. M. (1974). *Social Policy*, Allen & Unwin.

Toren, N. (1972). *Social Work—The Case of a Semi-Profession*, Sage.

Townsend, P. (1970). *The re-organisation of social policy, New Society*, 22 October.

Triseliotis, J. (1973). Issues in child care practice, *Child Adoption*, 73.

Truax, C. B. & Carkhuff, R. R. (1967). *Toward Effective Counselling and Psychotherapy*, Aldine.

Tunstall, J. (1966). *Old and Alone*, Routledge & Kegan Paul.

Tyerman, M. J. (1968). *Truancy*, University of London.

Vickery, A. (1973). Specialist, Generic: What next? *Social Work Today*, 4(2).

Warham, J. (1973). Abstracts, *British Journal of Social Work*, III 3.

West, D. J. & Farringdon, D. P. *Who Becomes Delinquent?* Heinemann.

White Paper (1965). *The Child, the Family and the Young Offender*, Cmnd 2742, HMSO.

White Paper (1966). *Social Work and the Community*, Cmnd 3065, HMSO.

White Paper (1974). *Children in Care in England and Wales,* Cmnd 5615, HMSO.

White Paper (1976). *The Children and Young Persons Act, 1969*, Cmnd 6494, HMSO, May.

Wilmott, P. & Young, M. (1957). *Family & Kinship in East London*, Penguin.

Woodroofe, D. (1962). *From Charity to Social Work*. Routledge & Kegan Paul.

Working Party, Ministry of Health (1959). *Social Workers in the Local Authority Health and Welfare Services*, HMSO.

Wright Mills, C. (1947). *The Sociological Imagination*, Oxford.

Wynn, M. (1964). *Fatherless Families*, Michael Joseph.

Younger Committee (1974). Report of Advisory Council on the Penal System.

Younghusband, E. (1951). A. The Training and Deployment of Social Work, Carnegie UK Trust.

Younghusband, E. (1951). B. *Social Work in Britain*, Carnegie UK Trust.

Younghusband, E. (1970). Editor, *Living with Handicap*, National Children's Bureau.

Younghusband, E. (1973). The future of social work, *Social Work Today*, 4(2).

A Guide to Further Reading

INTRODUCTION

For a general historical study of the development of the social services, reference should be made to:

M. Bruce: *The Coming of the Welfare State*, Batsford, 1961 and to the various editions, up to 1975, of
Penelope Hall's Social Services of England and Wales, edited by J. Mays or A. Forder, Routledge & Kegan Paul.

Policy issues in the development and administration of the social services are discussed by:

T. H. Marshall: *Social Policy*, Hutchinson, 1965.
R. M. Titmuss: *Essays and the Welfare State*, Allen & Unwin, 1958. and *Commitment to Welfare*, Allen & Unwin, 1968.
P. Hall *et al.*: *Change, Choice and Conflict in Social Policy*, Heinemann, 1975.

and in a collection of readings edited by:

E. Butterworth & R. Holman: *Social Welfare in Modern Britain*. Collins (Fontana paperback), 1975, especially Chapters 1, 4 & 5.

The relationship between policy making and political and social ideologies is discussed by:

K. Bell: *Disequilibrium in Welfare*, Newcastle University Press, 1973.
D. V. Donnison, V. Chapman *et al.*: *Social Policy and Administration Revisited*, Allen & Unwin, 1975.
J. L. M. Eyden: *Social Policy in Action*, Routledge & Kegan Paul, 1969.
R. Pinker: *Social Theory and Social Policy*, Heinemann, 1970.
M. Rein: *Social Policy*, Random House (New York), 1970.

K. M. Slack: *Social Administration and the Citizen*, Michael Joseph, 1966.

Other works concerned with social and political values are:

T. H. Marshall: Value problems of welfare–capitalism, *Journal of Social Policy* 1 (1), 1972.

D. V. Donnison: Ideologies and policies, *Journal of Social Policy* 1 (1), 1972.

G. Myrdal: Place of values in social policy, *Journal of Social Policy* 1 (1), 1972.

A summary of alternative social philosophies and their implications for social policy and services has been made by:

V. George & P. Wilding: *Ideology and Social Welfare*, Routledge & Kegan Paul, 1976.

PART I

In addition to the books suggested as relevant to the introduction, general studies of the development and functions of component services in the welfare state may be found in:

M. Brown: *Introduction to Social Administration in Britain*, Hutchinson, 1970.

P. Willmott: *Consumers' Guide to the British Social Services*, Penguin Books, 1975.

J. Stroud: *Where to Get Help*, Ward Lock, 1975 (which contains some short case studies of social work).

The growth of the personal social services is described by:

P. Seed: *The Expansion of Social Work in Britain*, Routledge & Kegan Paul, 1973.

Reference should be made to:

R. M. Titmuss: *Problems of Social Policy*, HMSO and Longmans, 1950, for a study of the changes in social policy before and during the second world war culminating in the 'welfare state' legislation. A brief statement of these policy changes is contained also in A. Forder's Introduction to the eighth edition of: *Penelope Hall's Social Services of England and Wales* (ed. A. Forder), Routledge & Kegan Paul, 1971.

A current statement of the philosophy of social policy is in:

J. Parker: *Social Policy and Citizenship*, Macmillan, 1975, particularly in the following chapters: 1 (on models of welfare), 8 (the distribution of welfare), 9 (citizenship), and 10 (the implementation of policy). This book offers further references at the end of each chapter.

The complexity of objectives in the provision of the personal social services is illustrated by:

J. Carrier & I. Kendall: Social policy and social change, *Journal of Social Policy*, 2(3), 1973.

As has been suggested in the text, this complexity arises from difficulties in defining certain key words, particularly 'need', 'problem' and 'beneficiary', and determining the extent to which they form an adequate conceptual basis for identifying the purpose and scope of the personal social services. With regard to the concept of need, reference should be made to:

W. G. Runciman: *Relative Deprivation and Social Justice*, Penguin Books, 1972.
R. Olsen (ed.): *Management in the Social Services*, University College at Bangor, 1974.
G. Smith & R. Harris: Ideologies of need and the organization of Social Work Departments, *British Journal of Social Work*, 2(1), 1972.
J. Bradshaw: Taxonomy of social need, *Problems and Progress in Medical Care*, 1972.

The relationship between the work of the personal social services and the containment of social problems is considered by R. Pinker (see previous reference), and by:

H. L. Wilensky & C. N. Lebeaux: *Industrial Society and Social Welfare*, Free Press (New York), 1965.
B. J. Heraud: *Sociology and Social Work*, Pergamon Press, 1970.

These books, together with the article by Carrier & Kendall, illustrate also the difficulty of defining the beneficiaries of services. As the clients of services are frequently defined, in practice, as the primary beneficiaries, and as services are usually evaluated by criteria of change in the clients' behaviour and circumstances, further references to beneficiaries may be found in the context of Part III.

The 'rationing' of personal social services is discussed in general terms by:

R. A. Parker: Social administration and scarcity, *Social Work (UK)*, April 1967.

And with particular reference to the reception of service-users by:

A. S. Hall: *The Point of Entry*, Allen & Unwin, 1974 and Client reception in a social service agency, *Public Administration*, (49), 1971.

Further studies of the reception of clients are contained in:

M. N. Zald (ed.): *Social Welfare Institutions*, Wiley, 1965 (Part D on client relations).

The costs of services are analysed in:

R. Klein *et al.*: *Social Policy and Public Expenditure*, Centre for Studies in Social Policy, 1974.

A useful collection of papers relating to all these issues is:

Association of Directors of Social Services: *Proceedings of the First Study Conference*, April 1972.

PART II

Brief studies of the development of all the personal social services up to 1968 are contained in Appendix F of the Seebohm Report:

Report of the Committee on Local Authority and Allied Personal Social Services, HMSO 1968, Cmnd 3703.

An outline of the legislative responsibilities of the personal social services is provided by:

W. E. Baugh: *Introduction to the Social Services*, Macmillan 1973 and 1975, and in various editions of *Penelope Hall's Social Services of England and Wales* to which reference has been made in earlier sections.

The pattern of service-provision in a local area is described by:

B. Rodgers & J. Stevenson: *A New Portrait of Social Work*, Heinemann, 1974.

Child Care

A brief study of the development of child care provisions and the transition towards a family service is contained in a chapter by P. Boss (Child Care and the Development of a Family Service) in:

(ed.) A. Forder: *Penelope Hall's Social Services of England and Wales*, eighth edition, chapter 8, Routledge & Kegan Paul, 1971.

A fuller account may be found in:

J. Packman: *The Child's Generation*, Blackwell & Robertson, 1975.

The practice of child care by field social workers is described by:

J. Heywood: *Children in Care*, Routledge & Kegan Paul, 1965.

E. Pugh: *Social Work in Child Care*, Routledge & Kegan Paul, 1968.
J. H. Berry: *Social Work with Children*, Routledge & Kegan Paul, 1972.

Specific aspects of child care practice may be studied by reference to the following:

(1) Adoption:

J. Goodacre: *Adoption Policy and Practice*, Allen & Unwin, 1967.
Association of Child Care Officers: *Adoption—the Way Ahead*, ACCO, 1969.
Report of the *Departmental Committee on the Adoption of Children* (the Houghton Committee), HMSO, 1972.
J. Rowe & I. Lambert: *Children Who Wait*, Association of British Adoption Agencies, 1973.

Notes on the provisions and implementation of the Children Act 1975 are contained in the DHSS Circular (75) 21. Reference should be made to Sections 3 and 59 which state the principle that first consideration must be given in all situations to the welfare of the child; Section 108(6) sets out the grounds for dispensing with parents' consent to adoption; Section 20 provides for the appointment of Reporting Officers who will witness parental agreement to adoption applications and will report on applications for orders to free children for adoption; Sections 33–46 define Custodianship Orders. Section 57 sets out the rights of the Local Authority in assuming parental rights in respect of the welfare of a child; in particular, these rights will in future be available to local authorities where parents have failed to exercise care or interest for three years. Section 64 will make possible a separate legal representation of the child in Care Proceedings and other proceedings.
Reference should be made also to:

C. Andrews: The Children Act—how it works, *Social Work Today*, 6(21), 1976.

(2) Foster-care

V. George: *Foster Care*, Routledge & Kegan Paul, 1970.
G. Adamson: *The Caretakers*, Bookstall Services Publications, 1972.
R. A. Parker: *Decision in Child Care*, Allen & Unwin, 1966.
R. Dinnage & M. L. Kellmer Pringle: *Foster Home Care*, National Children's Bureau and Longmans Green, 1967.
R. Thorpe: Mum and Mrs So-and-So, *Social Work Today*, 4(22), 1974.
M. Fletcher: Short-stay foster parents, *Social Work Today*, 4(22), 1974.
R. Holman: The place of fostering in social work, *British Journal of Social Work*, 5(1), 1975.
E. Owen Jones: A study of those who cease to foster, *British Journal of Social Work*, 5(1), 1975.

H. Napier: Success and failure in foster care, *British Journal of Social Work*, 2(2), 1972.

(3) The use of financial resources:

J. Heywood & B. Allen: *Financial Help in Social Work,* Manchester University Press, 1971.
D. Piachaud: The Family Fund, *Social Work Today*, 4(23), 1974.

(4) The availability of general social resources for the care of children:

J. Packman: *Child Care—Needs and Numbers*, Allen & Unwin, 1968.
P. Wedge & H. Prosser: *Born to Fail*, Arrow Books, 1973.

(5) One-parent families:

M. Wynn: *Fatherless Families*, Michael Joseph, 1964.
V. George & P. Wilding: *Motherless Families*, Routledge & Kegan Paul, 1972.
The (Finer) Committee on One-Parent Families, HMSO, 1974.

(6) Delinquent children and the case for a family service:

Committee on *Children and Young Persons*, HMSO 1960, Cmnd 1191.
The Child the Family and the Young Offender, HMSO 1965, Cmnd 2742.
P. Boss: *Social Policy and the Young Delinquent*, Routledge & Kegan Paul, 1967.
Children in Trouble, HMSO 1968.
Committee on *Children and Young Persons* (Scotland), HMSO 1964, Cmnd 2306.
Social Work and the Community, HMSO 1966, Cmnd 3065.
D. Thorpe: A half-hearted Act of Treatment (on the CYP Act 1969), *Community Care*, 20 January 1976.

(7) Intermediate treatment

Intermediate Treatment: HMSO (for DHSS) 1972.
T. Bamford *et al.*: Intermediate treatment, *Social Work Today*, 3(4), 1972.
D. Thorpe; Working with young people, *Social Work Today*, 3(23), 1973.
D. Haxby: Children in trouble, *Social Work Today*, 3(22), 1973.
G. Aplin & R. Bamber: Groupwork counselling, *Social Work Today*, 3(22), 1973.

(8) Social work with families:

A. Needham: Working with the family as a group, *Social Work Today*, 3(3), 1972.
G. Gorrell Barnes: Working with the Family Group, *Social Work Today*, 4(3), 1973.
A. C. R. Skynner: Indications for and against conjoint family therapy, *Social Work Today*, 2(7), 1971; A group-analytic approach to conjoint

family therapy, *Social Work Today*, 2(8), 1971; Minimum sufficient network, *Social Work Today*, 2(9), 1971.

C. Pritchard: An analysis of parental attitudes towards the treatment of maladjusted children, *British Journal of Social Work*, 2(1), 1972.

(9) The use of supervision orders in matrimonial and guardianship cases:

E. Griew & A. Bissett-Johnson: Supervision Orders . . . *Social Work Today*, 6(11), 1975.

(10) Non-accidental injury to children:

K. L. Castle & A. M. Kerr: *Suspected Child Abuse*, NSPCC 1972.

A. E. Skinner & K. L. Castle: *78 Battered Children*, NSPCC 1969.

Report of the *Committee of Inquiry into the Care and Supervision Provided in Relation to Maria Colwell*, HMSO 1974.

C. Andrews: The Maria Colwell enquiry, *Social Work Today*, 4(20), 1974.

C. Andrews: Non-accidental injury to children *and* Violence in the home, *Social Work Today*, 5(4), 1974.

BASW working party: Violence in the Home, *Social Work Today*, 6(13), 1975.

(11) Residential child care:

R. Dinnage & M. L. Kellmer Pringle: *Residential Child Care*, National Children's Bureau and Longmans Green, 1967.

C. Beedell: *Residential Life with Children*, Routledge & Kegan Paul, 1970.

J. H. Berry: *Daily Experience in Residential Life*, Routledge & Kegan Paul, 1975.

B. Dockar-Drysdale: *Consultation in Child Care*, Longmans, 1973.

Care and Treatment in a Planned Environment, HMSO, 1970.

R. King, N. Raynes & J. Tizard: *Patterns of Residential Care*, Routledge & Kegan Paul, 1971.

D. Wills: *Spare the Child*, Penguin Books, 1971.

Residential Care and Treatment, Advisory Council on Child Care, Home Office, 1970.

E. Butlin: Institutionalization, management structure and therapy in residential work . . . *British Journal of Social Work*, 5(3), 1975.

Education welfare provisions and practices have been studied recently by:

L. F. Davis: Education welfare—the patchwork service, *Community Care*, 18 February 1976.

M. Saltmarsh: Misalliance? *Social Work Today*, 4(6), 1973.

M. Davies: The use of volunteers in school social work, *Social Work Today*, 6(4), 1975.

See also

C. Pritchard & R. Ward: The family dynamics of school phobics, *British*

Journal of Social Work, 4(1), 1974.

The Care of the Mentally Disordered

The legislative procedures relating to the care of the mentally disordered are summarized in:

Procedural Requirements under the Mental Health Act, Shaw & Sons, 1974.

A definitive history of social policy and services for the mentally disordered up to the present day has been undertaken by:

K. Jones: *Law, Lunacy and Conscience*, Routledge & Kegan Paul, 1955.

And the thinking behind current legislation is also recorded in the:

Report of the Royal Commission on *The Law Relating to Mental Illness and Mental Deficiency*, HMSO 1957, Cmnd 169.

Reference should be made also to the White Papers:

Better Services for the Mentally Ill, HMSO 1975, Cmnd 6233.
Better Services for the Mentally Handicapped, HMSO 1971, Cmnd 4683.

(This is summarized, with a useful critical commentary, in:

B. Watkin: *Documents on Health and Social Services*, Methuen, 1975.)

And to

A. Maynard & R. Tingle: Objectives and performance of the mental in the 1960's, *Journal of Social Policy*, 4(2), 1975.

The provision of social work help to the mentally disordered and their families is at present described in two ways: by reference to specific professional skills and to the development of community care. The effectiveness of both approaches is interdependent, though this interdependence has yet to be fully explored. Studies of professional skills may be found in:

J. Nursten: *Process of Casework*, Pitman, 1974.
D. Jehu *et al.*: *Behaviour Modification in Social Work*, Wiley, 1972.
G. Gorell Barnes: Working with the Family Group, *Social Work Today*, 4(3), 1973.
I. Salzberger-Wittenberg: *Psychoanalytic Insight and Relationship*, Routledge & Kegan Paul, 1970.
C. Truax & R. Carkhuff: *Toward Effective Counselling and Psychotherapy*, Aldine Press, 1967.
D. Williams: Helping the Mentally Handicapped, *Social Work Today*, 2(ii), 1971.

The development of community care as an essential aspect of social service provision is argued by:

M. J. Bayley: *Mental Handicap and Community Care*, Routledge & Kegan Paul, 1973.
K. Soddy & R. H. Ahrenfeldt (ed.): *Mental Health is a Changing World*, Tavistock Publications, 1965.
DHSS: *National Health Service Reorganisation, England*, HMSO 1972, Cmnd 5055.
DHSS: *Better Services for the Mentally Ill*, HMSO.
DHSS: *Better Services for the Mentally Handicapped*, HMSO, Cmnd 4683.
D. M. Boswell & J. M. Wingrove: *The Handicapped Person in the Community*, Tavistock and Open University, 1974.
J. D. Sutherland: *Towards Community Mental Health*, Tavistock, 1971.
P. McCowen & J. Wilder: *The Life Style of 100 Psychiatric Patients*, Psychiatric Rehabilitation Association, London, 1975.
S. Hewett, P. Ryan & J. Wing: Living without the mental hospitals, *Journal of Social Policy*, 4(4), 1975.

A brief study of the work of community-based hostels for the mentally ill may be found in:

P. Ryan & S. Hewett: A pilot study of hostels, *Social Work Today*, 6(25), 1976.

An indication of the ways in which in-patient treatment may reinforce a lifestyle of illness is presented by:

T. J. Scheff: *On Being Mentally Ill*, Weidenfeld & Nicolson, 1964.

The attitudes of social workers both to psychiatrists and to a treatment-model of social work are examined in the broad context of current social science theories by:

G. Pearson: *The Deviant Imagination*, Macmillan, 1975, who offers a comprehensive guide to further reading.

Problems and inadequacies, both administrative and professional, in the provision of services are usefully summarized by:

K. Jones: *Health and Social Service Merry-Go-Round*, Occasional Paper No. 1, MIND.

An example of service breakdown may be found in:

B. Watkins: *Documents on Health and Social Services*, Methuen, 1975, which contains a summary of the Report of the Committee of Inquiry into Whittingham Hospital.

See also:

C. Creer: Living with schizophrenia, *Social Work Today*, 6(1), 1975.
B. Hudson: Working with schizophrenia, *Social Work Today*, 6(1), 1975.
R. Olsen: The non-contribution of drugs, *Social Work Today*, 6(1), 1975.
D. Hepworth: Tribunal discharge from Rampton, *Social Work Today*, 6(1), 1975.

The Care of the Physically Handicapped:

An outline of services in this field is contained in:

W. E. Baugh: *Introduction to the Social Services*, Macmillan, 1975.

And in

C. A. Hogan, W. Blair & N. J. Smith: Adults with Special Needs in
A. Forder (ed.): *Penelope Hall's Social Services of England and Wales*, Routledge & Kegan Paul (8th edition), 1971.

The extent of need is analysed in:

A. I. Harris: *Handicapped and Impaired in Great Britain*, Office of Population Censuses and Survey, HMSO, 1971.

And the extent to which services are adequate to meet needs is considered in:

E. Topliss: *Provision for the Disabled*, Basil Blackwell, 1975.
J. Hilbourne: On Disabling the Normal, *British Journal of Social Work*, 3(4), 1973.

Social Work in Clinical Practice

The development and functions of medical and psychiatric social work have been recorded in:

C. Morris (ed.): *Social Casework in Britain*, Faber, 1951.

The appointment of social workers in clinical practice was transferred from the Health Service to the local authorities in 1974. Both before and after this transfer, the advantages and disadvantages were described in a range of articles and reports. Reference may be made to the following in *Social Work Today* and the *British Journal of Social Work*

D. T. Carter: Attitudes of MSWs towards re-organization, *BJSW*, 1(3), 1971.
BASW News, incorporated in *SWT*, 2(22), 1972 and 3(12), 1972.
BASW Conference: *The Future of Health Service Social Workers, SWT*,

3(1), 1972.

T. Moss: Health Service Social Work, *SWT*, 3(25), 1973.

J. Baraclough: Social Work Support for the Health Service, *SWT*, 5(4), 1974.

References to the practice of social work in relation to mental and physical ill-health are made elsewhere. In addition, examples of the use made of social workers and of their skills may be found in:

D. T. Carter: The deployment of medical social workers, *SWT*, 2(11), 1971.

D. T. Carter and J. A. Jinks: The next step in medical social work, *SWT*, 2(19), 1972.

S. McMullen: Illness as a focus for social work help, *BJSW*, 2(3), 1972.

A. Miles: Social Workers in psychiatric hospitals, *SWT*, 2(21), 1972.

M. Chambers: Social Work on a cancer unit, *BJSW*, 4(2), 1974.

J. M. Spoor: Terminal Illness, *SWT*, 5(23), 1975.

C. P. Brearley: Social Work in a geriatric hospital, *SWT*, 6(8), 1975.

Particularly since the transfer of medical social workers to social services departments, some use has been made of the attachment of social workers to general practitioners. Studies of social work in general practice have been made by:

J. Collins: *Social Casework in General Medical Practice*, Pitman, 1965.

J. A. S. Forman & E. M. Fairbairn: *Social Casework in General Practice*, Oxford University Press, 1968.

E. M. Goldberg & J. E. Neill: *Social Work in General Practice*, Allen & Unwin, 1972.

This book offers references to other studies: see Chapter 1.

See also

DHSS: *The Reorganisation of Group Practice*, HMSO, 1971.

The Elderly

A general review of services for this group is reported in:

DHSS: *Social Work Service*, December 1973.

And reviews of the attitudes of old people to the services provided are reported in:

Age Concern: *On the Place of the Retired and Elderly in Modern Society 1975* and *Attitudes of the Retired and Elderly*, 1975.

Examples of studies of the needs and provisions for the elderly are:

P. Townsend: *The Family Life of Old People*, Penguin Books, 1973.
E. M. Goldberg: *Helping the Aged*, Allen & Unwin, 1970.
P. Townsend & D. Wedderburn: *The Aged in the Welfare State*, Bell, 1965.
D. B. Bromley: *The Psychology of Human Ageing*, Penguin Books, 1966.
J. Turnstall: *Old and Alone*, Routledge & Kegan Paul, 1966.

The quality of residential care has been examined by:

P. Townsend: *The Last Refuge*, Routledge & Kegan Paul, 1962.
B. Robb (ed.): *Sans Everything*, Nelson, 1967.

A general study of residential care provision for all client groups was made by:

NCSS: *Caring for People*, Allen & Unwin, 1967.

The problem of allocating residential places and the determination of priority of need is studied by:

I. Duncan & R. Davies: A Matter of Choice, *Community Care*, 11 February 1976.

Probation and After-care and Services to Offenders

A standard work on the probation service, which sets out its history, structure and professional purpose, is:

J. E. S. King: *The Probation Service*, Butterworth, 1968.

A further review of the work of the service may be found in Report of the *Departmental Committee on the Probation Service* (the Morison Report), HMSO 1962, Cmnd 1650, and in
Report of the Departmental Committee on the *Business of the Criminal Courts* (the Streatfeild Report), HMSO 1961, Cmnd 1289.

Social work practices in the probation service are described by:

P. Parsloe: *The Work of the Probation and Aftercare Officer*, Routledge & Kegan Paul, 1967.
M. Monger: *Casework in Probation*, Butterworth, 1965, and *Casework in Aftercare*, Butterworth, 1967.

Since these books were published, new responsibilities have been added to the work of the service; these are reviewed, with particular reference to the responses of officers, by:

P. Parsloe: Through the Eyes of the Probation Officer, *British Journal of Social Work*, 2(1), 1972.

M. Davies: The objectives of the Probation Service, *British Journal of Social Work*, 2(3), 1972.

W. Jordan: Probation; in M. Cooper (ed.): *Social Policy*, Basil Blackwell, 1973.

BASW: Evidence to the Butterworth Enquiry on salaries, *Social Work Today*, 3(2), 1972.

D. Mathieson: Conflict and change in Probation, *Probation*, June 1975.

Reference should be made also to:

The Longford Report: *Crime—a challenge to us all*, 1964.

The Child, the Family and the Young Offender, HMSO 1965, Cmnd 2742.

Report of the Advisory Council on the Treatment of Offenders, HMSO, 1961.

Probation and After-care Department: *Probation Research—Implications for Staff and Management*, Home Office, 1976.

The Adult Offender, HMSO, 1965.

Advisory Council on Penal System: *Young Adult Offenders*, HMSO, 1974.

M. Davies: The Criminal Justice Act 1972 as an expression of social policy, *Social Work Today*, 4(7), 1973.

R. Ryall: Delinquency—the problem for treatment, *Social Work Today*, 5(4), 1974.

M. J. Power *et al.*: Delinquency and the Family, *British Journal of Social Work*, 4(1), 1974.

Prison welfare and problems of after-care:

M. Pratt: Stress and opportunity in the role of the prison welfare officer, *British Journal of Social Work*, 5(4), 1975.

P. Morris: Not just within these walls, *Community Care*, 10 March 1976.

W. McWilliams *et al.*: An assessment of prisoners' knowledge of the after-care services, *British Journal of Social Work*, 1(4), 1971.

M. Davies: *Prisoners of Society*, Routledge & Kegan Paul, 1974.

A study of Community Service Orders has been made by:

J. Harding (ed.): *Community Service by Offenders*, National Association for the Care and Resettlement of Offenders, 1974.

N. Hinton: Offenders as social workers, *Social Work Today*, 3(21), 1973.

How far present practices by the probation officers meet the broader community needs of offenders has been studied by:

M. Davies (Home Office Research Unit): *Social Work in the Environment*, HMSO, 1974.

A radical statement of the limitations of the treatment and rehabilitation ideals in services to offenders has been made by:

P. Bean: *Rehabilitation and Deviance*, Routledge & Kegan Paul, 1976.

The Voluntary Sector

References concerned with the relationship between voluntary organizations, volunteers and the statutory social services may be found in other parts of this book, in particular Part III (community care and citizen participation) and Part IV (community work and community action).

The development of voluntary societies has been studied by:

M. Rooff: *Voluntary Societies and Social Policy*, Routledge & Kegan Paul, 1957.

The relationship between voluntary societies and the statutory services in the promotion of welfare is defined by:

M. Broady: Community Power and Voluntary Initiative, *Social Service Quarterly*, 1964.
A. H. Katz: Self-help organisations and voluntary participation in social welfare, *Social Work (US)*, 1970.
G. Darvill: *Bargain or Barricade?* The Volunteer Centre, 1975.
J. Lansley: *Community Organisations and Local Government Reform* and *Voluntary Reorganisation*, both published by the Community Councils Development Group, March 1973 and July 1974.

Reference should be made also to:

G. Popplestone: The Ideology of Professional Community Workers, *British Journal of Social Work*, 1(1), 1971.

And to a study of the functions and structure of the Volunteer Centre in:

L. Brown: Which Way Now for the Volunteer Centre? *Community Care*, 17 March 1976.

The use, recruitment and preparation of volunteer helpers in the social services are exemplified in:

NCSS: *The Voluntary Worker in the Social Services (The Aves Report)*, Allen & Unwin, 1969.
M. Morris: *Voluntary Work in the Welfare State*, Routledge & Kegan Paul, 1969.
DHSS: Voluntary Activity and the Personal Social Services, *Social Work Service*, 1973.
M. Davies: *Volunteers with Families and Children in Special Schools*, Manchester University Press, 1974.

H. Barr: *Volunteers in Prison Aftercare*, Allen & Unwin, 1971.

T. Bamford: Volunteers in Probation, *Social Work Today*, 2(8), 1971.

M. F. Goldberg *et al.*: Volunteers in a Psychiatric Setting, *British Journal of Social Work*, 3(1), 1973.

PART III

The organization and management structures of the personal social services have been extensively studied since the publication of the Seebohm Report.

Examples of 'blue prints' for organization preceding the implementation of the Local Authority Social Services Act 1970 (q.v.) are:

R. Foren & M. Brown: *Planning for Service*, Charles Knight, 1971.

M. Kogan & J. Terry: *Organisation of a Social Services Department*, Bookstall Services Publications, 1969.

M. Kogan: Management, efficiency and the Social Services, *British Journal of Social Work*, 1971.

See also

R. Parker: The future of the Personal Social Services, *Political Quarterly*, 40(1), 1969.

Subsequent studies of management patterns in the social services have been undertaken by:

R. Rowbottom *et al.*: *Social Services Departments*, Heinemann, 1974.

J. Algie: Management and Organization in the Social Services, *British Hospital Journal*, LXXX, 1970.

G. Smith & R. Harris: Ideologies of Need and the Organization of Social Work Departments, *British Journal of Social Work*, 1972.

R. Olsen (ed.): *Management in the Social Services*, University College of Bangor, 1974.

DHSS: Social Services Departments, *Social Work Service*, 1975.

R. G. S. Brown: *The Management of Welfare*, Fontana, 1975.

Association of Directors of Social Services: *Proceedings of the First Study Conference*, April 1975.

G. Rose: Approaches to the analysis of social service organizations, *Journal of Social Policy*, 5(3), 1976.

Similar studies of management and practice in Scotland may be found in:

Social Work in Scotland—*Report of a Working Party on the Social Work (Scotland) Act 1968*, University of Edinburgh, 1969.

J. Gandy: *The delivery of Social Services at the Community Level in Scotland*, University of Toronto, 1971.

The size of organizations in manpower terms is recorded in:

S. Rosenbaum: Social services manpower; in Central Statistical Office: *Social Trends*, HMSO, 1971.

A general study of management processes and of the special characteristics of social service management has been made by:

J. Warham: *An Introduction to Administration for Social Workers* (revised edition), Routledge & Kegan Paul, 1976.

The deployment of staff, particularly at the level of the area team, has been the concern of many recent articles, particularly in respect of the difficulties of clients in approaching large organizations and the problems of main-grade staff in hierarchical structures. On the first matter, reference should be made to:

A. S. Hall: *The Point of Entry*, Allen & Unwin, 1974.

E. M. Goldberg *et al.*: Reactions to Integration, *Social Work Today*, 4 (1 November 1973).

M. Phillips & E. Birchall: Structuring an area office to meet client need, *Social Work Today*, 2 (1971).

W. Utting: *The Way Ahead in Social Services*; in H. H. Perlman *et al.*: *Casework within Social Work*, University of Newcastle, 1973.

General problems of stigma in the client's role are discussed in:

R. Pinker: *Social Theory and Social Policy*, Heinemann, 1970.

A. S. Hall: reference above.

The place of the main-grade social worker in hierarchical social services has been one of the principal considerations at the 1973 and 1974 Conferences of the British Association of Social Workers: see Conference Editions of *Social Work Today*, 1973, 1974. Reference should be made also to:

BASW: *Social Services—The Councillor's Task*, 1973.

A. Hey & R. Rowbottom: Task and supervision in Area Social Work, *British Journal of Social Work*, 1(4), 1971.

T. M. Duncan: Intake in an Integrated Team, *Health and Social Services Journal*, 10 February 1973.

These issues raise the more general dilemma of the role of professional employees in social services—of how far social workers are truly professional people, and how far they are public employees. Studies relevant to this dilemma are:

G. Smith: *Social Work and the Sociology of Organisations*, Routledge & Kegan Paul, 1970.

BASW: *Social Action*—a working party report set out in *Social Work Today*, 2(13), 1971.

A. Etzioni: *The Semi-Professions and their Organization*, Free Press (New York), 1969.

B. J. Heraud: *Sociology and Social Work,* Pergamon Press, 1970.

See further references for Part IV.

The determination of priorities in local authority services and how to ration resources appropriately: reference should be made to:

P. Townsend: The Re-organisation of Social Policy, *New Society*, 22 October 1970.

W. Robson and B. Crick: *The Future of the Social Services*, Penguin Books, 1970.

J. Algie & C. Miller: Deciding Social Services Priorities, *Social Work Today*, 6(22), 1976.

K. Judge: Expansion or equity, *Social Work Today*, 6(5), 1975.

Nottingham Social Services Department: a staff paper on Priorities for Social Workers (stencilled), 1975.

DHSS Circular to local authorities 35/72.

Bleddyn Davies: *Social Needs and Resources in Local Services*, Michael Joseph, 1968; *Variations in Services for the Aged*, Bell, 1971; *Variations in Children's Services*, Bell, 1972.

The relationship between the effectiveness of social work intervention and the manner and frequency of its use has hitherto been directly studied only in the United States. Reference should be made to:

D. Fahs Beck & M. A. Jones: *Progress on Family Problems*, Family Service Association of America, 1973. This comprehensive study draws attention to the importance of the first few interviews in determining the rate of later change, irrespective of the overall length of client–worker contact.

W. J. Reid & L. Epstein: *Task-Centred Casework*, Columbia University Press, 1972. This book defines the function of initial interviews, and relates this function to subsequent work-effectiveness.

Similarly, the importance of intensive work in crisis situations (i.e. in situations where the clients' normal patterns of problem-solving have proved to be inadequate) is argued by:

G. Caplan: *An Approach to Community Mental Health*, Tavistock Publications, 1961.

H. Parad (ed.): *Crisis Intervention*, FSAA, 1965.

Reference was made in this section to the establishment of 'intake teams' to ensure a speedy service to all newly referred clients. The work of these teams is described by:

M. Phillips & E. Birchall: Structuring an area office to meet client need, *Social Work Today*, 1971.
J. Jones: Intake structure in local authorities, *Social Work Today*, 6(23), 1976.
E. Corrie: Intake—friend or foe: *Social Work Today*, 6(23), 1976.
C. Loewenstein: An intake team in action, *British Journal of Social Work*, 4(2), 1974.

Examples of the wider use of team-models of social work practice are given by:

R. Barker & T. Briggs: *Using Teams to Deliver Social Services*, University of Syracuse, 1969.
D. Brieland, T. Briggs & P. Leuenberger: *The Team Model of Social Work Practice*, University of Syracuse, 1973.

It needs to be remembered, however, that the work of 'intake teams' depends partly on the performance of the receptionist.

See:

A. S. Hall: Client Reception in a Social Service Agency, *Public Administration*, 49, 1971; and *The Point of Entry*, Allen & Unwin, 1975.

Reference should be made also to:

R. Rowbottom: Organising Social Services, *Public Administration*, 51, 1973.
A. Sinfield: *Which Way for Social Work?*, Fabian Society Pamphlet, 1969.
M. Rein: *Social Policy*, Random House (New York), 1970.

all of whom draw attention to potential conflicts between the organization of services and the achievements of welfare tasks.

Examples of the ways in which the users of social services perceive their status may be found in:

J. Mayer & N. Timms: *The Client Speaks*, Routledge & Kegan Paul, 1970.
N. Timms: *The Receiving End*, Routledge & Kegan Paul, 1973.
E. Sainsbury: *Social Work with Families*, Routledge & Kegan Paul, 1975.
M. Bayley: *Mental Handicap and Community Care*, Routledge & Kegan Paul, 1973.
D. Marsden: *Mothers Alone*, Penguin Books, 1973.

A recent brief resume of the arguments for and against the specialization of social workers is provided by:

A. Vickery: Specialist, Generic, What Next? *Social Work Today*, 4(9), 1973.

Preventive work is defined by:

P. Leonard: The Challenge of Primary Prevention, *Social Work Today*, 2(5), 1971.

Examples of the importance given to preventive work and of its implementation may be found in:

M. Meacher: Before the Crunch Comes, *Social Work Today*, 6, 1976.

Reference should be made also to chapters 4 & 5 of:

E. Butterworth & R. Holman: *Social Welfare in Modern Britain*, Fontana paperback, 1975.

Community care as an operational concept is discussed by:

K. Jones: *History of the Mental Health Services*, Routledge & Kegan Paul, 1972.
M. J. Bayley: *Mental Handicap and Community Care*, Routledge & Kegan Paul, 1973.

Bayley's book draws particular attention to what 'community care' means in the experience of families with a permanently handicapped member.

Effective community care rests in part on the quality of relationships between statutory services, voluntary services and volunteers. The present state of these relationships is explored by:

G. Darvill: *Bargain or Barricade?* Volunteer Centre, 1975.
J. Ward: *Community Workers and the Social Services*, Bedford Square Press.
A. Lapping (ed.): *Community Action*, Fabian Society pamphlet, 1970.
D. Cheeseman *et al.*: *Neighbourhood Care and Old People*, Bedford Square Press, 1972.
National Council of Social Service: *Time to Care*, 1972.
J. Ferguson & P. McGone: *Towards Voluntary Action,* Manchester Council for Voluntary Action, 1974.
Age Concern: *Good Neighbours*, 1974.
L. Knight: Lady Bountiful's Successors, *Community Care*, 17 September 1975.

Community care implies also, as suggested in Part III, a consideration of the relationship between community work and the practice of social work. This is explored in the last chapter of:

P. Baldock: *Community Work and Social Work*, Routledge & Kegan Paul, 1975.

Citizen participation in policy-making and the planning of services has been widely advocated in recent years. Reference should be made to:

People and Planning: Report of the (Skeffington) Committee on Public Participation in Planning, HMSO, 1969.

Two reports sponsored by the Gulbenkian Foundation:

Community Work and Social Change, Longmans Green, 1968, and
Current Issues in Community Work, Routledge & Kegan Paul, 1973.

And to:

A. Sinfield: *Which Way for Social Work?* Fabian Society Pamphlet, 1969.

Public involvement in planning in local neighbourhoods is discussed by:

W. Hampton: *The Neighbourhood and the Future*, Association of Community Workers, 1973 and *Democracy and Community*, Oxford University Press, 1970.
M. Broady: Community Power and Voluntary Initiative, *Social Service Quarterly*, 1964.
G. Goetschius: *Working with Community Groups*, Routledge & Kegan Paul, 1969.
P. Marris & M. Rein: *Dilemmas of Social Reform*, Penguin Books, 1972.

The extent to which the users of services at present feel involved in the policies of agencies is indicated by:

A. McKay *et al.*: Consumers and a Social Services Department, *Social Work Today*, 4(6), 1973.
R. Holman: *Trading in Children*, Routledge & Kegan Paul, 1973.

Reference has been made in this section to the relationship between community work and political action, and to the role of the community worker in social change. The philosophical and strategic issues involved in this matter are explored by:

R. Lees: Politics and social deprivation, *Social Work Today*, 2(18), 1971 and Social action, *New Society*, 474, 1971.
R. Holman: *Power for the Powerless: the role of community action*, British Council of Churches, 1972.
BASW: *Social Action and Social Work*, 1974.

The possible risks of association between community work and political activist minorities are discussed by:

J. Morrish: The Relevance to Agency-Based Workers of Community Work, *Social Work Today*, 1(2), 1970.

Studies of community work may be found in:

A. Power: *I woke up this morning—the development of a London community project*. Community and Race Relations Unit, British Council of Churches, 1972, and
David and Goliath, Holloway Neighbourhood Law Centre, 1973.
R. Bryant: Play and Politics, *Social Work Today*, 4(7), 1973.
D. Jones and M. Mayo: *Community Work One* and *Community Work Two*, Routledge & Kegan Paul, 1974 and 1975.

The nature of community work as a professional activity is discussed by:

G. F. Thomason: *The Professional Approach to Community Work*, Sands & Co., 1969.
R. A. B. Leaper: *Community Work*, NCSS (Bedford Square Press), 1968.
P. Baldock: *Community Work and Social Work*, Routledge & Kegan Paul, 1975.

Research into the outcome of intervention: the problems and methods of research are explored by:

D. E. G. Plowman: What are the outcomes of Social Work? *Social Work (UK)*, 26(1), 1969.
E. M. Goldberg: *Research and Social Work*, BASW Monograph 4, 1970; *Research in the Personal Social Services*, NISW, 1968.
E. J. Mullen, J. R. Dumpson *et al.*: *The Evaluation of Social Intervention*, Jossey–Bass, 1972.
R. Lees: *Research Strategies in Social Welfare*, Routledge & Kegan Paul, 1975.
T. C. Puckett: Can social treatment be effective? *Social Work Today*, 4(6), 1973.

In addition to these technical problems, there is a further dilemma concerning the relationship between the views of service-users and the formulation of policies for the provision of services. A review of recent studies of the attitudes of service-users in which the policy implications are considered has been undertaken by

I. Shaw: Consumer Opinion and Social Policy, *Journal of Social Policy*, 5(1), 1976.

Examples of studies of the outcome of social work, measured by objective criteria, are:

H. Meyer: *Girls at Vocational High*, Russel Sage Foundation, 1965.
E. Powers & H. L. Witmer: *Experiment in the Prevention of Delinquency*, Columbia University Press, 1951.
G. E. Brown: *The Multi-Problem Dilemma*, Scarecrow Press, 1968. (This contains a useful debate on the criteria used and their relevance to social work practice.)
E. M. Goldberg: *Helping the Aged*, Allen & Unwin, 1970.

Examples of studies in which the criteria used are directly related to a professional formulation of social work purpose:

W. J. Reid and A. W. Shyne: *Brief and Extended Casework*, Columbia University Press, 1969. (This study compares the outcome of two modes of casework practice.)
J. Mayer & N. Timms: *The Client Speaks*, Routledge & Kegan Paul, 1971.
H. S. Maas: *Research in the Social Services*, National Association of Social Workers (USA), 1971.
Z. Butrym: *Social Work in Medical Care* Routledge & Kegan Paul, 1967.

Recent studies concerned with the attitudes and opinions of service-users in Britain are those of Goldberg, Bayley, Mayer and Timms (see earlier references) and:

A. McKay, E. M. Goldberg & D. J. Fruin: Consumers and a Social Services Department, *Social Work Today*, 4(6), 1973.
J. Triseliotis: *In Search of Origins*, Routledge and Kegan Paul, 1970.
D. Marsden: *Mothers Alone*, Penguin Books, 1973.
P. Morris, J. Cooper & A. Boyles: Public Attitudes to Problem Definition and Problem Solving, *British Journal of Social Work*, 3(3), 1973.
N. Timms: *The Receiving End*, Routledge & Kegan Paul, 1973.
E. Sainsbury: *Social Work with Families*, Routledge & Kegan Paul, 1975.
S. Hewett: *The Family and the Handicapped Child*, Allen & Unwin, 1970.

The differential use of social work skills has been studied by:

W. J. Reid & A. W. Shyne (see earlier reference).
W. J. Reid & L. Epstein: *Task Centred Casework*, Columbia University Press, 1972.
D. Fahs Beck & M. A. Jones: *Progress on Family Problems*, FSAA, 1973.
J. R. Schuerman: Do Family Services Help? *Social Service Review (Chicago)*, 1973.
C. Rogers: *Client-Centred Therapy*, Houghton–Mifflin, 1975.
C. B. Truax & R. R. Carkhuff: *Towards Effective Counseling and Psychotherapy*, Aldine, 1967.

The extent to which the clients' definition of task provides an adequate basis for regulating the intervention of social services and social workers is a matter of dispute. No study has been undertaken specifically on this matter, but the arguments may be traced in the work of Reid and Epstein (see earlier reference) and in:

W. Jordan: *Client–Worker Transactions*, Routledge & Kegan Paul, 1970. (A perceptive study of the reciprocal influences of client and worker on each other's behaviour and perceptions of need).

F. E. McDermott (ed.): *Self-Determination in Social Work*, Routledge & Kegan Paul, 1974.

R. Foren & R. Bailey: *Authority in Social Casework*, Pergamon Press, 1968.

PART IV

The history of the development of social work and the processes of its professionalization may be studied by reference to the following:

K. Woodroofe: *From Charity to Social Work*, Routledge & Kegan Paul, 1962.

E. Younghusband: the first essay in *Social Work and Social Change*, Allen & Unwin, 1964.

M. J. Smith: *Professional Education for Social Work in Britain*, Allen & Unwin, 1965.

P. Seed: *The Expansion of Social Work in Britain*, Routledge & Kegan Paul, 1973.

R. Bitensky: The Influence of Political Power in Determining the Theoretical Development of Social Work, *Journal of Social Policy*, 2(2), 1973.

The current legal responsibilities of social workers are set out in:

J. D. McClean: *The Legal Context of Social Work*, Butterworths, 1975.

The extent to which social work is (or may become) a profession is explored by:

A. Etzioni: *The Semi-Professions and their Organisation*, Free Press (NY), 1969.

N. Toren: *Social Work—the Case of a Semi Profession*, Sage, 1972.

The risks of professionalization, particularly that this process creates distance between worker and client and that perception may be dominated by pre-defined techniques of work, are stated succinctly by:

A. Sinfield: *Which Way for Social Work?* Fabian Society Pamphlet, 1969.

D. Briggs: De-clienting social work, *Social Work Today*, 3(21), 1973.

So much has been written about the theory and practice of social work that it is difficult to make a small selection. Traditionally, social work has been described in terms of its methods: i.e. casework, groupwork, community work and residential care. (References to readings on residential care may be found elsewhere in this book.) Casework practice has made use of many different theories of human behaviour, and may be divided into a series of 'schools'. An excellent guide to all the schools is:

R. W. Roberts & R. H. Nee (ed.): *Theories of Social Casework*, University of Chicago Press, 1970, in which references for more detailed study may be found.

Casework theories are examined also by:

J. Moffett: *Concepts in Casework Treatment*, Routledge & Kegan Paul, 1968.
D. Jehu: *Learning Theory and Social Work*, Routledge & Kegan Paul, 1967.

and in the following collections of essays:

E. Younghusband (ed.): *New Developments in Casework* and *Social Work and Social Values*, Allen & Unwin, 1966 & 1967.

And in:

F. J. Bruno: *Trends in Social Work Practice 1874–1956*, Columbia University Press, 1957.

Group work practice may be studied by reference to:

B. Davies: *The Use of Group Work in Social Work Practice*, Routledge & Kegan Paul, 1975.
J. Klein: *Working with Groups*, Hutchinson, 1963.
S. Bernstein: *Explorations in Group Work* and *Further Explorations in Group Work*, Bookstall Services Publications, 1972.
T. Douglas: *Group Work Practice*, Tavistock, 1976.

Readings on community work practice have been mentioned elsewhere. The nature of community work and the techniques of practice are studied by:

P. Baldock: *Community Work and Social Work*, Routledge & Kegan Paul, 1974.
R. A. B. Leaper: *Community Work*, NCSS (Bedford Square Press), 1968.
Gulbenkian Foundation: *Community Work and Social Changes*, Longmans, 1970.
G. W. Goetschius: *Working with Community Groups*, Routledge & Kegan Paul, 1967.

R. Bryant: Community Action, *British Journal of Social Work*, 2(2), 1972.

J. Cheetham & M. Hill: Community work—social realities and ethical dilemmas, *British Journal of Social Work*, 3(3), 1973.

S. Rees: Patronage and participation, *British Journal of Social Work*, 3(1), 1973.

During the 1970s attempts have been made to develop a unitary theory relevant to all forms of social work practice. These attempts recognize that the division of social work into 'methods' has distorted both the quality of service offered to clients and the structure of the profession. This theoretical development may be studied by reference to:

H. M. Bartlett: *The Common Base of Social Work Practice*, National Association of Social Workers (USA), 1970.

A. Pincus & A. Minahan: *Social Work Practice*, Peacock, 1973.

H. Goldstein: *Social Work Practice*, University of South Carolina Press, 1973.

A. Vickery: A systems approach to social work intervention, *British Journal of Social Work*, 4(4), 1974.

R. Baker: Towards Generic Social Work Practice, *British Journal of Social Work*, 5(2), 1975.

Related to this, a study of the adaptation of casework theory to meet new challenges in practice has been made by:

C. Meyer: *Social Work Practice—a response to the Urban Crisis*, Free Press (New York), 1970.

J. Fitzjohn: An interactionist view of the social work interview, *British Journal of Social Work*, 4(4), 1974.

Politically radical views of social work practice are defined and illustrated by:

G. Pearson: Social work as the privatized solution to public ills, *British Journal of Social Work*, 3(2), 1973.

P. Leonard: *Poverty, Consciousness and Action*, BASW, 1976.

R. Bailey (ed.): *Radical Social Work*, Arnold, 1975.

see also:

H. Rose: Who can de-label the claimant? (on tribunals), *Social Work Today*, 4(13), 1973.

The present crisis in social work hinges principally on issues of value and accountability. A traditional expression of the values implicit in worker–client relationships is that of:

F. B. Biestek: *The Casework Relationship*, Allen & Unwin, 1961.

but this should be read in conjunction with a critique by:

R. Plant: *Social and Moral Theory in Casework*, Routledge & Kegan Paul, 1970.

and with

H. Prins: Motivation in Social Work, *Social Work Today*, 5(2), 1974.

The current state of the debate about values and accountability may be studied in:

H. Jones (ed.): *Towards the New Social Work*, Routledge & Kegan Paul, 1975.

A. Kahn (ed.): *Shaping the New Social Work*, Columbia University Press, 1974.

B. H. Knott: Social Conflict, *British Journal of Social Work*, 2(4), 1972.

And, in relation to the social and medical sciences, in:

P. Halmos: *The Faith of the Counsellors*, Constable, 1968.

R. Pinker: *Social Theory and Social Policy*, Heinemann, 1971.

G. Pearson: *The Deviant Imagination*, Macmillan, 1975.

See also:

A. W. Gouldner: *The Coming Crisis of Western Sociology*, Basic Books, 1970, and

E. Fromm: *The Crisis of Psychoanalysis*, Penguin Books, 1973.

Problems of accountability are raised also by:

B. Glastonbury: Social workers—cannon fodder in an age of administration, *Social Work Today*, 6(10), 1975.

T. J. Robinson: The Tarnished Image of Social Work, *Community Care*, 8 January, 1975.

J. Warham: Abstracts, *British Journal of Social Work*, 3(3), 1973.

R. Pinker: Social policy and social justice, *Journal of Social Policy*, 3(1), 1974.

J. Romanyshyn: *Social Welfare*, Random House, 1971.

W. Jordan: *Paupers*, Routledge & Kegan Paul, 1973.

R. Lees: *Politics in Social Work*, Routledge and Kegan Paul, 1972.

A. Sinfield: *Which Way for Social Work?* Fabian Society Pamphlet, 1969.

B. Lynch: Setting Priorities—a political or professional decision, *Social Work Today*, 6(24), 1976.

Part of the process of professionalization in social work has been concerned with the development of a code of ethics. Following considerable debate and drafting, the BASW published:

Code of Ethics for Social Work, set out in *Social Work Today*, 6(12), 1975 with a commentary by J. Baraclough, Assistant General Secretary.

Reference may be made also to:

W. J. Patterson: *Social Work's Theory of Man*, University of Ulster, 1975.

A brief guide to the development of social work training in Britain may be found in:

E. Younghusband: *The Training and Development of Social Workers*, Carnegie UK Trust, 1951.
Social Workers in the Local Authority Health and Welfare Services, HMSO, 1959.
E. Sainsbury: Education for Social Work, *International Social Work*, 1968.
The first and second reports of the CCETSW: *Setting the Course for Social Work Education 1971–3; A Year of Consolidation and Progress 1973–4*, available from CCETSW.
Education and Training for Social Work, Paper No. 10, CCETSW, 1976.

The expansion of social work training to cover residential care and day care services is discussed in

Residential Work is Social Work, CCETSW, Paper 1, 1973.
Day Services, CCETSW, Paper 12, 1975.

Future trends in the training programme for social workers are indicated in the Report of the Manpower Working Party, DHSS, 1976; these trends are summarized and evaluated in *Community Care*, 4 August 1976.

PART V

See references in the text.

Index